Law Enforcement Information Technology

A Managerial, Operational, and Practitioner Guide

Law Enforcement Information Technology

A Managerial, Operational, and Practitioner Guide

Jim Chu

CRC Press

Boca Raton   London   New York   Washington, D.C.

Library of Congress Cataloging-in-Publication Data

Chu, Jim, 1959-
     Law enforcement information technology : a managerial, operational,
and practical guide / by Jim Chu.
             p.   cm.
     Includes bibliographical references.
     ISBN 0-8493-1089-X (alk. paper)
     1. Law enforcement—Data processing. 2. Criminal
investigation—Data processing. 3. Information storage and retrieval
systems—Criminal investigation. 4. Police communication systems. I.
Title.
HV7936.A8 C48 2001
363.25′0285—dc21   2001035736

Visit the CRC Press Web site at www.crcpress.com

© 2001 by CRC Press LLC

No claim to original U.S. Government works
International Standard Book Number 0-8493-1089-X
Library of Congress Card Number 2001035736
Printed in the United States of America   2 3 4 5 6 7 8 9 0
Printed on acid-free paper

Preface ("Chapter 0")

In 1997, I was working as a watch commander in Vancouver, B.C., Canada in my first assignment at the management rank of Inspector. Due to a sudden retirement, I was abruptly transferred to a project that I knew very little about, and it appeared highly technical in scope. One of my first contacts was with a radio engineer who explained how our new wide-area digital-trunked radio system would be phased in over a number of years, and that the Vancouver Police Department would be the first phase. Instead of "Phase 1," they called it "Phase 0" because engineers like to start counting from zero.

I have borrowed this concept in starting this book, although I am not writing for engineers. On the contrary, I am aiming toward a non-technical audience — those thousands of managers, supervisors, and line officers working today in law enforcement that increasingly face new digital technologies in every facet of their operations. In addition, by illustrating how Information Technology (IT) can improve the processes in law enforcement, technical personnel, consultants, vendors, and developers, who may not know the business of policing very well, can gain more knowledge into how IT can add value to law enforcement organizations. I hesitated to use the term "modern" law enforcement organizations, because many police (the term "police" is used interchangeably with "law enforcement") agencies still employ decades-old manual business processes. Despite the obvious benefits, many agencies remain technology illiterate.

This book is about the applied use of IT in law enforcement. In my work, I took very seriously my leadership responsibilities on IT projects. Whenever a new facet arose, I sought out and studied additional readings and resources, so that I did not have to rely solely on what other experts told me. This enabled me to better articulate end-user needs in a realistic manner, and equipped me to challenge others who may not have had their facts correct or their homework done. As my knowledge base increased, it became obvious to me that I had reached a juncture in time where it seemed the logical course of action was to record my experiences and insights so that others following in a similar position could benefit. I was immersed in the challenges of delivering information systems to a consortium of small, medium, and large police organizations, as well as fire and emergency medical agencies.

Figure 1 Public safety officials from around the world have visited the E-Comm facility. It was opened in 1999.

I cannot state with certainty that all of our projects turned out as planned. I can say with certainty that if I knew then what I know now, they would have gone better.

The project and the quasi-municipal corporation that governed this consortium is called Emergency Communications for Southwest British Columbia, or E-Comm. In this assignment, I had the invaluable experiences of working closely with our own technical personnel, external consultants, and the new operations management team. It was an opportunity of a lifetime, and would have been beyond my wildest dreams (or nightmares) when I entered the Police Academy in 1979. Of some help to me was my rusty academic background in the passé field of management information systems.

The unique opportunity provided by E-Comm was that we were implementing many new technology projects at the same time. We brought in a new facility and call center (Figure 1), a new computer-aided dispatch system, a virtual private network, a new records management system, a state-of-the-art digital-trunked radio system, and a multi-jurisdictional Intranet. Our communications and information infrastructure converged. Doing it all at once allowed us to bring in advanced systems, but most importantly, to select and implement the systems using an integrated approach. Thinking constantly about the big picture allowed us to deliver valuable crime-fighting tools to the end users — the officers on the street who face the criminal element every day and have the important responsibility of protecting the public.

A very enjoyable part of my job was the opportunity to meet and brainstorm with colleagues from all over the world. At E-Comm, just some of the public safety leaders we hosted came from Finland, the United Arab Emirates,

Figure 2 The author, through an interpreter, instructing IT to police managers (rank of Lieutenant and above) at the Abu Dhabi Police Directorate Training Institute, United Arab Emirates, April 2000.

Hong Kong, Belfast, the People's Republic of China, the New Scotland Yard (London Metropolitan Police), the U.S. Department of Justice, Los Angeles Police, Honolulu Police, Austin (TX) Police, and the Federal Bureau of Investigation. In the course of product evaluations, I participated in conference calls to colleagues in Little Rock, AR, Springfield, MO, Boise, ID, Chicago, IL, and many other North American cities. Moreover, I had the opportunity to visit and observe firsthand law enforcement IT in over 30 agencies, located in 4 countries, and in North America, within 8 states and 4 Canadian provinces. In these travels, I encountered many knowledgeable police leaders and technical support managers who have excelled in bringing automation tools to the officers in their agencies. In fact, when I entered this field, I relied on these many contacts in the police community to bring myself up to speed on the constantly changing technologies.

I also obtained invaluable insights through speaking and participating at IT conferences — most notably the International Association of Chiefs of Police Law Enforcement Information Managers Conference. This provided networking opportunities where I had the opportunity to share observations and insights with colleagues and vendors from around the world (Figure 2).

In writing such a book, I have thought a great deal about the potential readers. As a police officer with a background in mostly operational areas, I have attempted to cover the concepts at a level that will allow the non-technical reader to become well versed in the latest terminology, products, and automation options. However, this is not just a survey work on computers and networks. The book also has a goal of describing the service parameters and the business processes that should and often already exist in law enforcement organizations. It is not only private businesses that must use IT strategically to support the enterprise.

In many small agencies that cannot afford high-priced assistance, it is often the street cop who knows how to install Windows and surf the Internet, who is assigned by the Chief to address automation. This book can help those officers in this position. For officers working in larger agencies, I offer this point: in today's environment, all police officers who aspire to a higher rank, or a specialty position such as a computer crime investigator, must be aware of how IT can help them in performing their jobs, and help their organizations.

I cannot overemphasize how important it is for current and future police leaders to understand the role of IT. This cannot be left solely with the technical data processing manager as it has been in the past. Chiefs of police, sheriffs, superintendents, executives and managers, section commanders, and unit supervisors must work with the technical resources in a partnership to improve the performance of the organization. MIT's John Rockart wrote in the *Harvard Business Review,* "Line managers are becoming more knowledgeable about IT as it becomes an increasingly valuable resource for managers at all levels."*

Technology can be both a catalyst and enabler. Maximizing the use of information, an asset that exists everywhere in all law enforcement agencies, will improve organizational performance. Furthermore, this information does not only exist in paper files and databases. Information exists in the heads of people, and newer concepts, in areas such as knowledge management, will have a profound influence on policing in the future.

When I started my assignment at E-Comm, I looked for material that could bring me up to speed on the recent changes and the application of new technologies in law enforcement. It was evident that very little in this area had been written. What I did locate was material from the 1970s and early 1980s.

In looking at the technical and academic side of IT in law enforcement, I believe that the nature of the work precludes many from knowing what is being implemented and how IT is being used. Law enforcement systems need to have high levels of security as a paramount consideration, and police and systems administrators are not going to let outsiders look at specifications and applications, let alone interview staff and observe systems.

---

* Rockart, Jack, Are CIOs obsolete? *Harvard Business Review,* March–April 2000.

Fortunately, the world of IT in policing opens up when the person making the inquiries carries a badge. I have visited many agencies and, in this book, I have been diligent in respecting the confidential areas of the IT systems I have seen. This book does not include any information that might assist system hackers. In addition, I made the conscious decision to provide kudos for agencies that are leaders and visionaries, and to anonymously refer to agencies that are engrossed in problems, or that I consider are seriously behind in IT.

The four parts of the book are:

Part I: Introduction — This introductory part emphasizes the critical importance of aligning IT to the mission and business strategies of a law enforcement agency. Chapter 1 outlines the economic and service-related reasons that relate to how and why IT is used. Concepts from government and commercial sources are described, and examples are used to illustrate their importance and relevance. The importance of IT knowledge as a basic managerial competency is emphasized. Chapter 2 describes how IT use in the past has not always led to desirable results, and we must learn from these past mistakes. IT systems must be implemented to support the strategic direction of the organization. For the foreseeable future, these directions are focused on community policing, and Chapter 2 provides many examples of how IT supports the philosophy of community policing and why police officers must be considered knowledge workers. Many cutting-edge uses of the Internet are highlighted.

Part II: Management — This part of the book is focused on the management concepts surrounding the planning and implementation of IT. Many IT projects fail. If systems are not properly implemented, significant amounts of time and money are needed to deliver the originally specified functionality. Chapter 3 addresses strategic planning and the important change practices associated with business process reengineering. Chapter 4 discusses how to prepare a business case to justify an IT project, and also covers procurement and project management. Case studies on the acquisition of IT are provided from the London Metropolitan Police Service and the Western Australia Police Service.

Part III: Major Applications — The chapters in this part describe the major IT systems used in law enforcement. Chapter 5 covers databases and concludes with case studies of regional information-sharing projects. This will set the stage for Chapters 6, 7, and 8 which cover the major law enforcement IT applications, computer-aided dispatch, records management systems, and mobile computing.

Table 1 Chapter Content and the Target Reader

	Chapter and Content	Managerial	Operational	Practitioner
Part I: Introduction	1. The Strategic Significance of IT	High	High	High
	2. IT in Support of Community Policing	High	High	High
Part II: Management	3. Strategic Planning and Reengineering Operations	High		
	4. The Acquisition of IT	High		
Part III: Major Applications	5. Databases and Information		High	
	6. Computer Aided Dispatch		High	
	7. Records Management Systems		High	
	8. Mobile Computing		High	
Part IV: Technology Infrastructure	9. Wireline Infrastructure			High
	10. Wireless Voice IT Infrastructure			High
	11. Wireless Data IT Infrastructure			High

Part IV: Technology Infrastructure — Chapters 9, 10, and 11 cover wireline and wireless IT infrastructure. These discussions are very technical at times and a key point to remember is that many modern, and perhaps trendy, IT terms will be bandied about by technicians, vendors, and consultants. These chapters are helpful in anchoring the applied context of a particular technology term.

Another way to look at the organization of this book is depicted in Table 1, which correlates the chapters with reader backgrounds. Law enforcement executives should focus on the first two parts of the book and may want to skim the remainder. Criminology and general law enforcement administration/management students should also focus on the first two parts of the book in order to understand the underlying theories of IT use in police operations. Parts III and IV of the book are targeted toward practitioners who are on the frontlines implementing IT systems, and for the readers who want to achieve an advanced level of understanding of the applied technical components of IT.

A work such as this could not have been produced without the assistance and input from many key individuals. I would especially like to thank, in alphabetical order:

Captain Jon Arnold, Huntington Beach Police Department
Mr. Keith Bandy, P. Eng., Planetworks Consulting
Chief Paul Battershill, Victoria Police Department
Chief Inspector Steve Benn, London Metropolitan Police Service
Superintendent Glenn Crannage, Western Australian Police Service
Mr. Warren Loomis, Vice President, Versaterm Inc.
Constable Keiron McConnell, Vancouver Police Department
Sergeant Kevin McQuiggin, Vancouver Police Department
Mr. Ron Meyer, President, Versaterm Inc.
Mr. Tom Steele, Chief Information and Communications Officer, Maryland State Police
Mr. Mark Stiegemeier, Chairman and CEO, MEGG Associates Inc.
Mr. Matt Snyder, IACP Technology Center and Technical Assistance Program Administrator, LEIM Section Liaison

I accept responsibility for all errors and opinions in this work and I welcome comments, suggestions, and criticisms. They can be e-mailed to: jim_chu@city.vancouver.bc.ca or jim.chu@lawenfit.com.

In conclusion, there is no other field that is expanding as rapidly, and changing as fast, as the IT business. In order to keep this work as current and relevant as possible, I have created a companion Website to provide supplemental information for each chapter and to provide links to the latest resources on the Web. Similar to what is provided in many DVD movie releases, I even provide chapter commentaries, related anecdotes that the book did not have space for, and additional information and opinions from other experts.

I encourage all readers to visit the companion portal to this book at www.lawenfit.com.

Jim Chu
Vancouver, B.C.
2001

The Author

Inspector Jim Chu began his career with the Vancouver Police in 1979. Positions he has held include: patrol constable, school liaison officer, robbery squad detective, patrol sergeant, and duty officer (watch commander). He holds a Bachelor of Business Administration from Simon Fraser University and a Master of Business Administration from the University of British Columbia. He has taught criminology at the college level.

Since 1997, he has been the Vancouver Police project manager for the Emergency Communications for Southwest BC (E-Comm) project. This involves partnerships among police and other public safety agencies for consolidated dispatch, computer-aided dispatch, digital trunked radio, and records management systems. He has been a featured speaker at police and technology conferences and seminars throughout North America, Europe, and the Middle East.

Jim can be contacted at:

jim.chu@lawenfit.com   or   jim_chu@city.vancouver.bc.ca

Table of Contents

Part II: Management 49

3   Strategic Planning and Reengineering
Operations 51

4   The Acquistion of IT 69

Part III: Major Applications 95

5 Databases and Information 97

Introduction

I

Chapter 1 provides a framework for understanding why IT is important in law enforcement. Examples and concepts are taken from business, economic, and service-sector research and are used to illustrate how and why IT can enhance the delivery of efficient and effective law enforcement services. Chapter 2 describes past mistakes in implementing IT and emphasizes the need to align IT with the mission and strategic objectives associated with community policing.

Chapter 2 outlines why the decentralization of services is an important facet of community policing. Wireless connectivity for mobile workstation computers facilitates decentralization. All Vancouver Police notebook computers are equipped with integrated Sierra Wireless SB 300 CDPD modems, and this allows police officers to remain in their communities longer, as they can remotely access and contribute to databases.

The Strategic Significance of IT

1

1.1 IT Is Important

Information Technology (IT) has made inroads in all law enforcement organizations. Some agencies have embraced automation tools and technologies while others have been slower in bringing in what they perceive to be costly, complex, and unjustifiable systems. What is clear is that IT will play an integral and increasingly significant role in policing. Tom Steele has been a commander in the Alexandria (VA) Police Department and is currently the chief information and communications officer for the Maryland State Police. He is also a founding member of the International Association of Chiefs of Police, Law Enforcement Information Managers Section. In 2000, he stated:

> We are just beginning to realize the significance of what is happening. There is not one — I repeat not one — area of the enforcement culture that will go untouched. The very essence of how we do business has been impacted through greater communications and information sharing. Over the next 15 to 20 years you will see the greatest redirection, reorganization and modification of policing since Sir Robert Peel and the Metropolitan Police.

Luddites in policing beware: the train is leaving the station. In fact, the IT train has jumped the rail tracks and has taken off on the information superhighway. It is imperative that IT becomes a prime consideration in all aspects of the public safety service delivery chain. Properly implemented systems will:

- Increase the ability of the police to respond to, and provide assistance in, emergency and non-emergency situations
- Increase police officer safety
- Increase the numbers of criminals being identified, apprehended, and convicted
- Decrease administration and operating costs

If these opportunities seem improbable, then an examination of the commercial sector, where key implementations of IT have resulted in significant competitive advantages, can be used as evidence. For example:

3

1. The Internet — Dell Computer has implemented a ordering process that eliminates selling sales overhead. It even designs customized Websites for large customers that allow purchases to be made at negotiated custom discounts. This allows customers to deploy new technologies faster and more efficiently. Combined with this is a sophisticated, just-in-time delivery process where an Internet order is delivered to the factory floor and the product is built almost immediately. Dell can receive customer payments before it has to pay its suppliers — literally unheard of for a manufacturing company. Customer service is further enhanced through online support.
2. Data Warehouse — Wal-Mart utilizes a high capacity data network that overnight amalgamates all of its sales information into a multi-terabyte data warehouse. The information is combined with local community demographics and answers the key questions of who is buying what, where, and when. Over 5000 manufacturers participate in Wal-Mart's Retail Link system over the Internet, and some even handle their own distribution.
3. Mobile Computing — Prudential Insurance Company provided laptop computers to over 11,000 insurance agents and field managers at a cost of about $100 million. Selling policies, updating policies, reporting payments, settling claims, and keeping up with industry news all are accomplished more quickly and more efficiently with computers in the field.

What do these examples have to do with law enforcement? This book will outline several examples that parallel the commercial applications. For example:

1. The Internet — Many law enforcement agencies have public information posted on their Websites. In addition to programs and crime statistics, some even allow queries into their operational systems. The Hillsborough County Sheriff's Office (Tampa, FL) provides real-time motor vehicle accident updates and the Website also allows access to its jail records database (Figure 1.1). Any Internet user can make an inquiry as to who is currently in jail and if a specific individual has been arrested in the county. Even if only a partial name is available, the Web page will return a list of inmates matching the criteria specified in the search.
2. Data Warehouse — The Los Angeles County Consolidated Criminal History Reporting System (CCHRS) employs a data warehouse with over 200 million records. It serves over 10,000 users and can retrieve a complete criminal history in less than 2.5 seconds. The system receives inputs from over 50 law enforcement agencies, 62 additional authorities (railroad and university patrols), 21 city attorney/prosecutor offices, and

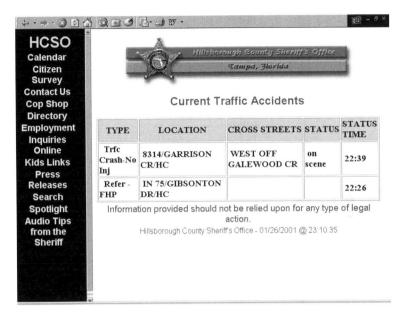

Figure 1.1 The Hillsborough County Sheriff's Office has a Website that shows current traffic accident locations.

24 municipal court districts. Criminal courts can assemble complete case histories. On the street level, investigators can query the massive database with partial descriptions as well as learn if another agency is investigating the subject.

3. Mobile Computing — In order to alleviate the congestion on its voice channels, the Philadelphia Police Department installed over 700 fixed-mount laptop computers equipped with wireless connectivity to law enforcement databases. Instead of having to wait for a dispatcher to respond, the officers on the street have "anytime, anywhere" access to data. In Nashville, the laptop computer software permits digital mug-shots to be accessed from police cruisers. Mobile computer work-stations are fast becoming a vehicle equipment standard, just as universal as the siren, the light bar, and the radio.

1.2   The Need to Understand IT

Clearly, there is a need for many in a police organization to understand IT and the ramifications for the law enforcement business process. The police manager in charge of information systems needs to know how to efficiently collect, store, and disseminate the vast stores of occurrence information captured every minute. The police supervisor must be able to articulate to the technical staff the needs of the beat officers who may be frustrated by the peculiarities of an application. The IT technical manager has a need for understanding how calls for service are handled and where streamlining can occur. For many small police agencies, one individual (the Chief) may fill all three of the above roles, in addition to many other operational duties. This book will cover many concepts which all revolve around the electronic capture, processing, storage, and access of information.

Specific reasons for why police leaders must be knowledgeable about IT include:

- Policing is no different than any other commercial or non-profit field. The general administrative component (bookkeeping, inventory, and human resource management) will increasingly be IT based.
- More and more policing tools have microprocessors built into them. Digital radios are fast becoming a standard. A newer example is the "smart" handgun, which uses an embedded microchip to determine if someone is authorized to pull the trigger.
- The Internet is fast supplanting the telephone network as the most practical and popular way for people and organizations to connect. The Web empowers the six "A's" of computing: Access Anywere, Anytime, to Anyone Authorized and Able.
- Computing supports knowledge work. Law enforcement officers need to collect information, share it with others, mine and analyze it, and use the knowledge for decision-making and problem-solving.

1.3   Information Is an Asset

In all organizations, skilled people are the most important resource. However, in order to carry out their mission, organizations also must utilize resources such as money, physical property, time, and information. For example, the electric utility would place great value on physical property such as the hydroelectric dam they built. In law enforcement, the obvious physical assets include the headquarters building and the fleet of vehicles. However, it must never be forgotten that the most important asset is human resources. People bring a vast repository of abilities, experience, and skills to the workplace.

Information is the next most important asset in law enforcement because information allows people to work smarter and faster. In fact, the combination of people and information becomes knowledge, and the concepts of knowledge management are further explored in Chapter 2 when community policing and IT are covered.

Despite the importance of IT, police agencies have lagged behind the private sector in bringing in new systems, and many still rely on labor-intensive paper processes. There is often a strong commitment to maintaining the paper-based workflows, and in the pre-digital era, these processes became entrenched as a means of keeping control of the daily occurrences and other activities.

It does not take a long-serving crime investigator to reach this conclusion: retrieving information from file cabinets full of paper reports is very cumbersome. While some information may be indexed, significant amounts of information are not. For example, an investigator may want to search for all instances of the words "Ford Pinto" because one was used as a suspect vehicle in a homicide. No stones can be left unturned in a major case, and there are not many suspects driving such a vehicle today. It is important to note that the homicide detective will not just search for violent suspects related to such a vehicle. The suspect may have been a witness or a victim in another occurrence. Notable examples of how related occurrences can result in the capture of criminals include:

- Son of Sam killer David Berkowitz, who was identified through a linkage to a parking ticket placed on his car after one of his murders.
- Oklahoma City bomber Timothy McVeigh, who was located after FBI agents ran his name on the federal U.S. criminal database, NCIC. The query returned information that he was under arrest in nearby Perry, OK, after a routine traffic stop led to a possession-of-handgun charge. He was just about to be released when FBI agents determined that he had rented the Ryder truck used in the bombing.

It seems that paperwork and policing are synonymous and this is a state of affairs that must be changed, given the many technology options that are not even cutting edge anymore. With paper, critical assets to policing — such as occurrence information — are being stored in a manner that inhibits their use. Too many reports are stored in different ways and are obtained from different sources. Many a police officer has received a look of aversion after asking an overworked records clerk for a file. It's a look of "I haven't time to get you what you need because I'm too busy typing, cataloging, and filing."

The fault does not lie with these harangued records personnel. There needs to be recognition among police administrators that the information police officers spend so much time collecting must be processed and archived in a manner that maximizes its subsequent use. In the pre-digital era, index cards were the answer. With today's technology being affordable and robust, information must be collected as digital text and be searchable by pre-defined fields, as well as through ad hoc queries.

In Practice: The Cost of Not Sharing Information

The Charlotte-Mecklenburg Police Department has an annual budget of over $110 million and employs 1400 officers. It has been a leader in the field of law enforcement IT and projects received high level sponsorship from former Chief Dennis Nowicki. At the managerial level, Major Piper Charles has spearheaded many initiatives. In 1998, with the participation of the University of North Carolina–Charlotte (UNCC), a survey was conducted of 600 line officers to determine what information sharing gaps exist. They determined:

- 75% need more information about felonies occurring in their area
- 90% state they get little feedback on case status or whether the suspect was identified, arrested, or prosecuted
- 50% feel they could improve their performance if they were better informed re: felony occurrences
- 60% claim that the data collected are not completely relevant to their needs
- 80% say they cannot easily access offense report data

Excerpts from the UNCC report written by Dr. Maureen Brown, UNCC, stated:

… the current systems are dysfunctional for meeting key business needs … Roughly three-quarters of a million dollars are spent annually to support the inefficient and ineffective technological infrastructure … In short, the current technology thwarts any ability to deliver efficient and effective policing services ….

Source: Charles, Piper, Aligning Information Technology with Community Policing Initiatives, Presentation at IACP Law Enforcement Information Managers Conference, 1998.

Despite today's technology environment, many manual processes still exist in law enforcement. Perhaps this is attributable to the slow pace of innovation in policing, and another factor may be the high costs of IT. Borrowing again the refrain from the community policing movement, the train is leaving the station — but it is not too late to get on board.

A law enforcement agency that does not consider the strategic importance of IT will soon be considered mismanaged. It is more costly — in terms of wasted staff hours and missed opportunities to identify criminals — to not automate.

1.4 Barriers to Information Use

There is a caveat attached to electronic information storage. Not only can these systems give employees easier access to information, but they open the door for other interested parties, such as defense lawyers, organized criminals, and disgruntled current and former employees, to quickly obtain large amounts of information which can be easily distributed. For this reason, law enforcement officers will have a natural reluctance to freely contribute all of their information.

In the past, truly sensitive information could be stored under literal "lock and key." As information becomes digitized, this is not a viable option unless there is a desire for no one to ever use it. Hackers are also a major risk as formerly physically isolated systems now have e-mail and Internet gateways that can be exploited. A common refrain from the U.S. National Infrastructure Protection Center (NIPC) is "the only completely secure system is the system that cannot be accessed by anyone." In addition to hardware and software protections (firewalls, network intrusion detectors), security rules are needed such as right to know (adequate security clearance) and need to know (a legitimate reason for viewing the information), and audit trails are important since it is often people who are the weakest security link.

While workers in the private sector regularly use collaborative tools such as Lotus Notes to exchange ideas and conclusions, there is an inherent reluctance for crime investigators (at least today) to engage in similar electronic discussions on crime suspects and criminal intelligence. Perhaps this can be attributed to the secretive and sensitive nature of police work. For example, there are many channels that can be used to facilitate information sharing other than a face-to-face meeting. The options include e-mail, fax, written letters, voice mail, electronic bulletin boards, and videoconferencing. However, the unique characteristics of law enforcement, and perhaps the slow pace of change, mean that face-to-face meetings have remained as the most accepted method of exchanging certain types of information.

There are many organizations that have made partial progress in bringing in automated systems for sharing information. In his book, *The Crime Fighter,* former New York Police Deputy Commissioner Jack Maple commented on the number of unconnected systems that were in existence in the New York Police Department.

> In the NYPD of early 1994, not many detectives had access to all nineteen data systems due in part to concerns that corrupt cops might sell information back to the criminals, but mostly because catching crooks was not the Department's top priority.

Maple felt that that the NYPD's Management Information Services Division lived up to its reputation as "an enemy of management, information, and service" since it held back system access codes (passwords and user IDs). At one point, he ordered that the codes be distributed and found out that the MIS division only released codes to the Midtown precinct. The other 75 precincts were left in the "dark ages." Maple did not solely blame the MIS division for the problems. He found fault with end users as well and commented:

> You would think that detectives would not have to be told that information already captured somewhere else in the criminal justice system could be useful to an investigation, but they often don't know what's in these systems and they are almost never trained how to go in and get it. That's why in every city I go to, one of the first things I do is find out what kind of systems are available to the police and whether anybody is using them. Not only do we then distribute a summary of what's on the computers, but the checklists we give to the detectives include check-offs for the systems that should be used in each type of investigation.

1.5   The Scope of IT

For the purposes of this book, IT will encompass:

1. **Hardware** — computers, workstations, printers, laptops, wireless and wireline networks, personal digital assistants (PDAs), routers, storage devices, and other physical things that process information
2. **Software** — end-user applications and operating systems (an example is a word processor for keying in an occurrence report)
3. **Systems** — an integrated combination of software and hardware that allows an organization to automate a business process

Basic IT functions that span the above three areas can be illustrated through the example of the serving of a traffic citation as illustrated in Table 1.1.

1.6   The Structure of IT Resources

Examinations of annual reports and police agency Websites frequently show a traditional approach to organizing the technology departments. The traditional separation of the line departments follows functional areas such as:

Table 1.1   Current and Cutting-Edge Applications in Law Enforcement

Function	Current	Cutting Edge
Capture		
Obtain information	An officer relays information verbally to a dispatcher who types the information into a terminal	A bar code on a driver's license is scanned and the details are automatically recorded into pre-defined fields on a mobile computer deployed in the police vehicle
Transmit		
Move information from one location to another	Information is sent from the dispatcher terminal, over a local network, to the state or provincial switch which is connected to local and federal databases	The information is automatically sent from the vehicle through a wireless connection. Results are returned (registered owner of a vehicle) and the results are used to spawn new queries (NCIC or CPIC query on the registered owner). The location of the stop is determined from an automatic vehicle location (AVL) system
Store		
Save information on a disk drive for later retrieval	The traffic stop details are recorded in the computer-aided dispatch (CAD)	The offender details are sent to a regional data warehouse which serves as a multi-jurisdictional investigative information repository
Retrieve		
Find the information needed from the disk drive	Users from the same agency access the data stored in the CAD system	The "islands of information" that exist in many areas are eliminated as investigators quickly access regional, state, and federal databases to narrow the search for suspects to a crime
Manipulate		
Computer processor performs calculations	A query is made to find all traffic stops that fit a user-specified criterion	Data mining techniques correlate CAD data with other sources (traffic flow, accident locations) to help identify patterns and areas requiring targeted enforcement
Display		
Show the information on a screen or printout	Lists of CAD incidents are printed and passed around	Electronic presentations, including maps and other graphics, are assembled for high level executive briefings, and the material is also posted to an agency intranet for comments by others

- Communications — The 911 and non-emergency call-taking centers were responsible for working with the telephone companies, handling systems such as private branch exchanges, and acquiring and implementing voice radio and CAD systems.

- Information or Records — The masses of paper collected daily by law enforcement agencies would be sent to a centralized unit that would sort, perhaps enter data, route, and file the endless streams of reports. Some agencies use a "call in" dictation method of reporting, and data entry operators must be continually on standby.
- Technology — Computers are ubiquitous in most police agencies. They may or may not be networked and the application software may be simply common, off-the-shelf end-user productivity tools. Word processing and electronic mail are important tools. Technology managers usually come from technical disciplines such as engineering or computer science.

1.7   The Chief Information Officer (CIO)

In today's environment of converging technologies, the traditional separation just described will encounter difficulties in serving the organization as a whole. All facets of computing and telecommunications should fall under a broad IT umbrella. For example, radio communications, which traditionally have been delivered as part of the dispatch and call-taking center operations, must be included under IT. Moreover, the business processes, which encompass document flows, work assignments, and operating procedures, must also be considered under the scope of IT.

In business, this has been recognized by the introduction of CIOs who have backgrounds in general management and business operations, rather than in technology. These executives have responsibilities such as to:

- Understand the business
- Formulate information policy — developing and approving IT strategies
- Evaluate technology directions — understanding trends and their impact on the firm's business
- Introduce new technology
- Facilitate organizational change
- Find new ways to do business better
- Establish an IT infrastructure
- Implement an information vision and architecture
- Develop and nurture relationships with internal and external clients

Policing agencies are reaching the same conclusion on the need for CIOs. Organizations such as the Broward County Sheriff's Office (FL) and the

RCMP have formally appointed a CIO. In other agencies, the senior commander, who is in charge of the functional areas, is the de facto CIO, although the incumbent may not know this. In the computing field, there has been convergence with voice and data systems. In law enforcement, a similar convergence is needed in terms of the functional responsibilities. As an example, mobile computing involves linkages among CAD, radio, and information systems.

In Practice: A New CIO Is Announced

OTTAWA, May 7, 1999 — Demonstrating leadership in police information management, the Royal Canadian Mounted Police today named a chief information officer to its senior ranks. The RCMP is among only a few police organizations in North America to take this progressive step toward managing information as well as the technology, which supports its use. Assistant Commissioner John L'Abbé was appointed to the position and will be responsible for the task of helping police officers better access and use information.

"You can't fight organized crime — or any other crime — without organized information," said RCMP Commissioner Philip Murray. "Our new CIO is going to make sure that our information systems are compatible. In the past, information technology simply captured information. Today, we have to be able to extract the exact information we need easily."

Source: RCMP Website: www.rcmp-grc.ca.

1.8   How and Why IT Is Used

There are underlying service characteristics associated with law enforcement that explain how and why a process was automated. In addition, economic and business policy theories, specifically Michael Porter's value chain concept, help provide an underlying rationale for automation in policing.

1.8.1   The Service Sector

Whether it is law enforcement or any other line of business, the implementation of IT can be categorized under a framework that answers the question, "why was this process automated?" According to the National Research Council publication, *Information Technology in the Service Society,* these uses are:

1.   Basic Infrastructure for Communications and Data Handling — This has often been approached as "the cost of being in business." At a basic

level, people need to be able to phone the police for assistance. The system needed may range from a single 7-digit business phone line to a multiple-trunked digital 911 switch with automatic call distribution and other capabilities. On the administration side, staff need word-processing facilities, e-mail, and other personal productivity software packages. Almost all agencies require links to national crime databases such as NLETS, NCIC, and CPIC. There is wide interpretation as to what is basic and what is not. Many agencies see a CAD system as being a basic need while others still rely on paper dispatch cards.

2. Mandated Systems — All agencies are required to submit statistical data (UCR/NIBRS), as well as retain occurrence records. Given these needs, IT investment was seen as a means of reducing the costs associated with reporting compliance.

3. Cost Reduction — Automating repetitive transactions such as in large record-keeping functions can save money with reduced clerical staff. Reduced errors also save money.

4. Specific New Products or Opportunities — IT can enable the creation of new products or services. For example, a database registry of private business and residential alarm installations can be seen as a new service for a police agency. Not only are problem alarms identified, but costs can be charged to repeat false alarm offenders thus making it more compelling for these businesses to repair faulty alarms and reduce their false alarm calls to the police. Chapter 2 outlines the possibilities for increased public involvement (community policing) using the Internet.

5. Improvements in Quality — Crime victims may be phoning to inquire about the status of their cases. A records management system can allow for an immediate response. Paper files require time to access and are more time consuming to find, review, and forward. A word-processed report, with call-pathing (based on the incident, the officer is prompted to describe critical elements), is more accurate and useful than an inconsistent, handwritten report.

6. Major Strategic Innovations — A relatively recent development is the pervasiveness and global networking of the Internet. With it brings an opportunity for new citizen contact processes. This ranges from "calling" the police through an Internet e-mail, to a feedback mechanism where information can be obtained in relation to a complaint, before human interactions need to occur. Examples are logging on a Web page with the particulars of a problem, and waiting for an e-mail response back.

In Practice: The Legal and Societal Context of Policing and IT Priorities

In egalitarian Finland, the amount of traffic fine is determined by the wealth of an offender. In 2000, a Finnish mobile Internet entrepreneur made headlines all over the world when he was fined the equivalent of $70,000 U.S. for speeding in his Ferrari. His public comment was, "The road was wide and I was feeling good. All I can do now is hope that my fine is used wisely."

To enable Finnish police officers to determine traffic penalties quickly, a speeding fine calculator with a link to the tax administrator's database has been developed. The system uses a short message service (SMS)-enabled mobile phone that has access to the European GSM public cellular network. Text messages of up to 140 to 160 characters are stored and forwarded from SMS centers. When an officer stops an offender, details such as social security number and date of birth are obtained. These are entered by an officer into the mobile phone and in 10 to 20 seconds, data are returned on the offender such as salary, the value of personal assets, and dependents. Based on this information, the size of the fine is calculated. The Finnish police deploy 2500 mobile phones and in 2000, 302,700 traffic fine calculator queries were made.

Sources: Rippa, Heikki and Sillanpaa, Juhani, Making the Business Case for E-Commerce in Police and Public Safety Services, Presentation at World e-Police Conference, London, England, January 29, 2001; Brown-Humes, Christopher, Flying Finn pays for life in the fast lane, *Financial Times*, November 24, 2000, Website: www.ft.com.

1.8.2   The Value Chain, and Lessons from the Commercial Sector

In his book, *Competitive Advantage,* Michael Porter proposed the concept of the value chain, which describes how a firm can take raw inputs and turn them into a product that others will demand. His theories have relevance to why IT is important in public safety. One of his main ideas is that a firm can create a competitive advantage by performing its value activities at a lower cost than its rivals, or in a way that provides its customers with an added value or service. Organizations must have distinct value activities in order to support the business. These can be considered as inbound and outbound, as well as primary and support. The primary activities include obtaining supplies, manufacturing a product, delivering the product to customers, promoting the product, and repairing and maintaining the product. The support activities provide the organizational, human resources, and technologies that support the primary activities (see Figure 1.2).

IT can support an organization in all of the value activities. For primary activities, an automated warehouse system can support materials handling, a manufacturing control system can streamline the production process, and

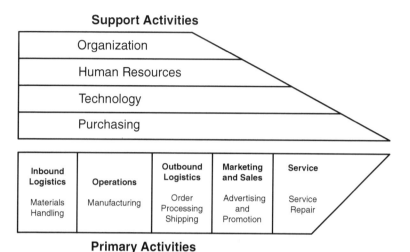

Figure 1.2 Support activities and the value chain.

data mining tools can focus the marketing efforts. With support activities, the use of e-mail and personal productivity applications will improve organizational operations, a skills database will improve human resources practices, and online links to suppliers will improve procurements. According to Porter, the three ways to create and sustain competitive advantage are through:

1. Low cost leadership — The firm has lower production costs.
2. Product differentiation — A product has a better image, quality level, or service level.
3. Market specialization — A firm is able to concentrate on a specific niche market.

Commercial organizations have adopted IT in order to survive and prosper. Those that are successful have used their information-based strategies to achieve dominance in their market segments. Those that have lagged have seen their market positions eroded or wiped out, and they are often swallowed up by the strong firms or go out of business.

The applicability of Porter's concepts to the non-competitive environment of law enforcement may initially appear tenuous. First, it must be acknowledged that private security can be a competitor to law enforcement services. An example is the proliferation of gated communities, with their private guards and sophisticated electronic surveillance systems. Residents in these communities (the wealthier and more powerful) will be less inclined to see their taxes increased to fund general police services. Nonetheless, private security services must not be viewed as a threat or competitor that is completely analogous to what is found in the corporate for-profit world. If fact, many lower-level public protection tasks (random patrols, monitoring public places) can be more economically delivered using private security officers rather than through higher trained and higher paid law enforcement officers. In recognition of this, the Canadian CPIC network allows the public to make stolen property, vehicle, and license plate queries over the Internet (see Chapter 2, Figure 2.5). This is an important tool that private security firms utilize, especially when patrolling public parking lots, and this also reduces calls to the police for suspicious vehicles.

Second, although law enforcement agencies strive — at least in theory — to cooperate and assist each other, there have been examples of amalgamation or larger agencies swallowing up smaller ones. An automated and efficient agency can provide lower cost and higher quality police services to a community, than an agency stuck with inefficient manual processes. There have been many cases where police agencies have been merged, regionalized, or disbanded. This is quite similar to the commercial sector, where frequently, strong companies swallow up poorly performing competitors.

There are also many examples of how value activities in law enforcement are supported by IT. To begin with, every public sector agency has the same support activity needs as a private sector agency. In fact, many larger agencies have adopted enterprise resource planning systems, such as PeopleSoft or SAP, to automate financial planning and human resource management. In addition, e-mail and office suite applications are a must-have (word processing, spreadsheet, etc.). Table 1.2 illustrates the many IT applications used in law enforcement that support primary value activities.

In Practice: Inbound Logistics and Crime Intelligence Software

During a major investigation, many thousands of tips, leads, reports, and other fragments of information will stream in to the investigators. Michael Porter would call these inputs "raw materials." How they are handled will have an effect on the performance levels in the "Operations Activity" which is the deductive reasoning process that constitutes an investigation. Powerful software tools are used to manage the data flow. An example is the Special Investigative Unit Support System (SIUSS) which contains over 2000 data fields and screens. The analytical algorithms and database structure permit search methods and linkage analysis that would take hundreds of hours to produce manually. In addition, incident management tools and event chronologies allow investigators to analyze alibi and MO information. Graphical representations can be produced that depict relationships between suspects, associates, and event.

Source: www.anteon.com

Table 1.2   Law Enforcement Primary Value Activities

Primary Value Activity	Use of Information Technology
Inbound logistics	The raw materials that an officer utilizes to solve a community problem or a crime consist of information. In the case of a large-scale investigation, numerous reports and tips will cascade in and the sorting of the data into useful information can be supported through an IT database application.
Operations	Every day, many thousands of calls to 911 are received. Officers must be dispatched and coordinated in their responses, and computer-aided dispatch systems provide an efficient command and control structure.
Outbound logistics	The output from a patrol officer may be an occurrence report. This serves as the input for a follow-up investigator who will now have to assemble clues in order to identify the perpetrator. A records management system (RMS) facilitates the transfer and processing of an output from a patrol officer to the input for a detective.
Marketing and sales	The police do not just react to crimes. Public safety is a theme in most mission statements and crime prevention is a form of social behavior marketing with the objective of lowering crime. Websites can be used to disseminate crime prevention messages. The National Alliance for Gang Investigators Associations' Website (see Figure 1.3) includes tips for parents to combat gang recruitment.
After-sale service	An actual investigation may be concluded but the victim may be left wondering what transpired with the case. A modern RMS can provide an officer with a quick overview of what actions were taken, and by whom. The victim can be quickly advised of the outcome.

1.9   The Call-for-Service Process

The preceding discussions offered a perspective on why some operations are automated and why others are not. There are obvious reasons why an Automated Teller Machine can replace a bank teller, but this application cannot be transformed to a computerized kiosk replacing a neighborhood foot patrol officer.

In recapping the applications of IT, we can use an everyday process in law enforcement, calling for service (Figure 1.4), as a basis for illustrating how and why IT is used and how this book will address each topic. The example is chosen to illustrate where many technical concepts are located in this book.

The steps can be described as follows. A 911 call is received in the dispatch center. A call taker pre-fills a CAD system incident entry mask with information from the E-911 database, which includes location, calling number, and time. The incident is passed to a dispatcher with a CAD screen that shows radio system and map information. The CAD system references the

Figure 1.3 Prevention for Parents information on the National Alliance for Gang Investigators Associations' Website: www.nagai.org/kids_and_gangs.htm.

Figure 1.4 The call-for-service process.

status of units in the field with information updated through AVL transmitters and receivers integrated to the radio system. It also searches for units with special criteria based on the type of call (perhaps a dog handler is needed) and locates the unit closest to the call. The dispatcher confirms the CAD system recommendation and assigns a unit with a data message. The assigned field unit confirms the dispatcher notification by sending an "en route" message. Before arriving at the scene, the assigned unit reviews the premise history and requests a mug shot of the suspect. At the scene, the victim is interviewed and the report is data-entered at the source of the call and transmitted to the records system. The unit then indicates it is available for more calls. The dispatcher notes the location of the unit through the AVL and directs it to another patrol sector to balance field coverage.

Step 1   Call Received and Processed

This first stage of obtaining police assistance is addressed in Chapter 9 where wireline computing infrastructure is covered. For the past 80 years, the public-switched telephone network (PSTN) was the main entry point for public access to the police. Over the past 25 years, 911 and enhanced 911 systems were installed. Currently, wireline calls are fast becoming supplanted by cellular (wireless) 911 calls. Over the next 10 years, the reliance on the telephone may change as Internet-based technologies take hold. Modern networks have become essential in enabling information dissemination, and their uses are described.

Step 2   Officers Dispatched

Chapter 6 explains CAD. Chapters 10 and 11 cover wireless information transfer. Chapter 10 focuses on voice information (traditional land mobile radio systems) and Chapter 11 covers wireless data.

Step 3   Investigation and Report Completion
(Storing Information and Using Information)

Chapter 5 covers database technologies. The retention and access to information that is collected is an important part of IT and Chapter 7 covers RMSs. This sets the stage for Chapter 8, which provides an overview of mobile computing. A central theme in Chapter 8 is how anytime, anywhere access to IT resources will increase the efficiency of law enforcement agencies.

Of course none of these systems can be used unless managerial efforts are made to acquire and implement them. Chapter 3 covers the business process changes needed to capitalize on the investment in IT, and Chapter 4 addresses the acquisition and implementation of IT. Chapter 2 is perhaps the most important chapter in the book and addresses the use of IT in the support of community policing.

1.10   End-of-Chapter Comments

This chapter has outlined how law enforcement agencies must place great importance on their modernization efforts and not lag behind the private sector. Many of the commercial applications that have been implemented have already seen use in law enforcement. IT must be used to optimize the provision of services and there are many reasons for automation in the service sector. In addition, the theories associated with the value chain concept, which were originally based on for-profit enterprises, can also be applied as a means of understanding the non-profit police service delivery chain. It is clear that strategic uses of IT can lead to lower costs and higher quality work being performed.

References

Alter, Stephen, *Information Systems, A Management Perspective*, 2nd Edition, Benjamin/Cummings Publishing, Menlo Park, CA, 1996.

Anteon-CITI, LLC, Website (SIUSS): www.anteon.com.

Brown-Humes, Christopher, Flying Finn pays for life in the fast lane, *Financial Times*, November 24, 2000, Website: www.ft.com.

Charles, Piper, Aligning Information Technology with Community Policing Initiatives, Presentation at 1998 IACP Law Enforcement Information Managers Conference, San Diego, CA.

National Center for State Courts, *Court Technology Bulletin*, 9(2), 1997.

Hillsborough County Sheriff's Office, Website: www.hcso.tampa.fl.us/.

Holstein, William J., Sieder, Jill Jordan, et al., Data-crunching Santa, *U.S. News & World Report*, 125(24), 44, December 21, 1998.

Hulseberg, Paul, FBI Information Security and Cyber Crime Panel, International Association of Chiefs of Police, Law Enforcement Information Managers Conference, Denver, CO, May 25, 2000.

Information Technology in the Service Society, National Research Council, Washington, D.C., 1994.

Maple, Jack, *The Crime Fighter — Putting the Bad Guys Out of Business*, Doubleday, New York, 1999.

Mullholland, David, IACP's law enforcement information management section: technology training and education opportunities, *The Police Chief*, March 2000.

National Alliance for Gang Investigators Association, Website: www.nagai.org/kids_and_gangs.htm.

Porter, Michael, Competitive advantage, in *Competitive Advantage: Creating and Sustaining Superior Performance*, Free Press, New York, 1985.

RCMP, Website: www.rcmp-grc.ca.

Rippa, Heikki and Sillanpaa, Juhani, Making the Business Case for E-Commerce in Police and Public Safety Services, Presentation at World e-Police Conference, London, England, January 29, 2001.

The Weight of Evidence — Special Report/Oklahoma City, Vol. 149, No. 17, *Time Magazine*, April 28, 1997.

IT in Support of Community Policing

2

2.1 Introduction

Up until the 1980s, the "professional policing model" was the dominant approach to delivering police services. This involved a focus, if not a preoccupation, on responding to the ever-increasing number of 911 calls for service. The prevailing operational philosophy was for the police to act as detached professionals who would deter criminals through:

- Random patrols
- The associated capability of rapid response to calls for service achieved through technology tools such as 911, CAD, and mobile radio systems

Inherent problems with the professional policing model became apparent as higher workloads and crime rates overwhelmed the police — especially larger agencies — which drowned in the sea of 911 calls.

New types of thinking the community policing movement began to emerge in the early 1980s, led by academics such as Herman Goldstein, Robert Trojanowicz, and George Kelling, and law enforcement executives such as Lee Brown (Houston, TX, New York, NY), David Couper (Madison, WI), and Chris Braiden (Edmonton, Alberta).

Community policing was not a passing fad as many detractors predicted, and it remains the dominant model for service delivery for the foreseeable future. This chapter will outline the problems with past technology implementations, and will discuss how IT, when aligned with an organization's mission and service (business) strategies, can provide immense benefits in the community policing era.

2.2 The Roots of Modern Policing

Chapter 1 opened with a statement that asserted that IT will bring about the biggest changes to policing since Sir Robert Peel. The significance of this reference becomes apparent when it is considered that the form of policing that is practiced in North America and much of the Western world is derived from the nine principles of policing introduced in 1829 in London, England by Sir Robert Peel (the Appendix lists these nine principles). These principles have been resurrected recently by many community policing theorists and great attention has been paid to Peel's principles, two of which are:

1. The ability of the police to perform their duties is dependent on public approval of police existence, actions, behavior, and the ability of the police to secure and maintain public respect.
2. The test of police efficiency is the absence of crime and disorder, not the visible evidence of police action dealing with them.

Former Oakland Police Chief August Vollmer's policing philosophies from the 1920s and 1930s were similar to Peel's principles. Unfortunately, both Vollmer and Peel's ideas gave way in the 1940s to a different way of thinking. These theories are now referred to as the "reform style" or "professional policing model" and the movement was led by former Chicago Superintendent of Police, O.W. Wilson, who ironically was a Vollmer protégé. Wilson's ideas achieved dominance in the 20th century, until supplanted by community policing philosophies.

2.3   The Professional Policing Era

After World War II urban sprawl led to the greater utilization of police cars and radios. This was an appealing mobilization model and allowed police agencies to keep pace with their growing service areas. The main leaders of the professional policing era were also referred to as reformers. A notable reformer was O.W. Wilson who saw other benefits to mobilization. Wilson felt that preventative patrol (undirected patrol officer time) and rapid response would create a feeling among criminals and people of police omnipresence, and this view became widely accepted.

Wilson was not an advocate of people contact. He felt coziness with people bred graft and corruption and was quite happy to have officers stay in their cars with the windows rolled up. He encouraged policies such as frequent beat changes so that officers would not get to know people in their neighborhoods too well. The influential Wilson believed in tight central control and professionalism. The essential preoccupation of all police reformers was control, and to ensure that individual officers carried out the priorities of police departments, demand was channeled centrally through 911 call centers. The Boston Police introduced 911 in the late 1960s. When citizens persisted in calling the neighborhood precinct officers, the solution from the department was to cut off the lines.

In addition to 911 systems and mobile radio, IT in the professional policing era was used to design beats and calculate, using complex mathematical models, how many officers should be on duty and how many should be allocated per district. Programs such as the Patrol Car Allocation Model (PCAM) were developed through the Rand Institute. Beats were designed using complex models based on the queuing theory that were described by MIT Professor Richard Larsen in his book *Urban Police Patrol Analysis,* published in 1972. It was felt that the models would optimize the deployment of police officers and this would maximize the probability of catching criminals through preventative patrol, and minimize the police response times to priority and routine calls.

2.4   Questioning the Reformers

In the 1970s, research studies into response times began to appear, and they challenged the prevailing wisdom. One study showed that when the police arrive within 5 minutes of a call involving a crime, the probability of an arrest is 60%. When the response time exceeds 5 minutes, the probability drops to below 20%. Consequently, many law enforcement agencies made great efforts to ensure delays do not occur in the parts of the process they control. The thinking was that automated systems (911, ANI/ALI, and CAD) could reduce the dispatch delays, and that the optimal deployment of units engaging in random patrols would reduce the response times after the dispatch. As found by James Auten, the real delays occur in the part of the process that the police have no control over: the reporting process. Research in the Wilmington (DE) Bureau of Police showed a median reporting delay by victims and witnesses of 10 minutes. A similar study in the Syracuse (NY) Police Department showed that there was a delay of over 10 minutes in 70% of the calls. These studies were conducted prior to the widespread usage of cellular phones, and these calling delays may be less pronounced today.

The professional policing era was colorfully described by former Edmonton (AB) Police Superintendent Chris Braiden, who noted that the invention of the telephone contributed to the police becoming more alienated from the community. Before the telephone, when citizens needed a police officer, they had to actually go out and look for one, and most officers were deployed on routine foot patrol in neighborhoods. The telephone meant that the police could very easily be summoned to homes, and the police, instead of focusing on the order maintenance ideas that Sir Robert Peel talked about, became more embroiled in people's private lives. Officers began to encounter ordinary people less, and problem people more. The automobile and the mobile radio magnified this distance and the police had even less direct contact with ordinary people. Both officers and citizens missed out on the social benefits of normal, non-crisis interactions. This contributed to a greater sense of public alienation from the police, and police alienation from the public. The consequences of this were in direct contradiction of Peel's principle of the police needing to maintain public approval and support.

The introduction of CAD systems and in-vehicle computers was a key milestone of the professional policing era. Braiden noted with irony that the status code of "in service" meant being in the car, near the radio and the computer terminal. "Out of service" meant being away from the car, dealing with potential problems or spending time with witnesses and victims. The CAD systems could return detailed printouts on patrol activity including undirected patrol time. Many agencies tried to meet the professional policing era targets of 33 to 50% undirected time so that the officers could respond to calls more quickly and be ready for what Braiden called the "big catch." Consequently, "in service" was seen as good, and "out of service," which involved being away from the car and computer and dealing with people, was seen as bad. Technology contact became the primary focus and people contact was seen as secondary.

Another major driving force in the professional policing era was Uniform Crime Reporting (UCR) which provided statistical report cards on the performance of agencies. UCR gave rise to a crime-reporting mentality, and computer systems were used to generate a multitude of statistics such as response times, arrest rates, and crime rates. Criminologists Banas and Trojanowicz observed that UCR demands became a driver for technology changes. They noted:

> The Uniform Crime Reports and associated measures dictated forms of structural change and technological innovation which had little to do with the dynamic and boundless social environment of policing and much to do with the insular criteria as defined by command officers.

Former New York Commissioner William Bratton talked about the professional policing era thinking, which he encountered early in his career:

> In November 1976 when I was assigned to the commissioner's office, the latest concepts were rapid response, mobility, technology, and professionalism. The emergency number 911 had come into being in the early seventies and had completely changed the face of American policing, putting a premium on "the three R's: rapid response, random patrols, and reactive investigation.

Bratton lamented the increasing fear factor of citizens, and the distancing between the police and the community — yet reformers would point out that crime and response statistics showed the police were doing an excellent job. He talked about a repeat 911 caller and wrote:

We would send a two-man sector car, get there in five minutes, kick the kids off the corner, notify the dispatcher, and leave. The kids would come back and the old man (the reportee) would call — always anonymously — we would arrive ... 1300 times. Nobody ever tried to locate the caller or solve the problem.

While 911 and CAD systems had many benefits, the problems these IT tools brought with them were very significant.

Call-driven policing became the tail (IT) wagging the dog (police operations). If an officer did not respond promptly to a call, citizens would complain and newspaper headlines would report on the police failures. Consequently, many departments, particularly in larger jurisdictions, became primarily reactive with their officers focusing on the never-ending task of clearing the "call holding" queue that a CAD system can so vividly display.

Today, agencies must use these same technology tools to manage their work (business process reengineering) so that officer time is freed up for crime prevention and community interaction work. A CAD system can be used to offload non-priority calls in a differential service response model, and this will divert a large proportion of the demand for police services to quieter hours. This is an example of the proper use of IT: the dog (operations) wagging the tail (IT tools). Another option is to refer callers to community policing centers where the caller can interact with volunteers, or where they can make appointments with community-based police officers.

In Practice: Lee Brown and Community Policing in the Houston Police Department

In the early 1990s, Chief Lee Brown wanted to invent a new style of policing for the Houston Police Department. He stated, "The CAD system was designed, developed, and implemented to support the traditional style of policing. Not what we're in the process of doing." He questioned the effectiveness of the primary police tactics of random patrol and rapid response. "I don't want our officers driven by 911," he said. "I want a system that will let us manage our time." His changes drove him straight on a collision course with the new CAD which, according to Deputy Chief Betsy Watson, did not allow officers to work as intelligently and as flexibly as they ought to. Watson wanted beat cars to handle as many of their area's calls as possible, so officers would be familiar with local problems. CAD made that hard: it wanted calls answered fast and would call in cars from other beats if it had to. She wanted related calls to go to one unit but CAD would assign ten burglaries on the same block to ten different units. Beat cars couldn't even look at the calls holding since their access to the pending incidents queue was cut off to prevent "cherry picking" of calls.

In order to make the CAD more responsive to neighborhood policing, meetings were convened with data processing, dispatch, and field operations personnel who proposed call stacking to facilitate Neighborhood Oriented Policing (NOP). The data processing staff and the dispatchers were opposed to call stacking. One said, "Stacking calls doesn't allow the system to manage itself, it allows officers to manage the system," and agreement on the major issues could not be achieved. In 1991, Lee Brown left for New York and Betsy Watson became Chief. She stated that she wasn't sure CAD was salvageable. "It's a rigid system. There's no room for 'what ifs.' Each officer is in service or out of service. No dispatching system will ever make NOP happen. What we need to do is de-emphasize the system; it's far less important, in my mind, than what we've made it. What we need to do is retune our thinking and our priorities so that people drive what's happening and the system responds to it."

Source: Kennedy, David, Computer-Aided Dispatching in Houston, Texas, Case Study, Kennedy School of Government, Harvard College, 1990.

2.5 Community Policing Is Not Anti-Technology

Community policing has often been described as a return to the policing philosophies of Peel and Vollmer. Reformers thought that the police were liked because of their professionalism, rapid response and high clearance rates, and technology tools. These reasons meant little to the public, who liked the police for the human elements of talking and listening. Almost all law enforcement agencies have now instituted community policing and problem-solving philosophies, and it is important to note that IT has been proven as an enabler for the achievement of community policing goals.

In terms of overall research, there has not been a significant amount of attention focused on IT and community policing. However, criminologists David Carter and Robert Trojanowicz took pains to state that community policing is not anti-technology. They stated:

The goal should be to employ sophisticated and expensive technology where it will provide the greatest payback. The community policing officer is like the base of a funnel, using information filtered down from various "hi-tech" sources and providing information upward generated from his/her neighborhood beat. A misconception is that community policing is antithetical to hi-tech policing, that the two conflict, like fire and water. Instead, if functioning properly, they should mesh. For example, a technique like criminal profiling obviously falls into the hi-tech approach. Using sophisticated computers, the FBI can profile a likely perpetrator and create a description of what that person is like. Yet, obviously, that information still requires identifying the individual, finding out where he or she lives, and apprehending the suspect. Consider the advantage a community policing officer, so familiar with bad actors in his beat area, has in employing that information to make an arrest. Because of community trust, the officer will have information superior to that of a centralized agency like the Federal Bureau of Investigation.

William Bratton achieved international recognition for his community policing efforts in New York City, and he clearly understood the benefits of IT. When he became commissioner in Boston, he was told there was two million dollars available and the money could be used to put more officers on the street. He felt that without modern support the officers would not have an impact and he argued for systems over cops. He estimated that the equivalent of 80 more officers would accrue from technology and he considered this to be a priority in his community policing plan, along with neighborhood beat officers and other community-based policing projects.

2.6 IT Supports the Mission of Community Policing

There are many ways that IT can be used as an enabler for community policing. Many uses support individual officers since these are the practitioners and frontline linkages to the community. Some benefits are enablers for the whole organization. For example, almost all law enforcement organizations have mission statements that talk about how community policing promotes peace, order, and civility. The public needs a sense of security and also wants to be consulted about priorities. Many organizations have used Internet Web pages as a means of disseminating information on organizational priorities (annual reports, operational plans), and they obtain feedback through e-mails and interactive message boards.

In Practice: Chicago Police and Web Maps

In October 2000, the Chicago Police debuted an interactive Website that allows the public to view crime maps. The primary purpose of Citizen ICAM (Information Collection for Automated Mapping) was to get more people involved in community policing, and, in the first 2 weeks, 210,000 hits on the Website were recorded. The coordinator of the police technology unit, Sergeant Jonathan Levine, stated, "This reflects our commitment to citizens to give them access to information. One of the things we've been talking about is getting more tools for citizens to fight crime." A local member of a crime prevention board, Sandy Campbell, emphasized the need for the public to obtain information on crimes and stated, "Once you get this information, you can ask the police what they're doing to combat this. Are they beefing up patrols in the area? The whole idea is to identify problems and think of ways to cooperatively solve them. The police really do want citizens involved."

Source: Davis, Kevin, Web maps pinpoint crime activity, *USA Today*, November 6, 2000, Website: www.usatoday.com/life/cyber/tech/cti770.htm.

2.7   Process Reengineering Produces Resources for Community Policing

Many law enforcement managers argue that they do not have sufficient resources to deploy community-based officers. Workloads always seem to be going up while budgets remain the same or even shrink. While these managers may fail to see the long-term benefits, it is important to note that priority calls do need to be answered, and when arrests are made, the officers need sufficient time to process their cases. Technology can be used to increase the time officers spend on the frontlines, and in Chapter 8 applied examples of how mobile computing can enable this are described. In addition, Chapter 3 discusses process reengineering and will emphasize that one way to capitalize on the benefits of IT is to ensure slack resources that are freed up by IT are re-deployed elsewhere.

Former police administrator (and now consultant) James Lingerfelt calls technology a force multiplier. He notes that there are three ways to save time and money that can be applied to community policing:

1. Use technology to off-load work to other personnel. This could involve using a CAD system as the focal point of a call management program. Work can be sent to a telephone reporting unit that could handle complaints that do not require an actual police visit or immediate response.
2. Use technology to streamline work. Work can be moved to support services or it can be streamlined so it is more efficient and generates higher quality outputs.
3. Reduce the costs of support services and apply the savings (in people and dollars) to direct-service areas.

Administrative tasks can be automated. Law enforcement agencies have many services that consume staff time but also generate revenue. An example is a Freedom of Information request where a service fee could be charged using an online credit card payment process. An e-commerce capability streamlines the ordering and delivery process. Many jurisdictions, including

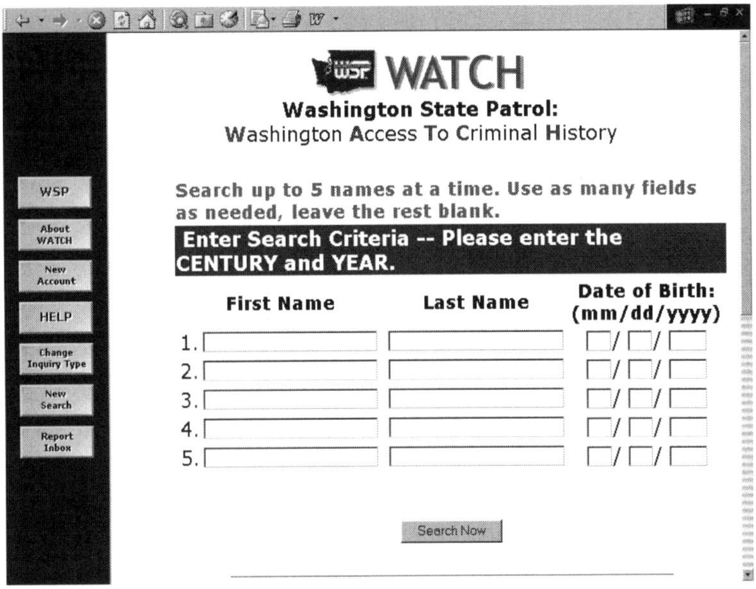

Figure 2.1 Washington State Patrol Website allows the public to make a $10.00 credit card payment and conduct a criminal record check: www.wa.gov/wsp/ reports/reports.htm.

North Carolina, Washington, and Texas, have implemented online e-commerce sites that allow the public to obtain criminal records after making a credit card payment (see Figure 2.1).

2.8 Law Enforcement Officers Are Knowledge Workers

The professional policing era concepts of "scientific management" were patterned after the writings of Frederick Taylor, who theorized that labor had little or no investment in work itself or the products. If left on their own, workers would malinger and/or get into trouble. Consequently, police work was routinized and officers had little or no discretion. Criminologist George Kelling wrote on how police reformers viewed line officers with disdain. While honesty, loyalty, and hard work were valued, intelligence was not. Most police agencies are still structured after Taylor's theories. For example, management in many organizations still wear white shirts while rank and file officers still wear blue.

The dawn of the information age has meant that the general work force is becoming knowledge-centered as opposed to physical labor-centered. The same trend is extended in law enforcement. Agencies that subscribe to community policing do not hire recruits based on their ability to run, shoot, and drive. They recruit officers for their education, intelligence, and interpersonal abilities. Problem solving, relationship building, counseling, and negotiation skills are now more important than physical strength and large size.

Community policing officers will need to establish a level of trust and acceptance in the communities they are assigned, and are expected to come up with order maintenance and crime prevention strategies that are not solely focused on apprehensions and arrests. They need to be able to function effectively with minimal supervision.

It was stated in Chapter 1 that people are the most important resource in law enforcement. Without people accessing it, data will remain in its original form of unused stacks of paper. The data only becomes information when it is accessible. Digitizing the text and permitting creative and remote online searches of the data are the best ways to create accessibility. Looking farther along this continuum, once the community officer, who is familiar with local trends, problems, and solutions, reviews and judges the information in a timely manner, it produces knowledge and wisdom.

2.8.1   Knowledge Work and Productivity

Community policing has led to a change in the work police officers perform. Compared to the professional policing era, where officers conducted random patrols waiting for the "big catch," far more officers today require access to information repositories so that they can make judgments on:

- Crime prevention activities that can be pursued
- Which problem resolution strategies are realistic
- What investigative avenues should be pursued
- Whether the actions taken have led to positive results

The greater percentage of knowledge workers in policing means that productivity is an important issue. In their article, "Knowledge Work Productivity," Davis and Naumann argue that knowledge workers have a set level of mental energy that is determined by their personal motivation levels and their work environment. If they spend significant amounts of time searching for information resources — such as pestering overworked records personnel for copies of paper reports — they have less mental energy remaining for performing knowledge work. Hence, the management challenge is to conserve scarce mental resources by automating and streamlining as much as possible the process for gathering information. This involves providing an appropriate IT infrastructure with knowledge work functions and features, establishing organizational processes and training plans that encourage productivity, and introducing evaluation and reward systems that recognize knowledge work productivity.

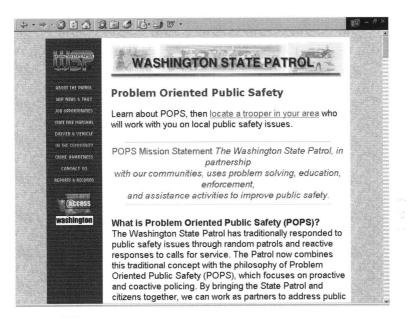

Figure 2.2 The Washington State Patrol Website discusses the principles of problem-oriented policing and invites the public to be involved in "proactive and coactive" policing. The names and contact information for numerous community policing troopers are posted on the Website: www.wa.gov/wsp/community/pops. htm.

2.8.2 Problem-Oriented Policing — Applying Knowledge

Problem-oriented policing (POP) has been widely cited as a completely different policing tactic as compared to the practices from the incident-driven, reactive crime-fighting thinking of the professional policing era (see Figure 2.2). POP focuses on identifying the root causes of a problem and attacking the problem so that crimes are stopped before they begin. The law enforcement executives that subscribe to community policing want every officer to be a POP practitioner, and this implicitly reinforces their role as knowledge workers. Professor Herman Goldstein developed the SARA (scanning, analysis, response, and assessment) method in the early 1990s and this approach has been widely adopted and successfully applied throughout the world.

Scanning — The POP practitioner, by working with local citizens, becomes aware of local concerns, issues, and priorities. The officer can verify community concerns by analyzing reports on incidents to see if they are repetitive, or if they have relationships to other incidents. In addition, exception reporting can alert the officer to a developing or new trend. During this stage, problems must be prioritized and IT resources can be used to track public concerns and assist in providing solvability factors.

Analysis — The POP practitioner may review CAD data (data mining) and analyze the time periods for a particular problem. Maps that depict "hot spots" can help in the understanding of the problem. Officers also need to be able to review the details of individual incidents in order to gain an intuitive understanding of the problem and related elements.

Response — The POP practitioner ideally should have access to a repository of similar problems and learn of special municipal ordinances or previous responses that can be used to address the problem. Ideally, a knowledge database, using an Intranet approach, is available. Perhaps a neighborhood discussion group on the Internet can be used for feedback or ideas.

Face-to-face contact is important. By being stationed in the community, the officer is also aware of community resources that can be used to address the problem. Community meetings are often held to enlist local support and resources. Presentations on the nature of the problem and recommended responses are necessary to obtain local community and police management support for a specific response.

Assessment — Following the response, RMS or CAD data can be used to assess whether the tactics were successful.

The characteristics of SARA can be compared with how Davis and Naumann describe knowledge work:

> Knowledge work results in useful information. It involves sets of activities for acquiring knowledge, designing analyses and solutions, making decisions, and communications. Examples of individual activities are scanning and monitoring information sources, searching from information, modelling problems and processes, planning, organizing, scheduling, authoring outputs, formulating problem definitions, performing analyses, selecting among alternatives, formulating action plans, presenting results of analysis, and persuading others to accept analyses and plans.

In Practice: Barriers to Solving Problems and Crimes

In 1998, Major Piper Charles, Charlotte-Mecklenburg Police, and Dr. Maureen Brown, University of North Carolina at Charlotte, conducted a study that surveyed 1767 police officers in 10 different police agencies that had adopted a community policing philosophy. They learned that:

- 55% claim they have little knowledge of what residents perceive to be their most pressing problem
- 50% claim they have little knowledge of resident involvement in problem-solving activities
- 40% claim that information is not available in a timely manner
- 55% lack information on suspects and felonies in their response area

- 75% get no feedback on case status
- 60% claim they frequently or always feel "at risk" due to a lack of timely and accurate information

The study assisted the Charlotte-Mecklenburg Police in acquiring funding for a $8.2 million technology modernization project. Major procurements included a new CAD, RMS, and laptop computer for every officer.

Source: Charles, Piper, Aligning Information Technology with Community Policing Initiatives, Presentation at 1998 IACP Law Enforcement Information Managers Conference, May 1998.

2.9 Community Policing Is Decentralization

The ending of the professional policing era is characterized by the return to neighborhood foot patrols and storefront offices (fancier callboxes?). This trend toward the decentralization of control and authority means that officers deployed in community precincts or storefronts need access to the right information, at the right time. There is a context to the information retrieval process, and having the right expert (the frontline officer) retrieve the information can lead to observations and conclusions not previously possible. As noted earlier, Carter and Trojanowicz felt that a community-based law enforcement officer may be the best person to judge whether a suspect is "the bad actor" that is wanted. The local officer can also cultivate and access information sources that others cannot.

Wireline and wireless networking (see Chapters 9 to 11) can facilitate a decentralized model of deployment without a sacrifice in information usage and sharing. Similar to the new economy knowledge workers, frontline police officers must be recognized and encouraged to develop skills such as creating relationships. These officers are the key contributors and will make or break community policing efforts. They need to be able to get out of their cars and into neighborhoods to build relationships, and that is why mobile computing is so critical (see Chapter 8). In addition, these knowledge workers must be provided with tools that support Internet and Intranet collaboration. Databases, discussion groups, and online experts can all be sources of information (see Chapter 5).

A key future aspect will be the knowledge portal, which brings people and knowledge together in a central area, accessible anytime, anywhere. For example, an officer may have documented an innovative problem-solving technique. The officer needs to know what to do with the document, where to put it, and what taxonomies to use so people can find it. Technology enables this, and the business process challenge is to get people to share their knowledge.

In Practice: Redmond (WA) Police and Streamlining the Sharing of Knowledge

The Redmond Police Department has implemented the automated Intranet application Xpedio Content Publisher. This allows end users to directly convert and publish on the Redmond Police Intranet documents, files, and photos. Employees in all divisions can now submit content to the Intranet directly from their desktops. The material is automatically converted to HTML and published on the Intranet with synchronization of content issues managed in the background. The Redmond Police also have mobile computers with wireless data capabilities and this means that officers can have immediate access to information, and can post new content remotely. Prior to the Intranet approach, officers would hand out or mail paper bulletins, and these were often posted on cluttered clipboards.

Source: The keyboard cops, *Knowledge Management World*, September 2000.

2.10   The Community Is More Than Just the Police

The professional policing era was epitomized by the image of Sgt. Joe Friday from the "Dragnet" police show telling a citizen to provide "just the facts ma'am." The police operated with a detached "lone ranger" approach, thinking that only the police could deal with a crime, and the only solution was to arrest the perpetrator. Today, it is recognized that many other social agencies can make valuable contributions to enhancing public order and safety.

As an example, youths that continually cause crime and disorder problems could be the focus of a joint agency response. Many young persons who are involved in crime or disorder problems are also known to social service agencies, probation officers, school administrators, and perhaps mental health agencies. Chapter 7 discusses how field interview reports are often submitted to document police contacts where there is no direct crime being committed. Partner agencies could use information in the field interview database to establish patterns of behavior, associates, and times of client contact. This knowledge could trigger an early intervention, and prevent later crime problems. In cases where there are large amounts of data, an Extranet application could be used to permit "read only" views of the portions of the database, depending on the access rights granted to a specific agency.

Up until recently, information sharing with external agencies (including other law enforcement) could only happen through time-consuming processes involving a police officer or other agency employee acting as an information intermediary. Now, shared systems based on Virtual Private Networks (see Chapter 9) make data connections robust, secure, and affordable for community partners such as social services and probation. Figure 2.3 depicts

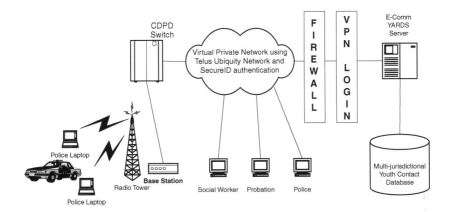

Figure 2.3 The B.C. Police Intranet piloted a Youth-at-Risk Database System (YARDS). This information-sharing project uses a virtual private network and Cellular Digital Packet Data (CDPD wireless data) services to enable mobile and remote access.

the architecture of a shared young offender information system that involves community partners.

In Practice: Technology Supports Community Policing Partnerships in Illinois

Recent high profile and tragic events in the U.S. and Canada have made school safety a high priority for all school administrators. In a forum held with police officers, teachers, counselors, and administrators in McLean County, IL, the participants identified the need to share information as a high priority. In response, a pilot project on youth violence information sharing has been initiated. In addition to the Normal and Bloomington Police Departments, partners include the McLean County State Attorney's Office, the juvenile division of the Illinois Department of County Court Services, the local division of the Department of Family and Children Services, and schools from two districts.

The project uses a "virtual private network" as the channel for the partners to communicate. An example would be if officers intervened in a fight among teens over the weekend. Principals could be alerted to the possibility of further problems in the schools Monday morning. The early warning capability of the system is seen as a major benefit. If a problem is flagged with an "at risk" youth early, it could be addressed through conferences with parents and administrators, counseling, or peer intervention. The project will institute strict access and confidentiality rules so that privacy laws are respected.

Source: Principals and police use Internet to track troubled teens, *e-School News*, February 1, 2000, Website: www.eschoolnews.com.

2.11   The New Community: The Internet

The Internet provides law enforcement agencies with an inexpensive way to connect to their constituencies. Many agencies have Websites and they can be categorized as:

Generation One: The Websites are simple "brochures-online" and provide addresses and telephone contact numbers.

Generation Two: The Internet becomes more sophisticated and graphical. Mission statements, messages from the Chief or Sheriff, and crime prevention tips are featured on the Websites. Public information on the organizational structure, community policing goals, and recruitment is posted.

Generation Three: These Websites have become interactive portals for the police-to-community and police-to-stakeholder transactions. Examples include:
   Dynamic information
   - online crime statistic databases (inlcuding crime mapping)
   - registered sex offender databases
   - inmate database
   - criminal records queries, with fee paid via credit cards
   - most wanted
   - unsolved crimes
   - current traffic accidents

   Static information
   - application forms
   - permit information, local laws
   - crime report forms

Generation Four: Generation four sites are similar to generation three sites, but behind the scenes, the various browsing habits of visitors are recorded for market research purposes. An example could be a person browsing a victim's information page on the subject of spousal abuse. An online chat session with a specially trained abuse counselor could be launched asking the person (perhaps a battered spouse) if she (or he) wished to discuss the particular site visit in more detail. Someone else who browses information on how to get to a public beach may have a banner ad pop up that warns the person to not bring alcohol to the beach, and outlines the large law enforcement presence at the beach.

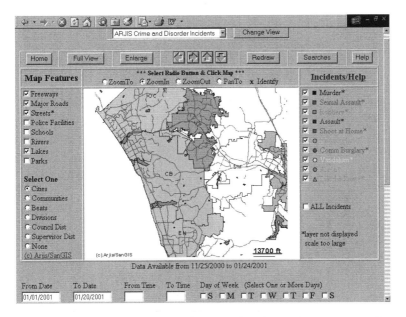

Figure 2.4 ARJIS and a crime map of Coronado, CA. Website: www.arjis.org.

2.12   Community Policing Websites

Some form of Web presence is almost standard for law enforcement agencies, and the Internet has given rise to other applications that the community can use to become more involved in the criminal justice system. A few notable examples follow.

2.12.1   Automated Regional Justice Information System (ARJIS)

The ARJIS Website in San Diego County provides crime statistics and mapping capabilities. The public can zero in on specific neighborhoods and examine crime patterns and locations. The public's interest and awareness of crime in their neighborhoods increase through the availability of this type of information (see Figure 2.4).

2.12.2   London, Ontario and P2S (Police to Stakeholder)

The London Police Service recognized that digital-trunked radio systems are a new frustration for the news media since they cannot monitor digitally encrypted transmissions. The London Police service implemented a paging system for the media on a temporary basis, and in 1999, they called the media to a meeting and agreed that an Internet-based solution would be pursued to provide dispatch information to the media. Benefits they saw were:

- There is access to this information by any authorized user on a 24-hour basis.
- Overnight information is available without having to phone a media officer.
- Better cooperation exists between the media and the police.
- The police can get important messages out to the media more quickly and easily.

The new media system links to the live CAD system and uploads the latest dispatch logs every 5 minutes to a City of London server through a firewall. Internet "push" technology is used to send updated information to a media agency's browser so that the users do not need to refresh their screens to get the latest information. In the event of a priority incident, the browser will display a colored alert and emit a tone. In addition, certain priority incidents are set with a longer display delay time so that the media do not respond to incidents that may be in progress.

2.12.3   Self-Serve Queries

The Canadian Police Information Center (CPIC) has a public Website (see Figure 2.5) that allows the public to search the entire national database of law enforcement records for the following stolen items:

- Vehicles
- License plates
- Firearms
- Boats
- Boat motors
- Bicycles

2.12.4   Self-Serve Police Reports

The County of St. Claire, IL has a Website with links to online forms. These allow community members to file non-emergency crime reports, forward complaints and compliments about police actions, and to request special attention on their premises for their vacation absences (see Figure 2.6).

2.12.5   Crime Prevention

One of Sir Robert Peel's more important principles of policing is that it is better to prevent crimes than to try to apprehend an offender after the fact.

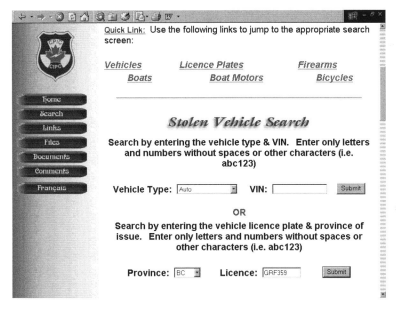

Figure 2.5 Canadian Police Information Center Website allows the public to conduct self-serve stolen property searches: www.nps.ca/english/search.html.

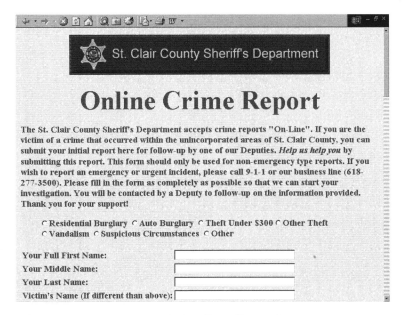

Figure 2.6 St. Claire County (IL) Sheriff's Office online non-emergency crime report. Website: www.sheriff.co.st-claire.il.us/olcr.htm.

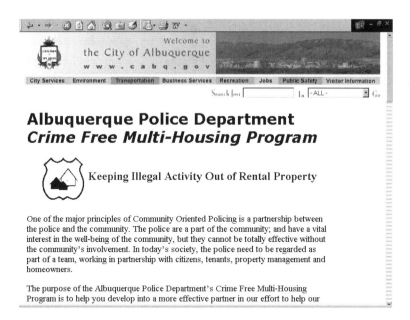

Figure 2.7 Crime prevention Website from Albuquerque, NM: www.cabq.gov/ police.

To facilitate this goal, many agencies post crime prevention tips on their Websites. In Figure 2.7, an example of a Website with crime prevention tips from the Albuquerque, NM police is shown.

2.12.6   The Community Bulletin Board

A principle of community policing is to obtain more public consultation in order to determine policing priorities. Gone are the days when the police were the professional crime fighters who paternally and singularly determined community needs. Gauging what the community actually wants can be difficult and a new resource for accessing public viewpoints is the Internet.

An example of this occurred in July 2000, when a civilian oversight board brought out a judgment against the Abbotsford (British Columbia) Police Chief and his Emergency Response Team after a drug raid resulted in a children's birthday party being interrupted and a family pet dog being shot. Media coverage was especially damning and citizens (apparently randomly chosen) were interviewed by the media on the streets and asked their opinions. All of the persons quoted by the media disagreed with the actions of the police, leading to the conclusion that there was an overwhelming condemnation of the police actions and the attention paid to drug investigations.

On the same day, a discussion question was posted on the MyBC Website, www.mybc.com, which is a community Website sponsored by the local telephone exchange carrier. In 2 days, 88 postings were made to this question:

Abbotsford's top cop is shouldering some of the blame as the result of a report, which damns the Abbotsford Police Department's tactical team's botched drug raid last year. A family dog was shot in front of children at a birthday party, while no drugs were found. What do you think can be done differently to avoid these problems?

Of the first 13 postings, all were supportive of the police actions. A sample posting was:

Once again the police are being blamed for doing their jobs. The criminals are again protected by our laws. So, no drugs were found, but I'll bet that if the police had gotten there a bit earlier there would have been drugs. It's a good bet that they did enter a "drug house." The police are damned if they do and damned if they don't. Regardless, the dog was attacking and chewing on the arm of a policeman. Nice people with nice dogs don't have dogs that attack people. How many people's lives have been ruined by the drugs that came out of that house?

Posting #14 was critical of the others and the police. Portions of what the writer stated were:

I am truly amazed at the closed mindedness of you all. You obviously watch too many American cop movies and have no compassion for your fellow man. Police are fully to blame and should be held accountable for this situation in Abbotsford. A 5-day suspension for endangering children's lives as well as causing irreversible psychological trauma reminds me of the Rodney King affair in the States.

A review of the remaining 84 postings showed a definite pro-police trend. Despite the negative news coverage, the public response on the Internet was overwhelmingly supportive of the police actions and priorities.

Section 3.3 in Chapter 3 outlines how IT can increase an agency's ability to handle complex issues. When there is access to all of the information available, better decision making will occur. This may prevent the mobilization of risky and expensive resources such as an Emergency Response Team, which is often deployed as a precautionary measure in the absence of information.

2.12.7   The Law Enforcement Agency Bulletin Board

The Milwaukee Police Department places a high value on community consultation. Information on department crime priorities, resource expenditures, and major strategies and policies are presented. An appeal is made for the community to become more aware of how police services are delivered

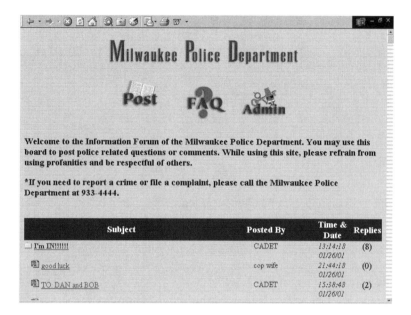

Figure 2.8 Milwaukee Police community information board. Website: www.milw-police. org/wwwboard2/wwwboard2.html.

and to share in the responsibility to work with the police. In his welcoming remarks on the Website, Chief Arthur Jones states:

> This information represents our latest effort to reach out to the community that we serve. Like all law enforcement agencies, we rely on the trust and cooperation of the public to successfully carry out our responsibilities. The frank exchange of information is an essential ingredient in our effort to enlist that trust and cooperation.

To further this objective, a community bulletin board (called an information forum) can be accessed on the Department's official Website and sergeants are assigned the tasks of moderating discussions and answering questions (see Figure 2.8).

2.12.8   Police to Public Communications

Law enforcement issues and problems are always topical and newsworthy in the eyes of the broadcast and print media. However, it is not just the police who assert that the media tends to sensationalize events and create controversy and conflict when none really exists. Nonetheless, a free press is a fundamental tenant of a democratic society and most members of the media believe that they report fairly and act in accordance with the public interest.

In the event of a perceived unfair story being reported, the traditional avenues of recourse for law enforcement leaders are to write a letter to the

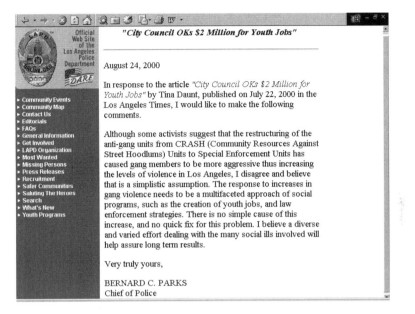

Figure 2.9 Commentary from Chief Bernard Parks, Los Angeles Police Department. Website: www.lapdonline.org/press_releases/editorials/2000.

editor, or contact a broadcast news director to protest. Unfortunately, even if a well-reasoned argument is presented that refutes the slant of a news story, more often than not the complaint would go unheeded. An expensive and rarely used option is to purchase advertising space for a rebuttal. In reality, most media articles that unfairly portray the police go essentially unchallenged.

With the advent of the Internet, police executives no longer have to suffer in silence. The existence of the Web now means that any organization can quickly and cheaply communicate to the public at large, and this bypasses the information gatekeeping role the media traditionally has held. On the Los Angeles Police Department Website (Figure 2.9), Chief Bernard Parks regularly publishes commentary that sheds greater light on topical issues, as well as refuting perceived unfair accusations in the media.

2.12.9 Recruiting the Knowledge Worker

There are many people with a glamorized and unrealistic view of what is involved in working as a law enforcement officer. In order to appeal to the right persons, as well as to save in the recruiting staff time spent on explaining to people what police work is really like, a realistic job preview can be published on the Web (Figure 2.10). In addition, the selection criteria, preferred qualifications, and selection process can provide candidates with information that helps them determine if they are a competitive applicant.

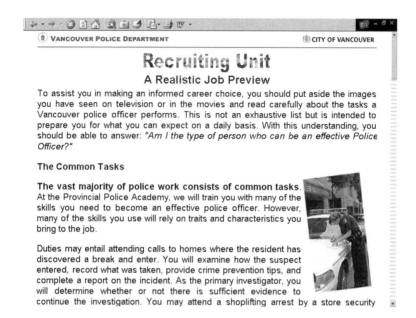

Figure 2.10 Recruitment information on the Vancouver Police Department Website: www.city.vancouver.bc.ca/police/recruiting.

2.12.10 Digital Wanted Pictures

The public can be directly involved in the search for fugitives. Many agencies will post pictures of wanted persons on their Internet sites. In addition, public assistance can be solicited to help determine the identity of unknown suspects. The use of video surveillance cameras in public and private premises is growing fast. Media footage of public events is often available. In addition, people with personal video cameras now film many private and public events. The availability of these video footage sources and the use of video imaging software can produce facial pictures of crime suspects literally caught in the act. These pictures can be posted on the Internet and video clips of the criminal acts can be posted to demonstrate the gravity of the crimes.

In Practice: Unknown Riot Suspects

In March 1999, the City of East Lansing, MI created a special Website with pictures taken during a riot that followed a basketball game. Significant property damage and violence occurred and other offenses included arson, felonious assault, disorderly conduct, and incitement to riot. The Website recorded 28,000 hits in the first week of operation.

Source: McDonough, Brian, Wanted, click here to view photos, *Government and Technology Magazine*, August 1999.

2.13   End-of-Chapter Comments

This chapter provided a historical overview of IT and its adoption in the professional policing and community policing eras. There are many ways that IT can facilitate better policing, and the new recruits that are coming into community policing organizations must be recognized as knowledge workers. If new officers don't demand and expect the best support tools, then the recruiting process itself needs an examination. The future of law enforcement is the subject of many conjectures but all theorists predict a greater role for technology. In our wired and wireless world, law enforcement must keep pace in order to remain relevant and effective.

Keeping current in IT is a fundamental leadership issue. Chiefs, sheriffs, and all senior administrators in law enforcement must be aware that an agency that is lagging in IT will be increasingly viewed as lagging in leadership.

References

Albuquerque Police, New Mexico, Website: www.cabq.gov/police.

Amoroso, Eldon, Internet based media release project, *Blueline Magazine*, October 1999.

Auten, James, Response time: what's the rush, *Law And Order*, November 1981.

Automated Regional Justice Information System Website: www.arjis.org.

Banas, Dennis and Trojanowicz, Robert, *Uniform Crime Reporting and Community Policing: A Historical Perspective*, National Center for Community Policing, 1985, Website: www.ssc.msu.edu/~cj/cp/uniform.htm.

Braiden, Chris, *Bank Robberies and Stolen Bicycles: Thoughts of a Street Cop*, Alberta Ministry of Attorney General, *circa* 1987.

Bratton, William, *Turnaround: How America's Top Cop Reversed the Crime Epidemic*, Random House, New York, 1998.

Canadian Police Information Center Website: www.nps.ca/english/search.html.

Carter, David and Trojanowicz, Robert, *The Philosophy and Role of Community Policing: A Historical Perspective*, National Center for Community Policing, 1988, Website: www.ssc.msu.edu/~cj/cp/uniform.htm.

Charles, Piper, Aligning Information Technology with Community Policing Initiatives, Presentation at IACP Law Enforcement Information Managers Conference, San Diego, CA, May 1998.

Davis, Kevin, Web maps pinpoint crime activity, *USA Today*, November 6, 2000, Website: www.usatoday.com/life/cyber/tech/cti770.htm.

Davis, Gordon and Naumann, J. David, *Knowledge Work Productivity, Features and Functions of Information Technologies, Emerging Information Technologies and Improving Decisions, Cooperation, and Infrastructure*, Sage Publications, London, 1999.

Goldstein, Herman, *Problem-Oriented Policing*, Temple University Press, Philadelphia, 1990.

Kelling, George, *Fixing Broken Windows*, Simon & Schuster, New York, 1996.

The keyboard cops, *Knowledge Management World*, September 2000.

Larsen, Richard, *Urban Police Patrol Analysis*, MIT Press, Cambridge, 1972.

Lingerfelt, James, Technology force multiplier, *The Police Chief*, August 1998.

Los Angeles Police Department Website:
www.lapdonline.org/press_releases/editorials/2000.

McDonough, Brian, Wanted, click here to view photos, *Government and Technology Magazine*, August 1999.

MyBC Website: www.mybc.com.

North Carolina Court Records Website: www.123nc.com.

Principals and police use Internet to track troubled teens, *e-School News*, February 1, 2000, Website: www.eschoolnews.com.

St. Claire County Sheriff's Office Website: www.sheriff.co.st-claire.il.us/olcr.htm.

Washington State Patrol Website: www.wa.gov/wsp/wsphome.htm.

Management

Chapter 3 addresses strategic planning and the important change practices associated with business process reengineering. Chapter 4 discusses how to prepare a business case to justify an IT project, and also covers acquisition, procurement, and project management issues.

Chapter 4 discusses the importance of good client/vendor relationships. In March 2001, Panasonic factory staff met with Vancouver Police project personnel to discuss the first worldwide rollout of the CF 28 Toughbook computer. Holding the CF 28 is Panasonic Personal Computers Division Director Yoshi Yamada. The Vancouver Police deployed 186 CF 28 notebooks, which feature magnesium alloy cases, a Pentium III 600 processor, 128 MD SDRAM, and a 20-GB gel-mounted HDD.

Strategic Planning and Reengineering Operations

3

3.1 Introduction

This chapter will cover the strategic planning and reengineering that has to occur prior to the successful implementation of new technology.

Many experts contend that there is no such thing as an IT project. There only exist business reengineering projects that include IT as an enabler.

Planning and process change concepts from the private sector and law enforcement will be highlighted. It is important again to note what an IT project should be, and what it is not. IT may be naively thought of as the automation of existing manual processes or the delivery of "toys" and "techno gadgets" to end users. It is imperative that IT projects be focused on the introduction of new ways of doing business that reflect the best practices possible with the new technology tools.

In Practice: A Drug Squad Detective and the Need for Automation?

In the mid-1980s when the IBM PC was first introduced, a detective responsible for intelligence analysis in the Vancouver Police Drug Squad approached a colleague of mine that was familiar with the new personal computers. He showed my colleague a card file box containing 3" by 5" cards that were arranged in alphabetical order. The individual cards listed the names of every suspect the Drug Squad had dealt with over the past several years. My colleague immediately assumed that the detective wanted a computer database set up, perhaps using Dbase II or Lotus 123. "No, no," responded the detective. "I want you to write a computer program that prints out nice name labels for these cards."

This anecdote is used to illustrate how many uninformed managers simplistically view the acquisition of new technology as what produces the benefits. I have seen this type of thinking in agencies that I have visited — some of which have spent hundreds of thousands of dollars on a new system with no appreciable gains in efficiency. Expressions I have heard that describe automation implemented without process reengineering include, "if you bought a jet, why are you still walking," and "all you are doing is paving the cow path."

3.2   Leading the Technology Project

While the position of IT manager is mentioned often in this chapter, this is not intended as a strict reference to a head of an IT section. These individuals typically are hired on the basis of their technical skills and knowledge and they are essential contributors to all IT projects. However, when large-scale projects are planned, and especially when bringing about major organizational change, the IT project leader should be a line manager with a detailed knowledge of police operations, administration, and the unique "cop culture" present in policing agencies. Again, this reflects the "business change" nature of an IT project, not the technology focus.

In Practice: The Technology Translator

Chief Robert Ford is from the Port Orange (FL) Police Department, and is a former Chair of the IACP Law Enforcement Information Managers Section. In an article in *The Police Chief* magazine, he wrote:

How often have you heard (or overheard) the MIS director or the City Administrator complain, "Cops should be on the street dealing with criminals. Computer programmers should be in the information center dealing with the information needs." This idea sounds reasonable but it just doesn't seem to work that way in the real world. Unless individuals with police experience are involved in pre-planning projects, directing installs, and either guiding operations or actually operating the information systems, these systems rarely realize their potential.

Chief Ford estimated that approximately 25% of new information technology installed in law enforcement does not work at all. He also recognized the valuable contributions a computer specialist can make after becoming knowledgeable about police operations.

Source: Ford, Robert, Can you keep what you got? Retaining the technically savvy officer, *The Police Chief*, May 1999.

3.3   Strategic Plans for IT

In the commercial sector, IT is used to support specially chosen business strategies, or to enable the development of new business strategies. This allows the firms to create or maintain the competitive advantages described in Chapter 1. In the non-profit sector, the technology initiatives must be linked to the overall mission and objectives of the agency. While most law enforcement agencies strive for a coherent and well thought-out approach, it is just as likely that the current IT systems have been implemented as separate, short-term fixes. This gives rise to the "silo" effect where information is stored in many places and access is difficult. Perhaps the most important aspect of strategic management is learning from the past, and it is never too late to adopt a more global and strategic view of IT.

In the overall strategic planning process for an agency, a situational analysis is necessary to provide a context and a starting point for future directions. An organization needs to know where is it now, before planning on where to go. Mission statements and goals and objectives arise from these planning efforts. The end objectives must be clearly defined. An often-repeated adage is *"If you do not know where you are headed, all roads lead there."*

The strategic plans that actually incorporate technology aspects often will state "more technology is better," and that "technology is important because we are forward thinking." However, what is preached is not often what is practiced. Limited resources often mean that other service areas are funded before IT projects.

A SWOT analysis (strengths, weaknesses, opportunities, threats) that is part of the larger planning effort is also useful when focusing on an IT strategic plan. The following issues should be considered:

- Current capabilities of the technology
- Economics of use
- Applications that are feasible
- Skills and abilities available to develop and use the applications
- Pressures from interest groups to improve performance
- Ability of the organization to make appropriate judgments on the deployment of IT

By also incorporating the inputs from line staff, plans should be developed that are easily understood. The plan must limit the technical terms and use of complex phrases. It should provide an overview of the big picture and how the objectives will be achieved.

Ideally, large projects are modularized so that early functionality is delivered. When long delays occur, skepticism can arise as to whether a product will actually ever be delivered. Furthermore, the plan should be flexible and readily adaptable. It must focus on the operational goals, not technical objectives, since these change constantly and rapidly. If not previously developed, the plan should incorporate standards in the areas of:

- Hardware and software
- Developing and implementing new applications
- Training and certifications
- Use and access policies
- Security and audit policies
- Roles and responsibilities
- A common data dictionary (see Chapter 5)

In summary, a plan can be considered sound if it answers the questions:

1. *What are we trying to do?*
   The answers here are usually found in the mission statement or broader strategic plan of the agency. Examples are:
   - Lowering crime rates.
   - Improving public perceptions of safety.
   - Increasing crime clearance rates.
2. *What are the goals necessary to accomplish the mission?*
   This specifies the success factors that must be delivered for the mission to be considered accomplished. Examples are:
   - Improvements in the quality of initial and follow-up investigation reports.
   - Increased officer time available for problem solving.
   - Reductions in the time it takes for a follow-up investigation to begin.
3. *What strategies will we use to achieve our goals?*
   There are many ways to achieve a goal and the strategy must incorporate budget and staff constraints, and must also be developed with employee input. Examples are:
   - Make all information available online.
   - Share information within the agency and with other law enforcement agencies in a timely manner.
   - Implement differential response processes so that occurrences that do not require a fast police response can be off-loaded to a neighborhood beat officer.

3.4   The Rationale for Business Process Reengineering

In looking at the non-competitive environment of policing, the key strategy concepts are related to increasing the productivity of the people resources, and arming them with information tools to enable better decision making. Achieving both objectives will lead to better services to the community using the same resource inputs. Central to this is the need to transform an agency. This involves a critical look at:

- What work is done
- Why the work is done
- How the work is done

Law enforcement leaders must continually ask themselves if their organizations are operating efficiently and effectively. Key questions must be posed such as, "Why do we do it this way?" If the only answer is, "We've always done it this way," then it is very likely the procedure or work method is outdated and inefficient. Unfortunately, when the reasons for a particular process are not well understood, there is a very real possibility of a change having undesirable impacts. Consequently, many are unwilling to bear the risks of initiating change.

Similar to private sector counterparts, police agencies have had their share of IT disasters that involved problems such as:

- More staff needed with the new system
- Increased complexity and time associated with performing work tasks
- Missed delivery dates
- Cost overruns
- Inadequate functionality

Very often, vendor and product problems are to blame — especially in the case of custom-developed solutions. However, similar implementations of a product or application can produce problems in one agency that are not experienced in another. In trying to explain why an IT project failed in one agency when it succeeded in another, the context of implementation must be considered. If the IT project simply tries to automate processes that evolved from old business processes or even legacy IT systems, then it is unlikely positive changes will arise. However, if the IT project is implemented in support of the vision and strategic reorientation of the agency, then significant benefits can and will accrue. IT is an enabler and catalyst of reengineering and organizational change. Leaders must understand that it is the business changes associated with IT that produce the benefits, not simply the automation process itself.

As an example, if an automated process results in less data entry work for records clerks, then efforts must be made to either deploy the slack resource to other duties, or to enlarge their current tasks. If this is not done, then the agency does not benefit from implementing the new technology. It is the indirect utilization of the slack resources IT produces that will provide the benefits, not simply IT itself.

Using the example of mobile report entry and data access, these benefits can be categorized as:

1. Efficiency improvement — Officers performing direct data entry do not need to drive to the police building to complete reports and will have more patrol time available. The clerical workload associated with the data entry of handwritten reports will dramatically decrease.

2. Quality improvement — A mobile computer allows officers to file reports sooner after an incident. Prompts in an automated system can guide officers through the data entry process thus producing higher quality reports. Under the paper-based "pen and notebook" system, officers would take notes and then try to remember other details many hours after the incident. Another example is in interviewing a witness who can only describe vaguely a suspect vehicle. An officer could scroll through an online database of vehicle pictures to assist in the identification of the make and model.

3. Improved capacity to handle complex issues — An officer with remote access to the agency database can examine the past history of calls to an address, and review all of the related reports. For example, a full-scale mobilization of an emergency response team (ERT) or SWAT team may occur because the field commander needs to err on the side of caution, due to the absence of information. Having the capability to review all police incident reports will lead to better conclusions and could negate the need for this expensive and risky force deployment option. Section 2.12.6 in Chapter 2 provided an example of the uproar that can result from the perceived misuse of force.

While implementations of IT will generate benefits in all three areas, the size of the impacts will depend on the application type. In addition, one benefit is not more important than another. What is important, though, is to understand that even though the initial focus may be to automate a task, the greater benefits may arise out of the information by-products.

3.5 Principles of Reengineering

Reengineering work requires law enforcement managers to challenge traditional assumptions and rethink their processes. IT must be used to make changes to processes that were never possible before. There will be tremendous opportunities to do things differently and to do different things. The thinking must depart from a traditional "top down" hierarchical structure to a lateral view. The terms "thinking vertically" or a "90 degree" view have been used. Rather than thinking about accountability and control, the approach must be focused on improving job performance by improving understanding of how the job gets done.

In their book, *Reengineering the Corporation,* Hammer and Champy emphasize that it is critical to look hard at the processes and ask if they are solving the right problems and if they need to be as complex as they are. A second principle is that if a job is split up into too many pieces and involves too many people, nobody can see the whole process. Finally, they point out that the more handoffs of activity in a process, the more points of failure. The lesson they offer is that IT should not be used to replace old business processes or even to replace legacy systems. New technology must be implemented with new workplace solutions.

To successfully reengineer, the following principles must be considered:

1. Organize around outcomes, not tasks — Assignments of work should be structured to conclude a task. The traditional process may involve a file being passed along an "assembly line" of patrol officer (report taker) to detective (investigator). Despite the commonsense notion of a suspect's "trail" getting colder, there may be a prevailing attitude to wait and pass on a case to a speciality unit, rather than immediately beginning the effort to identify and/or locate a perpetrator. In the redesign stage, attention should be given to increasing the task significance of a process stage. A data entry clerk that keyboards endless reports into a RMS will experience boredom. Allowing the clerk to also perform quality control will provide a greater sense of contribution since he or she now becomes responsible for information integrity, which will lead to improved investigative data access and analysis.

    In Practice: Robbery Investigations in the NYPD

    In his book *The Crime Fighter,* former New York Deputy Commissioner Jack Maple talked about the typical way a robbery is handled in a typical American police department.

    The call comes in to 911. One or two patrol officers in a radio car respond to the victim's call and take down a cursory description of the event. If these two cops are unusually sharp, they also get a phone number for the victim and type it accurately onto the report that will be forwarded to the detective squad. The patrol cops may be friendly; they may be rude, but either way they're likely to offer a grim prognostication before leaving. 'There's probably not much we can do.'

Maple felt that the long time delays before victims were shown mug shots of potential suspects was a big problem. This was caused by slow paper flow with reports getting to detectives one day to a week later. He wrote, "detectives generally spend more time trying to track down complainants than they do trying to track down crooks." Maple changed the NYPD robbery investigative process to a "same-day" service model where patrol officers would "market" the crime-fighting capabilities of the police and persuade victims to view suspect photos and see detectives immediately. The detectives also had to adapt their part of the investigative process. They had to be more diligent in their questions so that patterns of behavior could be established. In order to maintain consistency, Maple instituted checklists so that all questions and investigative avenues were covered in every case. He also worked to maintain more up-to-date photo files and found great success with digital mugshot systems and databases.

Source: Maple, Jack, *The Crime Fighter — Putting the Bad Guys Out of Business*, Doubleday, New York, 1999.

2. Have those who use the output of a process actually perform the process — A follow-up speciality squad investigator who is handed a poorly conducted primary investigation is faced with many obstacles. The report could be handed back to the originating member for more information, but this could take days to travel through the internal mail system. If the investigator is in a remote location, it may be difficult to find out what shift the primary investigator is working. Given these barriers, the most expedient option for the investigator is often to duplicate the ground previously covered (re-interview victims and witnesses). In a reengineered system, these inefficiencies could be eliminated. The primary officer could be given the responsibility for all follow-ups and the specialist investigator could monitor the progress online. Another example is if a report is improperly submitted. The investigator could view an online database to find the next shift the poorly performing primary investigator is on duty. Armed with this knowledge, the investigator could decide to e-mail the report (with a receipt confirmation request) back to the originating member's supervisor, directing that the primary investigator complete the investigation.

3. Treat geographically dispersed units as if they were centralized — The information retention and access procedure in many larger organizations often results in information that is difficult to access. There is a lack of knowledge about what kinds of information is retained, and who retains it. Redundancy and inefficiencies are prevalent. A shared RMS can provide immediate access to all of the information available.

4. Link parallel activities during the process, rather than the end of the process — Electronic communication systems can allow concurrent work to be reviewed, analyzed, and acted upon. For example, a shooting and homicide occurring in a crowded bar will result in many officers involved and potentially dozens of witnesses. If reports and statements can be electronically filed (uploaded) from the field, homicide investigators can immediately review the reports from patrol officers and forensic identification officers at the scene, and start to browse intelligence databases using the suspect descriptors uploaded. Under a paper reporting system, the investigators must wait until many hours later, before they can gather up all the handwritten reports.

5. Capture information once at the source — A significant problem with older information systems is that information is created, maintained, and used in many different places. A suspect's information may be captured in several databases which not only means repetitive data entry, but results in data integrity problems.

> **In Practice:** CIO Viewpoints on Process Reengineering
>
> In the December 2000 issue of *Government Technology* magazine, several CIOs had their comments on barriers to electronic government recorded as they spoke at a roundtable discussion on electronic government. Relevant views were expressed by:
>
> George Molaski, CIO Federal Transportation Department
>
> One of the problems is that techies talk to techies, and techies don't own the business process. When we get the programmatic people espousing the same things that CIOs espouse, then we'll see a big emphasis and move forward.
>
> Wendy Rayner, CIO State of New Jersey
>
> I defy any of us to say we're really doing process reengineering and transformation the way we'd like to. That's our challenge for the future.
>
> Alisoun Moore, CIO State of Maryland
>
> I've done internal process redesign — it's painful. It takes incredible management time and effort to change internal processes. You will get resistance every step of the way.
>
> Source: Hanson, Wayne, Toppling the stovepipes, *Government Technology*, December 14, 2000.

3.6　Process Mapping

A redesign of workflow can be achieved through process mapping which will yield three types of maps:

1. As-is: Depicts the process as it currently works.
2. Should-be: Provides a description of the new process, which is formulated to reduce waste and minimize cycle time and errors. Small changes can be achieved to conserve resources, improve cycle times, and improve outputs.
3. Could-be: The third type of map could also be described as the process vision. It describes a new process based on a major new customer demand, or if a resource enabler, such as IT, were available. The objectives relate to mid- to long-term change. Stretching goals, such as decreasing by 50% the time it takes to prepare a case for court, will challenge managers to imagine technologies that could be deployed.

Solutions to problems are far easier to identify if the process is fully described and presented visually (see Figure 3.1). In addition, the maps allow managers, often for the first time, to see the complexity and connections associated with familiar and apparently simple processes.

In a study conducted by members of the Police Executive Research Forum (PERF), it was found that many organizations assumed the end product will be the sum total of the value added at each stage of the process. If patrol officers conducted good primary investigations, and detectives conducted good follow-up investigations, then good prosecutable cases would arise. What process mappers found was that many officers took responsibility only for their part of the process, and not for the end product. Often, officers didn't even care about their part of the process since they were not responsible for prosecutions and had little feedback on cases that they started.

In Practice: Process Mapping and the Chicago Police Department

In 1994, Mayor Richard Daley asked several senior business executives how they thought Chicago's economic health could be improved. In reporting back to the Mayor, they stated that a major factor affecting Chicago's viability was crime and an offer of help was made through a proposal of using private sector strategies in the public sector. This initiative grew into the 21st Century Policing Project, which was an effort to understand core police processes better and to use that understanding to improve police departments' crime fighting abilities. The project was expanded to seven police departments: Chicago, IL, Phoenix, AZ, Arlington, TX, Naperville, IL, West Palm Beach, FL, and one British police force, Thames Valley.

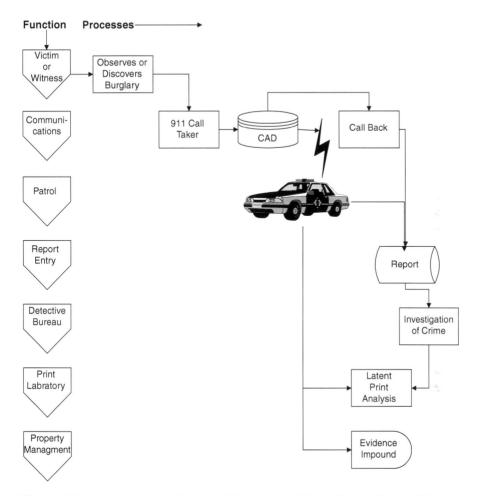

Figure 3.1 Process mapping diagram. (From Fraser, Craig, Scott, Michael, Heisey, John, and Wasserman, Robert, *Challenge to Change, The 21st Century Policing Project,* Police Executive Research Forum, 1998. Reprinted by permission of PERF.)

The PERF was selected to implement the vision of helping police departments discover methods to redesign core business processes to improve their capacity to prevent and control crime, violence, and disorder. The project focused on:

- Adapting "process mapping" techniques to the police environment and building departments' capacities to use these techniques to overcome obstacles to change.
- Applying process mapping techniques to police operations to help police agencies evaluate their systems and restructure their operations to support significant improvements in the delivery of service to citizens.
- Determining if the process mapping tool can be used to improve operations.

- Creating a complete understanding of core police organizational processes and discovering areas where adaptations and innovations can
  generate significant leaps in organizational performance.

An early success was realized with mugshots where it was found that the
procedures in place hampered rapid suspect identification. Process mapping
was also used to integrate IT applications such as CAD, AFIS, criminal
history system, and crime analysis system into the crime solution process.

Source: Fraser, Craig, Scott, Michael, Heisey, John, and Wasserman, Robert,
Challenge to Change, The 21st Century Policing Project, Police Executive
Research Forum, 1998.

3.7   The Agents of Process Change

Law enforcement officers are traditionally recruited from education backgrounds that are non-technical in nature. Education disciplines such as criminology, sociology, and psychology are more prevalent in recruits than fields
such as computer science, business administration, or engineering. For these
reasons, the implementation of technology projects may seem intimidating
or beyond the capabilities of the majority of managers. The fallacy of this
view is that while some previous training or education is helpful, the most
important attribute for leading an IT reengineering project is the understanding of the business itself.

In the book written by Bill Gates, *Business at the Speed of Thought,* Ralph
Larsen, CEO of Johnson & Johnson, offered views on process change. He
states that the most frequent cause of "spectacular failures" is that the business leaders turn over the big projects to their IT departments or outside
consultants "and then run because it's such hard work." He further argues
that, "You absolutely cannot do that. All the successes you see come because
of strong business-line ownership, not IT ownership. Business-line ownership with strong IT support. The project doesn't belong to the consultants
or to IT. It doesn't belong to anyone else but the business owner."

Bill Gates further asserts that, "It's impossible to reengineer a process
using technology without the oversight of someone who can bridge the
business and technical teams. This business process owner doesn't have to
be the most senior or the most technical person on the business side of your
organization, but the person does have to understand the business need and
how the technology will be used in actual work. The person must be respected
enough in the organization to make decisions stick. That's the person most
likely to have insight into developing newer, simpler processes and negotiat-
ing trade-offs between business and technical requirements."

In the case study on the Western Australian Police Service at the end of Chapter 4, a police executive-level sponsor and a police manager business owner are specifically named on their IT project overviews (see Table 4.1).

3.8 Managing Changes

There is no doubt that the pace of change in IT is occurring at breakneck speeds. In just trying to keep current, managers must continually invest significant amounts of time in reviewing materials and literature on IT developments. Keeping an organization current through the exploitation of new technologies means that change is a way of life for the IT manager.

With any change, there will be early adopters who will embrace new ways of working. There will also be early adopters who can readily recognize the benefits. Others will need more time before committing. There will also be laggards who simply resist change, despite the benefits. The IT manager must recognize these differences and use this knowledge to develop strategies to move the late adopters and laggards along, so that they do not hold back others or disrupt the project implementation. Some specific strategies to orchestrate organizational change include:

1. Obtain top management support — If the Chief and the senior executives want the benefits, they must be prepared to invest the resources and accept the project risks. In fact, their involvement and support will significantly reduce the project risks. They should act as sponsors of the project.

2. Create a need for the change — Clearly articulate to others the benefits of a new technology or process. Use examples obtained from other law enforcement agencies. For leading edge applications, apply examples from the private sector or other public services. While efficiency is often the most obvious benefit, do not lose sight of the overall purpose. Explain how the change will result in more criminals being apprehended, more officer time for community policing, or better service to the public.

3. Address fears up front — If there are going to be changes to a work unit because of automation, deal with them head-on and provide the organization's human resources policies. Ideally, full-time employees can be reassigned and any job losses will be through attrition only. There may be individuals that have something to lose with a new process and the potential resistance must be anticipated and dealt with.

4. Assign key managers to the business transformation roles — Major projects will have a critical impact on an agency and assigning a

manager, who is seen as upwardly mobile and has influence with peers, will increase the probability of commitment and collaboration. Consultants and some technology managers may have difficulty obtaining assistance and cooperation, as they likely will be unfamiliar with the police subculture. The IT leader must be adept at facilitating the emotional and psychological process of change. If top management truly believes that the IT project is important, then the manager assigned must be the manager that can't be spared.

5. Build task forces that involve representatives from line units — Ensure that the representatives are empowered by their managers or supervisors to provide input and information. Develop these individuals so they can be product champions. Many people will feel enthusiastic about being involved in a project that will improve on what they do. Moreover, the course that is chosen for now is not set in stone. No change is ever a final change and the input that is received can help chart the course for future directions.

6. Create interest and excitement about the change — Arrange site visits or functional demonstrations of the new technologies. Hold workshops and demonstrations that show how the tool can improve the work.

7. Utilize the training process to build acceptance — Select trainers for their instructional ability and personal credibility. Do not accept the fallacy that trainers need to be technically oriented. For end users, the best trainers are those that understand how a technology tool is used in an operational setting, not those that fully understand how it works in the background. Most vendors would rather conduct a "train the trainer" course than provide all end user training themselves.

8. Communicate regularly — People need to deal with the changes, and they can handle transition more effectively if they understand what is going on and how it affects them. The reasons to reengineer must be identified and communicated constantly and candidly.

9. People issues are prominent — Early in this book it was asserted that people are the greatest asset in a law enforcement agency. Changes affect people the most and while they may not explicitly state it, there will always be the thought of "what's in it for me" when confronted with something new. The most brilliant technology solution will be unsuccessful in implementation if users are unconvinced. If the people have low morale and feel disgruntled, then changes will be viewed with suspicion and resentment. Many will be passive or even destructive in their response. The challenge is to take into account the entire organizational climate and develop a plan that accounts for these situational factors. This issue is especially problematic for government agencies with entrenched civil service unions.

In Practice: A CIO's View of Reengineering Government Processes

In an article written for the Winter 2000 issue of *Electronic Government,* Alisoun Moore, CIO of the state of Maryland, offered a pessimistic outlook on implementing process change in government. She argued that reengineering often fails. When governments try to improve existing processes through the development of custom systems, problems such as "scope creep" arise, and training and reallocating existing staff require significant change–management finesse. The more common outcome is partial or complete project failure. Her reasons for the significant hurdles are:

- Governments at all levels have a protected civil service system.
- Agencies are themselves protected by statute, interest groups, and a diffused power structure that is a characteristic of democratic institutions.
- Government agencies are not subjected to the same market forces that would naturally require them to quickly adapt to an ever-changing environment.
- The combination of statue-based mandates and a diffused power structure makes change very difficult. Only in the most extreme cases where there is a complete failure of an organization to deliver service, or in the face of a crisis such as war, do the prospects for a successful reengineering improve.

With the advent of the new economy and the shift to Internet-based service delivery, Ms. Moore argues that existing internal processes should be completely bypassed. For example, governments are better off by instituting self-serve vehicle registrations over the Internet, rather than trying to retrain motor vehicle licensing staff on new processes. Ms. Moore calls the removal of the government middle layer the "disintermediation" of government. Chapter 2 provides examples of law enforcement agencies that have instituted self-service processes using the Internet.

Source: Moore, Alisoun, The disintermediation of government, *Electronic Government*, 1(4), Winter 2000.

Case Study: As-Is and To-Be at the Vancouver Police Department

The business process redesign effort in the Vancouver Police Department involved a change from a paper-based document management system to a fully electronic RMS and mobile reporting platform. Over 40 operational members were nominated by their managers to serve as operational unit coordinators. They were instructed to:

- Brief stakeholders in their units.
- Verify their decision-making authority.
- Obtain peer comments and "sign off" on the work they produced.

Their initial task was to complete an "as-is" workflow assignment to examine how information is received, processed, managed, shared, and stored in their units. Some questions were:

- Information Received — From whom, and how (e-mail, hardcopy, verbal)?
- Information Processing — What do you do with the information? What forms do you use?
- Information Management — What IT systems do you use? Identify all unit databases. Who has access to the information? Do you forward the information to anyone (who and how)?
- Storage — How do you store active records? Inactive? Concluded? Consider both hard copy records and electronic records.

As-Is

An "as-is" review of the patrol division reporting function was conducted. This involves the recording, filing, and access of reports from police investigations. Every month, over 10,000 reports are produced in a cumbersome process. The steps are:

1. Citizen John Doe phones in a break-in to his home. The call-taker enters Mr. Doe's information into the CAD system.
2. The incident is passed (electronically) to a radio dispatcher who relays the information by voice, and likely transmits it at the same time to a mobile data terminal. The officer in the car transcribes the address and victim information to a notebook. The officer then attends the location and records more information in a notebook.
3. The next step is to retrieve a paper form and transcribe the information again. For lengthy reports, the officer will spend time driving to the police station to access support systems and avoid writing in the car. Moreover, 50% of officers prefer to complete their reports by word processor and use computers in the police stations. The unintended consequence of providing word-processing facilities (a support value

activity) is that officers want to leave their beat areas and sit in the police station to data enter their reports. If the case involves an arrest, the officer must drive to another facility so that reports can be immediately photocopied and given to the jail.

4. Paper reports are collected once a day and taken to Quality Control where a Clerk III looks up the Statistics Canada (UCR) coding from a large binder, and identifies routing for photocopies (example: Sexual Offense squad for "peeping tom" reports). The report is next sent to Data Entry, where a clerk enters incident and Mr. Doe's personal information into the RMS. The narrative text is not entered because of time/cost constraints.

Characteristics of this process are:

- Four-time data entry of incident and Mr. Doe's personal particulars.
- Valuable officer time utilized in driving to report-writing locations which are away from assigned patrol areas.
- Inaccurate RMS information arising from data entry clerks guessing what an officer may have handwritten.
- No electronic access to narrative information because it is not entered into RMS. Digital text is printed on paper and treated as if it were handwritten.

To-Be

An intial "to-be" vision was to have a mobile reporting platform integrated to a CAD and the RMS. The electronic reporting process can yield benefits such as:

- A largely paperless occurrence management system which almost eliminates filing and copying duties. There is one-time data entry, occurring close to the source with CAD integrated to mobile workstations. Information is much more accurate.
- Automatic routing (workflow management) and immediate access for reports.
- More officer time in the community as reports can be submitted remotely using wireless transmissions.
- Improved human resource management practices arising from the enhanced capability to review the quality and quantity of work.
- Improved investigative and crime analysis capabilities as data queries and search engines are deployed to access the vast quantities of information that are collected.

3.9   End-of-Chapter Comments

This chapter provided insights into the management of change and improving operations. The ideas behind reengineering have roots in concepts such as total quality management and industrial design. Change processes are an integral aspect of any project involving IT, and leaders and managers also need to recognize and plan for human factors such as fear and resistance. In law enforcement, the uniqueness of the "cop" culture is an additional reason to designate a line manager (an operationally knowledgeable officer) to lead major IT projects.

References

Ford, Robert, Can you keep what you got? Retaining the technically savvy officer, *The Police Chief*, May 1999.

Fraser, Craig, Scott, Michael, Heisey, John, and Wasserman, Robert, *Challenge to Change, The 21st Century Policing Project*, Police Executive Research Forum, 1998.

Gates, William, *Business at the Speed of Thought*, Warner Books Inc., New York, 1999.

Goman, Carol, *The Human Side of High-Tech, Lessons from the Technology Frontier*, John Wiley & Sons, New York, 2000.

Hammer, Michael and Champy, James, *Reengineering the Corporation: A Manifesto for Business Revolution*, Rev. Ed., Harper Business, New York, 1997.

Lingerfelt, James, *Strategic Planning for Information Technology*, IBM Public Safety and Justice, Paper presented at the Canadian Police College Police and IT Conference, May 2000.

Maple, Jack, *The Crime Fighter — Putting the Bad Guys Out of Business*, Doubleday, New York, 1999.

Moore, Alisoun, The disintermediation of government, *Electronic Government*, 1(4), Winter 2000.

Warboys, Brian, Kawalek, Peter, Roberston, Ian, and Greenwood, Mark, *Business Information Systems: A Process Approach*, McGraw-Hill International (U.K.) Ltd., London, 1999.

Ward, John and Griffiths, Pat, *Strategic Planning for Information Systems*, John Wiley & Sons, New York, 1996.

The Acquisition of IT

4

4.1 Introduction

The decision to acquire IT resources may involve an investment of a few hundred dollars to tens of millions of dollars. A stand-alone database program, running on a single PC, can be procured for under $1000. A regional radio system can end up costing well over $100 million. In acquiring IT systems, an early decision is whether to make or buy. This chapter will cover current practices and will also discuss system procurement practices and how to obtain funding for IT projects.

4.2 The Business Case for IT

In developing the budgets and cost proposals for obtaining IT, many decision points need to be considered so that the investment can be justified. An early question is whether the agency has capital funds available. Often, a large systems acquisition (such as wide area radio) will require a local referendum for project approval. In other cases, local and federal grants must be sought out. In justifying a budget need for an IT project, the following rationales can be used.

4.2.1 Added Value

Improvements in the quality of work being performed may be hard to translate into dollars, but may be the most important reason for an investment in IT. For example, the organization may have the key strategic objective of crime prevention. Instituting a Web-based facility for access to crime prevention information could assist in meeting this organizational objective. The system could "push" news on recent frauds to all businesses, as well as "pushing" intelligence on seasonal crime trends to homeowners. In addition, the names and addresses of convicted child sexual offenders can be listed for parents to review.

Service enhancements in other areas are also possible. Under a paper filing system, a citizen may have to wait days before an officer can respond with a case status. In an automated system, cases can be accessed instantaneously. In addition, error rates can be lowered through quality control

69

measures instituted in data entry screens. The quality of reports will increase with word-processed rather than handwritten reports. In a criminal court case, a higher quality report will generate a higher probability of a successful prosecution.

4.2.2 Intangible Value

There are improvements in service that are not quantifiable in terms of financial paybacks. A law enforcement agency may want to be seen as having a progressive image by using the latest crime-fighting equipment. Equipping officers with the latest available tools enhances officer morale, can assist in recruiting efforts, and furthers the agency's image as modern and forward thinking. A community that is confident their police service is managed efficiently and progressively will have a greater sense of safety and security.

4.2.3 Return on Investment (ROI), Net Present Value (NPV), and Payback

The majority of law enforcement IT projects can be justified on the basis of financial savings. The concepts of NPV and ROI are related and involve costs savings being achieved through the benefits of IT. For example, an IT project could have characteristics such as:

- A 10-year project life
- 8% cost of capital
- Saves $100,000 per year
- Has a $500,000 capital cost

The following financial figures can be produced:

1. ROI = $100,000/$500,000 or 20%
2. NPV = Capital cost plus discounted 10-year cash flow of $100,000 per year at 8%, or (−$500,000) plus $671,008 = $171,008
3. Payback = $500,000 divided by $100,000 equals a 5-year payback period

Another example of a payback calculation can be illustrated by looking at mobile computing projects, which are often funded in the U.S. through COPS MORE technology grants. The objective of the MORE (making officer redeployment effective) program is to increase the number of law enforcement officers interacting directly with members of the community. A technology application can be translated into timesavings through redeployment.

For example, the following calculations may be used for a hypothetical agency with 20 officers that averages 1824 hours of work per year per officer. The example is taken from a COPS MORE grant application discussion:

1. Calculate hours expended baseline before IT implementation

    3.67 hours per shift writing reports
    1.8 hours spent on records checks
    = 5.47 hours per shift

2. Calculate hours expended after IT implementations

    3.13 hours per shift writing reports
    1.5 hours spent on records checks
    = 4.63 hours per shift

3. Calculate cumulative hours saved

    5.47 hours – 4.63 hours = 0.84 hours saved per shift with technology
    multiply by 20 officers
    multiply by 228 shifts worked by each officer per year
    = 3,830 hours saved

4. Calculate full-time equivalent (FTE) savings

    3,830 hours/1824 hours worked by a full-time officer
    = 2.1 FTE

    Each FTE costs $60,000 salaries and benefits

    Total annual savings equals $60,000 × 2.1 FTE = $126,000

If the IT application costs $300,000, the payback period is 2 years and 4.5 months (28.57 months).

In Practice: Funding for a RMS in the Vancouver Police Department

The following excerpt is taken from a report to Vancouver City Council justifying the new annual Police RMS expenditure of $575,000 per year:

Based on experience of other policing agencies, the move to an electronic-based RMS will result in significant cost savings. The Vancouver Police department anticipates that up to 33% of the 93 staff positions in the Information Section could be redundant with system implementation. This suggests savings in the Information Section as follows:

93 records staff × average salary of $35,805 = $3,329,865
Potential annual savings (based on a 33% reduction) = $1,098,855

These savings do not include the productivity benefits among sworn staff as a result of the improved enforcement tools that will be available to officers on the street which could result in sworn staff cost savings in the future.

In order to just offset the annual costs of the new system, it is anticipated that a budget reduction of $575,000 will be required, or just half the anticipated savings. This is the minimum saving to which the department is prepared to commit if Council agrees to participate in the project. It is recommended that the disposition of additional savings be the subject of discussion between the Chief Constable and Council prior to the go-live date for the new system.

Source: Inspector Jim Chu (author), Administrative Report, Vancouver City Council, September 21, 1999, Vancouver Police Department.

4.3   The Acquisition of Software

There are many ways to acquire IT resources and the options in all organizations involve procuring commercial products, as well as in-house development.

4.3.1   Custom-Developed Software

In law enforcement, the systems needs are not unique to an agency and it is becoming more common to buy an "off-the-shelf" software application vs. developing an expensive custom-written system. There are many examples of older applications, still running on mini- or mainframe computers that were completely developed by in-house data processing staff, or programmers contracted to write the code. In the case of an older CAD system, the execution speed that was necessary meant that a low level programming language such as assembler was used. Later on, increases in processing power allowed third-generation languages such as Cobol to be used. These older programs are characterized by monochrome character-based screens. The trend with modern application programs is to use graphical user interfaces with full color support and windowing.

   Software application development is a perilous and intimidating proposition. The thousands of lines of code that have to be produced, and the challenge of ensuring the software is stable and reliable, mean that few law enforcement agencies can afford the project risk. While changing a line of code may appear easy to do, understanding the change's consequences, especially with large programs, is difficult. Hence, the larger and more complex the software program, the more inflexible and arduous it is to change. Predictions on the final costs of a programming project tend to be too modest. There is a high demand for qualified staff in the corporate world, and finding and retaining programmers and system developers can be challenging. Governments cannot grant perks such as stock options, which private companies use to attract and retain top talent.

4.3.2   Commercial Off-the-Shelf Software

The law enforcement marketplace has many application vendors, particularly in the areas of CAD, RMS, and mobile computing. These vendors often received their initial start by engaging in an alliance with an existing law enforcement agency and developing the application on a partnership basis. The development costs could then be shared by the commercial partner who would recoup its costs through the sale of the software to other police agencies. As stated, most law enforcement agencies have similar needs. They enforce similar laws and may even deal with the same criminals. Unless there is a large size disparity, what works in one agency should work in another. The early versions of a CAD product initially developed for the Los Angeles Police and L.A. County Sheriff's dispatch centers were successfully marketed in hundreds of other law enforcement agencies.

In Practice: Commercial Off-the-Shelf (COTS) or Reengineer and Write Code

Is it better to reengineer a process or to install a software package and rework the processes around COTS software? Some reengineering advocates argue that you should start with a clean slate of paper, design the process that makes sense, and buy software that fits the new process, or write new software.

The COTS advocates argue that it is unlikely you would find a package that exactly meets the newly identified needs. In addition, software coding is expensive and risky. They argue that if you had a COTS package that met 80% of your needs, why spend the time redesigning or reinventing the wheel? They argue that COTS packages are less expensive and can be dropped in faster than a new process.

If there are some unique agency needs, such as with specialized law enforcement, custom-developed software is perhaps the only viable option. For example, the U.S. DOJ Web page used to list over 60 different system applications in use. For local law enforcement, it makes little sense to custom-develop common applications such as CAD and RMS.

Source: Cordata, James, *Best Practices in Information Technology,* Prentice-Hall, Englewood Cliffs, NJ, 1998.

4.3.3 Application Service Providers

An application service provider (ASP) is a newer example of procurement from a commercial vendor. Basically, an ASP provides access to a software application for use over the Internet (likely a virtual private network connection). By logging on to an ASP site, a standard Web browser will provide full access to a product that in the past would have been installed on an in-house server or network. ASPs could prove to be beneficial for small police agencies that cannot afford the expense of managing large and complex applications or that do not have the in-house expertise to manage a complicated system. The acceptance of this type of outsourcing in public safety still remains to be determined. This is because of the mission-critical nature and online performance demands of most public safety applications.

4.4 Outsourcing

Outsourcing involves an outside firm using its staff to provide services previously performed by in-house agency staff. Having the firm handle major acquisition and implementation details can allow an agency to keep current with technologies, without the significant internal investments and risk. The major reasons for outsourcing are:

Focus on Core Business — Major IT projects may drain an agency's resources on work that is outside the management competency areas. In addition, a smaller agency may have only low-level technical support available.

Reduction of Risk — In the case of a fixed-price contract, the outsourcer will assume a larger risk than with a time-and-materials contract. However, this risk is usually priced into the contract value by the vendor to allow for contingencies. A well-written agreement will specify the deliverables that must be provided and ensure that the systems meet the reliability and performance requirements, as well as ensuring the proper vendor support people are available at the necessary times.

Center of Expertise — Larger outsourcing firms will have more familiarity with new technologies. For example, a wireless data service such as CDPD may only be recently available in a given area. However, a larger firm may have significant experience gained from another client's installation. Consulting expertise, assistance in hardware and software evaluations, and project management assistance are all services that can be obtained on an "as needed" or temporary basis. Furthermore, internal IT staff may not be abreast of the latest technologies and the involvement of outside experts can lead to a positive knowledge transfer.

In Practice: Outsourcing in the Pittsburgh Bureau of Police

The City of Pittsburgh police department contracted with Paradigm4 to obtain wireless services for its officers. The electronic messaging system between police stations, patrol cars, and their supervisors substantially reduced the estimated 3 hours officers spend each day doing paperwork. In addition, the wireless data network services allow officers to connect to local, state, and national databases. The system uses CDPD and the encrypted data are transported over frame relay to Paradigm4's Stratus message server located in Harrisburg, PA. The value of the contract was over $1.3 million, and funds were obtained by the city through the Department of Justice COPS MORE program. Costs are paid on a monthly, per-user basis instead of the city having to buy equipment up-front and maintain it in-house.

Source: Hurley, Hanna, Car 101.1.0.54, Where are you? *Network Magazine*, March 1998.

4.5   Purchasing Systems

There are many purchasing rules that may be applicable at the local government level, that will determine the procurement path and methodologies. In general terms, buying IT can be conducted through competitive and non-competitive methods.

4.5.1   Sole Source Agreement

There are two variations of sole source procurement. In the first case, a contract has already been awarded to a vendor through a competitive procurement process. Later on, there is a need for compatible or upgraded products and it makes sense to return to the same vendor. For example, a software system may be substantially upgraded but still retains the business logic in the previous version. The agency has a large investment in training and employee experience and it makes sense to simply procure the upgraded software.

In the second case, there is a consensus that a vendor has the correct product and that there is little to be gained by going through the detailed work associated with an request for proposal (RFP). In a smaller agency, a RFP would generate little or no interest from the vendor community. Vendors would have to be sought out, most likely by studying products in similar-sized agencies. Local procurement rules will be the determinant of whether this is an available option.

Other reasons for justifying why a product should be procured in a sole source agreement include:

- The choice of a system is driven by what is being used successfully in an adjoining agency and there is a desire to partner, or to share data; or
- There is a product successfully implemented in another similar agency and there is a desire to move quickly and to save the expense of a bid process. There are some successful vendors that have sufficient business on hand and do not choose to expend the time and money on responding to RFPs.

4.5.2   Contract for Operational Services

In the past, building a private wireless data network often involved a competitive bid process. However, wireless data options, such as CDPD, ARDIS, or Mobitex, are provided as services from local commercial carriers. Consequently, what used to be categorized as a capital investment can now be viewed as a contracted service, similar to cellular and pager services.

4.6   Request for Information

Prior to the start of a competitive process, an agency may choose to gather material on the latest ideas and technologies in the marketplace, what vendors are actively seeking contracts, and what types of budgetary expenditures are to be expected. By issuing a RFI, vendor creativity can be solicited and vendors are not constrained by the narrower response guidelines in the RFP.

In Practice: LAPD Mobile Data Computer RFI

On January 19, 2000, the Los Angeles Police Department issued an RFI (Figure 4.1) with the stated objectives to:

- Inform vendors of our intent to acquire and integrate a mobile data computer system for the LAPD.
- Provide vendors with background information about the project and system requirements.
- Identify a pool of vendors interested in providing the MDC system.
- Determine vendor areas of interest: the hardware, software, or services in which vendors have knowledge and experience.
- Gather information from vendors on important issues, for use in developing a follow-on request for qualifications (RFQ).
- Solicit a statement of interest and basic corporate and product information, for use in disqualifying vendors who are not interested or whose products are unsuitable.

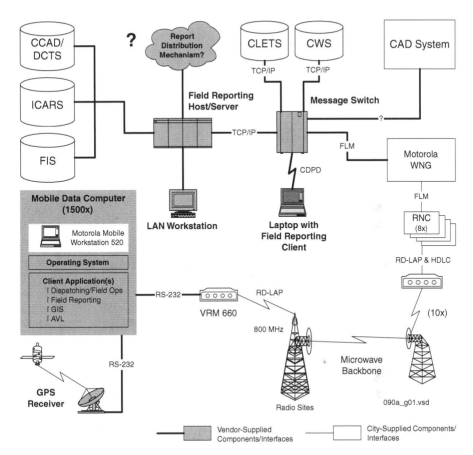

Figure 4.1 LAPD RFI diagram. Motorola MW 520 terminals, used with the Motorola DataTAC communications system, were selected in September 2000. The contract award was $21.7 million.

A proposed system architecture was provided to vendors so they could review the implementation environment for their product.

Source: City of Los Angeles, Los Angeles Police Department, 90-Day MDC Vendor Selection Study, Version 1.0, January 19, 2000, Doc. No. 090a.

4.7   Request for Quotation

A RFQ is usually issued to purchase commodity items that have little flexibility with respect to specifications and requirements. Hardware is an example of a procurement that would be awarded primarily on the basis of low bid and availability.

4.8   Request for Proposal

A RFP is used for procuring systems that are complex in design and scope. Because there are many variables in what a vendor can provide, the selection criteria cannot be based solely on lowest price. Developing an RFP is a painstaking and laborious process, and assembling one is not as simple as cutting and pasting from the work of other RFPs. The uniqueness of each agency means that some business process details need to be researched and documented so that vendors have a clear understanding of the objectives. There are excellent references available for managing competitive procurements using RFPs. This chapter will only summarize the key points.

In Practice: The Complexity of Law Enforcment RPFs

The March 2000 issue of *Government Technology Magazine* featured an article researched as part of the U.S. Department's Technology Acquisition Project. Author Raymond Dussault argued that the explosion of new technologies has brought on new challenges previously not faced by law enforcement managers. In government, vendors have always had the edge. In law enforcement, the advantage is increased. He notes, "As the individual leading a law enforcement procurement, you are at a disadvantage, since most systems are acquired only every few years. That cycle makes it difficult to learn from experience and become better at the procurement process." Dussault encourages line officers to learn from other jurisdictions, network among officers at conferences, and develop contacts through vendor customer lists.

Source: Dussault, Raymond, The RFP document: a map to success, *Government Technology Magazine,* April 2000, 42.

4.8.1   Developing the RFP

As stated, there are many examples of publicly available RFPs, which were written for the purposes of acquiring private radio, CAD, RMS, and AFIS systems. The three main parts in a RFP are:

1. Instructions to Bidders — This should include all the information that the bidder needs to respond to the proposal. Bidders must be given a format for their responses so that time is not wasted searching through hundreds of text pages for a particular response. The selection criteria and contract payment provisions should be outlined. A proposal schedule should include deadline dates for the submission of written questions, a date for the finalists to be announced, and a structure and timetable for oral presentations and site visits. Finally, the contract award date should be specified.

In Practice: The City OF Arvada CAD/RMS RFP Timetable

The City of Arvada, CO CA/RMS RFP was released on June 30th, 2000. Significant dates are:

1. Announcement of RFP availability	June 23, 2000
2. RFP date of issue	June 30, 9:00 A.M.
3. Due date for written questions	July 7, 3:00 P.M.
4. Mandatory pre-proposal conference	July 17, 9:00 A.M.
5. Final amendments or clarifications	July 21, 3:00 P.M.
6. Proposals due	August 4 by 3:00 P.M.
7. Complete final evaluation	October 2
8. Complete contract negotiations	November 10
9. Project kick-off	December 4

Source: Requests for Proposals for a Police Computer Aided Dispatch and Records Management System, City of Arvada, CO, June 30, 2000.

2. General Contractual Conditions — This section includes the legal conditions relating to the purchase and payments. A provision for default of contract may be included such as a letter of credit or a performance bond which can be utilized by the agency in the event payments are made and performance is deemed inadequate.

In Practice: Letter of Credit in a Contract

A public safety organization in a large urban center became embroiled in problems with a software vendor who repeatedly missed delivery dates. In addition, the code that was eventually delivered was not adequately tested and the agency began to feel that they were the quality control process for the vendor. Agency personnel continually found errors that led to functions and commands operating incorrectly. The tight integration required in the software code resulted in one bug fix creating problems in another area of the system that previously operated correctly. The contract with the vendor called for letters of credit, drawn on a local bank, to be provided whenever a payment was made. In order to recoup agency costs arising from the late delivery, a draw down was made on the letter of credit, which was actually provided by the vendor's parent company. The vendor was legally obligated to top up the letter of credit amount after the draw down and this proved instrumental in getting the vendor's attention and forcing it to direct more resources to this particular project.

3. Technical Specifications — The information in this section must be written by individuals who have a complete understanding of the business process and specific needs. The technical specifications in the RFP should describe:
    - Organizational characteristics
    - Technical environment
    - Business concerns
    - Strategic directions
    - Desired benefits
    - Standards of service (system response time, training, delivery schedule)

    In Practice: RFP Requirements

    In the RFP, it is worthwhile to distinguish between items in terms of their importance. In the Vancouver Police/E-Comm RMS RFP, categories used were:

    Mandatory — Vendors must respond to all RFP items identified as "mandatory." Requirements identified as mandatory are classified as critical to the operation of the records management system. They represent features that the participating police agencies cannot function without. Failure to respond to requirements in the "mandatory" category will result in elimination of the vendor's proposal due to non-compliance. The vendor **must** include the cost of meeting mandatory requirements in the bid price.

    Highly Desirable — Requirements identified as highly desirable are classified as important to the operation of the RMS system, but on a level of less criticality than those requirements identified as "mandatory." If the vendor and/or its product does not presently meet a highly desirable requirement, then the vendor must indicate whether a solution is being developed to meet the requirement and will be incorporated as part of the standard product or whether the solution is considered as a customization. If the latter, then the vendor must provide the estimate for meeting this requirement, and the cost estimates **must** be included in the total bid price.

    Desirable — Requirements identified as desirable are not critical to the operation of the participating agencies, but would represent helpful or convenient features that would be of operational or administrative benefit to the project participants. If the vendor and/or its product does not presently meet a desirable requirement, then the vendor should indicate whether a solution is being developed to meet the requirement and will be incorporated as part of the standard product or whether the solution is considered customization. If the

Figure 4.2 The evaluation team resources.

latter, then the vendor must provide the estimate for meeting this requirement, but the estimates **must not** be included in the total bid price.

Request for Information — This category incorporates options where specific information for a particular item is requested. The vendor is not required to provide cost estimates. If estimates are provided, they **must not** be included in the total bid price.

Source: E-Comm Police RMS RFP, September 1998.

4.8.2   Evaluation of Responses

The key to a fair and rigorous evaluation process is to combine the opinions and insights from the three main resource areas, and assemble an overall picture of which bid provides the best value.

Operations Expertise — At the top of the triangle in Figure 4.2 is Operational Expertise. This is the most important component of the evaluation team and selecting the right persons to provide the operational input is critical. The key here is not knowledge about computers or systems, but expertise that is current on the core functions in the law enforcement agency. Moreover, a broad base of knowledge must be included. For example, in an evaluation of a CAD, dispatchers may favor performance speed and simplicity. However, law enforcement managers and crime analysts may view analytical and reporting tools as being greater in importance. Obviously, trade-offs and compromise will have to be made.

Technical Expertise — The bidders may propose operating systems or technology solutions that are dated or proprietary. They may provide performance standards that are inadequate for the number of simultaneous users that have to be supported. In addition, response time, stability, and peripheral costs need to be costed. Total life cycle costs are a major consideration. For example, a system with a low initial purchase price may come with a high annual maintenance fee. One vendor may have to support a product remotely while another may have a local staff support presence.

Procurement and Legal Expertise — IT contracts are complex and confusing to the lay person. A specialist in this area is required in order to evaluate a bidder's compliance with the general contract conditions and to assess the inevitable counterproposals. For example, vendors will have to incur costs to purchase a performance bond. They may propose a price reduction if the bond requirement is dropped. In this case, a careful assessment is needed of the product stability and bidder's track record of delivery. Financial records, credit reports, and general company information must be obtained and interpreted. These specialists need to be involved early so that they are fully prepared for the contract negotiation stage.

In Practice: The City of Arvada CAD/RMS RFP Evaluation Process

The Evaluation Section of the RFP states:

1. Proposal responses will first be evaluated for their completeness and adherence to the form and format requirements.
2. Proposals will then be objectively evaluated by a qualified team based on the evaluation criteria in this Chapter, Section 5.5.2 [of the RFP].
3. Based on their scores, the city will select up to four finalists for further evaluation.
4. In the second phase finalists will be asked to make on-site oral presentations, answer questions, and demonstrate their products to selected members of the APD. Vendors will be granted from one to two days at the city's discretion, for these on-site demonstrations.
5. Following the on-site demonstrations the city will select two to three vendors for further evaluation. During this third phase the city will conduct due diligence evaluations of each vendor's reliability and performance on other public safety projects. In addition the city may choose to visit sites where the proposed system is installed, visit the proposer's headquarters, or conduct other evaluations as the city deems useful in their evaluation.
6. After Phase Three evaluations have been completed the evaluation committee will rank the finalists according to their proposal score,

their past history as a supplier of public safety systems, and the committee's evaluation of which proposed system will best meet the city's near- and long-term requirements.

7. Contract negotiations with the highest ranked vendor will begin immediately.

Proposals will be scored according to the following criteria:

Category	Maximum Points
Software functionality	30
System architecture and hardware functionality	15
Qualifications and references	15
Implementation plan	15
Warranty and service program	15
Price proposal	10
Total	100

Source: City of Arvada (CO) Police Department CAD and RMS RFP, 2000.

4.8.3   Reference Checks and Site Visits

A detailed study has to be undertaken as to the financial health, the staff availability, and the past performance of the vendor. Lists of current customers must be obtained along with the agency contacts. While these individuals can serve as a starting point for information, other personnel in the agency should be contacted. For example, if a contact person is listed as an IT department head, an operational manager should be sought out for information.

Site visits are extremely useful in this stage. Many agencies have seen the demonstration of the product in a clean office environment. A different reality may appear when it is viewed in a field scenario. In addition, end user comments are helpful from an evaluation, as well as a future implementation, viewpoint. A point to remember is that the manager who recommended the purchase of a particular system will likely have an emotional and professional attachment, and may not be able to provide a fully objective assessment of vendor performance and the functionality delivered. Comments from other knowledgeable users and managers are essential and, often, a site visit is the only way to obtain candid opinions.

In Practice: E-Comm and Vancouver Police Reference Site Visits

During the summer of 1998, project personnel from the E-Comm CAD procurement team conducted a site visit at a public safety dispatch center located in the northern U.S. The agency representatives made the following comments about their current vendor:

- Based on current experience, they are not confident about any of the time lines being met. The vendor has not focused resources on the project. They were seen as "quick to charge, and slow to deliver."
- Twice, the contract was defaulted and renegotiated.
- They discussed the extensive time they had to devote to the project. A total of ten people had to be really committed. They had to go to the vendor headquarters one week every two months.
- The IT manager was told during contract negotiations that three other sites would be installed first, and that they would not be a beta site. They since learned they are the beta site.
- They felt that they had gone too far to stop now.

The agency eventually accepted the CAD product but the RMS project was halted and a lawsuit was launched. In early 2000, an out-of-court settlement was reached between the county and the vendor.

4.9   The Contract

Many IT contracts are multi-year in duration and are broken into deliberate phases. The contract must be well defined since the persons who developed and agreed on the contract may not be the ones interpreting and working with it in the future. Changing business needs and personnel will result in future disagreements or misunderstandings. The contract becomes absolutely necessary to ensure both sides function within the project scope.

The expression "good fences makes good neighbors" has been used to describe the importance of the contract. In order to bridge the legalese in the contract with the actual desired outputs from a project, some contracts attach a Statement of Work (SOW) as an addendum. The SOW outlines day-to-day responsibilities, performance measures, and actual hardware and software to be used and is very helpful to operational personnel who may be unfamiliar with legal concepts such as liabilities, remedies, termination clauses, and warranties. In addition, a project plan is necessary to describe in detail who does what and by when.

In Practice: Who owns what?

A large law enforcement agency completely funded the development of an interface that fed information from a CAD system to its records system. A message switch was built to handle the transactions with a well-defined Application Programming Interface (API). When the time came to integrate a third product into the records system, the software firm pointed out that they owned the interface, not the agency that paid for it. Consequently, the only option for the agency was to pay for the right to access the API, despite the fact they funded 100% of the original development, and in fact were the only users.

The contract must include a project schedule, and payments should be tied to milestones and deliverables. Holdback amounts should be specified and retained until the entire project is complete. Change orders will likely arise and procedures are needed for handling project amendments. The "must haves" and the "nice to haves" must be placed on the table. A "nice to have" may come with an unjustifiable price tag and may need to be dropped. One potential benefit may have to be substituted for another.

There are many interpersonal roles that can be used in negotiations (e.g., good guy and bad guy roles) and they must be used with the knowledge that the other side may be equally familiar with these roles. The negotiation of contracts requires special skills that can be hard to come by. Obviously, price concessions are a desired outcome but not at all costs. A contract cannot be so rigid and unfair that a vendor cannot earn an acceptable profit margin. An agency may feel smug in grinding out a rock-bottom, potentially money-losing for the vendor contract price, but any vendor that allows itself to fall into this trap may not be around for much longer, and what agency wants to contract with such a company? On the other hand, many agencies have complained about the "Jekyll and Hyde" behavior of a vendor. Before the contract is signed, the vendor cannot do enough to "schmooze" and placate the potential customer. Once the contract is signed, the context changes to a business relationship. The vendor now becomes focused on delivering as little as possible to meet the terms of the contract.

4.10 Project Management

Both the agency and the successful vendor will need to have project managers that are willing to communicate regularly and outside of the project meeting schedules. They must be versed in project management concepts; this is the subject of numerous other books and courses of study. An agency project manager assumes responsibility for the completion of systems design and implementation activities within time and budget constraints. Project team members need to be supervised, training plans and staff allocations need to be developed, and users must be involved in the implementation planning.

Software packages, such as Microsoft Project, can be used to assist in maintaining control of the numerous intricacies, dependencies, and linkages between various activities. Tools such as Gantt charts and the critical path method (CPM) are useful to track start and end dates for major tasks.

Case Study: Project Management — The Seven Deadly Sins

Studies have revealed that between two thirds and three quarters of all IT projects are completed over budget or behind schedule or fail altogether. The Center for Project Management, www.center4pm.com, lists seven deadly sins that have been identified as primary reasons for why projects fail. They are listed below with an accompanying factual law enforcement example:

1. Mistaking half-baked ideas as projects

    A newly appointed chief of police was under severe pressure to lower property crime rates. An alert vendor made a presentation to the Chief of an "expert-based" analytical system that could be used to examine detailed patterns of residential and commercial break-ins. Despite the objections of the department's IT staff and the line patrol managers, the system was purchased and deployed. The main problem with the application was not its usefulness or functionality, but the enormous data collection requirements that officers in the field now faced, and the high data entry workload that this generated. The agency was still operating on a paper-based reporting process and data entry clerks were already functioning at their capacity levels. Many patrol officers openly disregarded the new data collection rules and their supervisors turned a blind eye because they did not like the higher patrol officer investigative times that the new system required. They felt the patrol division was already overextended with work. As a short-term fix to the data entry problem, police officers in the crime analysis unit were directed to keyboard the data elements into the new stand-alone system. This left them with little time for their real job of analyzing data. For other reasons, the Chief's tenure was short lived, and the system was abandoned immediately after his departure.

2. Dictating unrealistic deadlines

    A senior police administrator with responsibility for IT projects announced a clearly unrealistic deadline for a new RMS to be implemented. It immediately cast a pall of failure over the project since the project team knew they could not meet the schedule. It also was perceived as a misguided attempt to make them work harder. Very early in the project, he was forced to accept a more realistic "go-live" date from his staff.

3. Poor sponsorship

    It is argued that a sponsor is the single most influential ingredient for project success. Many projects are faced with hidden agendas, scope creep, changing requirements, and technology changes. The sponsor is needed to champion the project and must be able to break down the inevitable barriers that the project manager will face. A large law enforcement agency named an IT analyst to launch an Intranet project. The analyst made many presentations and consistently received the message from end users that an Intranet was the only way to go. Despite the compelling benefits that were identified, her immediate superior never pushed the project with senior management. The project could not get past the study stage and the agency was later seen as lagging severely in a "no brainer" of a technology project.

4. Underskilled project managers

    In a heavily populated jurisdiction in North America, five police agencies combined efforts on a major shared technology procurement. Initially, the agencies enjoyed the warm feelings of partnership and working together, and looked forward to the economies of scale. In order to avoid one agency being dominant, a federal agency was asked to provide a project manager. The individual had little knowledge of local law enforcement and had been a technical lead on mainframe applications for the majority of his career. The main qualification that he brought was that he did not work for one of the five partnering agencies. The project quickly became mired in cost overruns and missed delivery dates. Political infighting set in and agencies started to bring lawyers to meetings. Some agencies decided to cut their losses and bought their way out of the project.

5. Not monitoring the vital signs

    Vital signs that need to be tracked continually include the status of the critical path, milestone hit rate, deliverables hit rate, and costs. One agency made the decision to custom-develop a RMS from the ground up. During the functional design stage, many promises were made to end users about the functionality that would be delivered. The senior police officer in charge of the project, a deputy chief, was front and center and extolled the virtues of the new system. After 15 months, the first clue that the project was in trouble was that the project manager would lock himself in the office. He avoided contact with others and told his project sponsor that he was very busy working on the system. It was eventually determined that this manager was in fact hiding. The project was seriously late, and there was little to show for the funding that was used up. The entire project was sent to the scrap heap and a COTS RMS product was procured several years later.

6. Failing to deploy a robust project process architecture
    IT projects require detailed planning, solid cost estimates, and well-thought-out schedules. Moreover, the technology must be merged with new business processes. In one police agency, the first milestone activity in the new RMS rollout was to procure and ship end-user workstations. At the time, 486 processors were standard. Unfortunately, the software vendor had a 2-year development delay due to staff resources being re-deployed on another major project. The vendor finished developing the product on Pentium workstations. When the software was installed at the agency, the 486 processors could not handle the computational loads. Moreover, the business process that the police agency adopted was simply to replicate their current workflow. There was no mobile computing capability so officers still handwrote reports or used word processors. The data entry clerks then entered the "front page" tombstone data into the new RMS and used a separate database application to store scanned images of the narrative pages. Despite the major investment, the operational benefits were minimal.

7. Not formulating a comprehensive project portfolio
    All projects compete for scarce funding. Law enforcement agencies must automate what is important, not what is easiest to automate. A medium-sized police agency in a rural area expended significant funds on laptop computers for police vehicles. The area they policed had no commercial wireless data services and a "sneaker net" (diskette system) was used to transfer files. Many officers grumbled about the IT priorities. The voice radio system was an old patchwork network and there were many coverage gaps. Many felt that the radio system should have been upgraded first and this could also have provided the wireless data capability that the agency needed.

Case Study: Project Justifications and the Western Australia Police Service

The Western Australia Police Service (WAPS) embarked on a 5-year $124 million capital plan in 1998 to reengineer inefficient and ineffective policing practices and processes, and to replace aging and ineffective systems.

The approach chosen was to "fuse" IT and make technology an intricate part of the business. The WAPS called the approach the "Delta Communications and Technology Program" (DCAT), and there were three phases with associated components. By following the DCAT approach, the WAPS have delivered all planned projects on time, and within budget. The phases are

Phase 1 — Staying in Business: The WAPS identified as priorities IT projects that enabled effective and efficient delivery of police services. They are:
- Network infrastructure upgrade
- Resource management information systems
- Commencement of mobile computing
- Computer-aided dispatch
- Automatic vehicle location
- Digital-trunk radio network

Phase 2 — Front-Line Policing Systems: The WAPS brought in systems that enabled their officers to work smarter and faster.
- Pattern analysis system
- Custody and court brief system
- Intelligence management
- Incident management system
- Major crime case management

Phase 3 — Community Access & e-Policing: The new technologies of the wired world were reviewed and opportunities were identified that connected the WAPS to the communities they served.
- e-Business
- Online services
- Information center
- Operations support
- Records management

In the early planning stages, they determined that the existing IT support structure (several hundred staff), which was built to manage a monolithic mainframe, would have difficulty assisting the police in the transition to "business at the speed of thought." More and more, the IT staff evolved from an in-house development group to a core group of integrators who worked closely with consultants, contractors, vendors, outsource service providers, and new partners.

In order to assess adequately the priority, purpose, and rationale for a project, the WAPS adopted a "candidate investment approach" which documented the following four parts:

1. Project overview — This describes:
   - Intended project outcomes
   - Key elements of the proposed solution (or scope)
   - The current agency status or situation that the investment addresses

- Which broad program or activity of work the project or investment falls within
- The business area accountable, or responsible for the investment and outcomes

2. Financial summary — This part outlines the broad cost and benefit profile and includes capital and recurrent costs. The benefits include notional, real, or one-time savings. If applicable, a payback period is determined to indicate the "relative" financial viability of the project including NPV modeling.

3. Strategic drivers — Strategic drivers identify those external and internal drivers that resulted in this investment or project being considered. These drivers would evolve over time as the external and internal business environment change.

4. Benefit summary — This section provides a more detailed summary of the identified benefits area. In particular, the quantified benefits are broken into the key benefit areas for the WA Police Service. Key unquantifiable benefits are listed for completeness.

Table 4.1   An Example of a "Candidate Submission Form" from the Western Australian Police Service

Project Overview	
Scope	**Target** • Replace numerous homegrown applications which provide limited functionality and are not integrated • Reduce administrative time for Patrol Staff, OICs, and others to obtain, collate, and summarize the time and activity data • Reduce administrative time for Patrol Staff by eliminating the need to complete periodic activity surveys conducted by Strategic Planning Services (SPS) • Support district and regional reporting needs • Be easy to use, both for data input and retrieval/searches
Current Status	Pilot project has been successfully completed
Program	Delta Change and Technology Program (DCAT)
Sponsor	A/Commissioner Smith
Business Owner	Superintendent Jones

Financial Summary			
Cost Profile	Amount	Return Profile	Amount
Capital	$500,000	Real savings	$10,000
Recurrent (per annum)	$100,000	Notional savings	$400,000
Once-Off Revenue	$20,000	Payback period	<18 months

Table 4.1   An Example of a "Candidate Submission Form" from the Western Australian Police Service (continued)

Strategic Drivers Summary							
External Drivers				Internal Drivers			
Statutory	Regulatory	Government Policy	National Obligation	Cost Savings	Reinvestment	Infra- Structure	Enabling Project
				Yes	Yes		
Benefit Summary							
Quantified Benefits			Contribution			$ Contribution	
Sworn FTE						$0	
Unsworn FTE						$0	
Time Savings			10,000 hours			$150,000	
Cost Savings			$5,000			$5,000	
			Per annum total			$400,000	
			$0			$0	
Unquantified Benefits:							
Note: Dollar and time amounts in this example are for illustrative purposes only and have been changed from the real figures, and the names of police executives have been altered for confidentiality reasons.							

Case Study: Outsourcing and the New Scotland Yard (London Metropolitan Police Service)

The London Metropolitan Police Service (MPS) began a project in 1997 to outsource the running of its emergency call centers to a private firm or consortium of suppliers. The MPS foresaw an integrated service based on the elements of switchboard, call receipt, routing calls to its Public Service Bureau, and supporting field officers. Internal studies showed that 999 service was being delivered well, but the non-emergency call handling process was poor. In addition, physical space constraints, the unavailability of timely information for field officers, old equipment, and increasing service demands by the public were seen as impediments to delivering the desired level of service. An early decision was to consolidate the many scattered "control rooms" into one larger center. The project was called Command, Control, and Communications and Information (C3i). In describing this initiative, MPS Commissioner Sir Paul Condon stated:

> C3i is the largest and certainly boldest project that the MPS has ever undertaken. No other police service is actively considering such an initiative. We believe it to be an ideal opportunity to seek the assistance of the private sector, through the Private Finance Initiative, and to secure an equally bold partner to develop and then deliver the required accommodation, technology, personnel, training, and processes.

The MPS sought a supplier to deliver the C3i service through the:

- Provision of facilities
- Provision of technology systems
- Provision of staffing for management and operations
- Integration with existing MPS technology and systems
- Design and development of new and existing business processes and procedures in conjunction with the MPS
- Ongoing operation

Selection parameters for their selection of a business partner included:

- Deliver long-term business benefits to both parties
- Be financially viable
- Be fit for purpose
- Be delivered on time
- Have a manageable risk framework
- Accommodate future changes to the Metropolitan Police business
- Treat staff fairly

The contract award was scheduled for the end of 2000 and an implementation completion date for C3i was projected to be January 2003.

4.11   End-of-Chapter Comments

This chapter summarized many acquisition and procurement concepts. IT leaders need familiarity with the practices and should draw upon the expertise of procurement and contracting experts when significant dollars are at stake. For smaller purchases, often word of mouth, through consultations with previous and existing customers, can provide a comfort level as to whether the vendor makes promises that it will keep, and is committed to ensuring the customers are satisfied. In fact, even for large dollar contracts, the same client satisfaction references are important.

Even though contracts can be structured with numerous penalty clauses and detailed performance requirements, a project that has to resort to communications through lawyers and threatened court action is a good sign that the IT project is in trouble — if not doomed.

Another book that contains more perspectives on IT acquisition than what has been covered in this chapter was written by Charles Drescher, a former Commander of Automated Systems in the Los Angeles Police Department, and Martin Zaworski, CIO of the Broward County Sheriff's Office. *The Design of Information Systems for Law Enforcement, A Guide for Executives* is published by Charles C Thomas Publishing, Ltd., Website: www.ccthomas.com.

References

Chapman, Robert, COPS MORE Technology: Program Overview and Grant Requirements, IACP LEIM Conference Presentation, May 2000.

C3i Memorandum of Information, London Metropolitan Police C3i Project, 1998.

Chu, Jim, Vancouver Police Department, Administrative Report, Vancouver City Council, September 21, 1999.

City of Los Angeles, Los Angeles Police Department, 90-Day MDC Vendor Selection Study, Version 1.0, January 19, 2000, Doc. No. 090a.

Cordata, James, *Best Practices in Information Technology*, Prentice-Hall, Englewood Cliffs, NJ, 1998.

Crannage, Glenn, Building the Digital Nervous System, Presentation by Western Australian Police Service to Alphawest, 2000.

Dussault, Raymond, Managing the pressure: the RFP process in law enforcement acquisitions, *Government Technology Magazine*, March 2000, 42.

Dussault, Raymond, The RFP document: a map to success, *Government Technology Magazine*, April 2000, 42.

E-Comm, Emergency Communications for Southwest British Columbia Incorporated, Request for Proposals for a Police Records Management System for the Province of British Columbia, September 1998.

Hurley, Hanna, Car 101.1.0.54, where are you? *Network Magazine*, March 1998.

Imel, Kathy and Hart, James, Understanding Wireless Communications in Public Safety, A Guidebook to Technology, Issues, Planning, and Management, The National Law Enforcement and Corrections Technology Center (Rocky Mountain Region), Rockville, MD, 2000.

Kapur, Gopal, Project mismanagement: the 7 deadly sins, *Electronic Government*, September 2000.

Oakie, William, *Outsourcing, a CIO's Perspective*, St. Lucie Press, Boca Raton, FL, 1998.

Requests for Proposals for a Police Computer Aided Dispatch and Records Management System, City of Arvada, CO, June 30, 2000.

Major Applications

In law enforcement, the similar operating purposes and environments have resulted in the standardization of the types of software applications that are adopted. The applications predominantly support information gathering, storage, and the timely access to the information. Chapter 5 describes the basic underpinnings of database technology. Examples of specialized databases, and case studies of regional information sharing initiatives, are provided. Chapter 6 covers computer-aided dispatch and Chapter 7 covers records management systems. These systems are almost always procured from commercial vendors, and products from selected vendors are featured. Chapter 8, Mobile Computing, describes hardware platforms and concludes with several case studies.

A computer-aided dispatch system is an essential law enforcement technology. The E-Comm center is capable of deploying 60 call-taking stations and 24 dispatch stations. The layout of the E-Comm center can be contrasted with the picture in Chapter 6, Figure 6.1 which shows a pre-CAD mechanical conveyor belt from the previous Vancouver Police call center.

Databases and Information 5

5.1 Introduction

Police work and paperwork are two terms often used synonymously by weary officers who thought they had entered a career of excitement and action. Instead, they learn very early that the meticulous and time-consuming documentation of arrests, occurrences, crime reports, and other citizen contacts is a large and necessary part of the job.

Many chiefs also find themselves complaining about a new regulation or statute that makes the job of the frontline officers more difficult as the new law or regulation adds to the mountain of report writing duties. While the complaining is common, there is a tacit acknowledgment among all that there is a vital need to adequately document crimes and assemble information so that other officers (detectives) can solve cases and crime analysts can identify problems and trends.

The functionality provided in a modern database management system (DBMS) is a fundamental tool for the storing and accessing of information. A DBMS allows for the logical storage of information so that key facts or records can be retrieved from the voluminous amount of reports and other data that are captured and retained for later use. A computer can make the accessing of text records and other digital records, such as images and sound files, quick and powerful. This chapter will cover how a DBMS is structured, common terms used, and some of the many law enforcement systems that rely on DBMS functionality.

5.2 Card File Indexes

Before the advent of computerized indexes and databases, the primary tool for cataloging a seemingly endless stack of paper reports was to assemble an alphabetized paper card index. The card would contain cursory (tombstone) information on a specific file such as:

- Name of person
- Type of occurrence and relationship
- File number

A sample layout is shown in Figure 5.1.

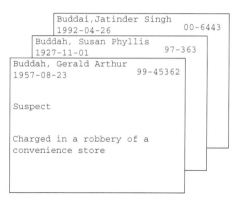

Figure 5.1 Examples of the information contained in a card file.

An important field on the card was the file (incident or case) number, which would allow an investigator to go to a shelf of reports and retrieve the report and any other associated documents. In many respects, the card file in a police records section is similar to the card file in a local library. In both cases, the use of computers has improved the access to the records.

The card file had many uses, especially for specialty units who wanted their own repositories of data. For example, the Fraud Unit would keep a card file of the well-known "bad check" artists. The Vice Squad would keep a card file of known pimps and prostitutes. The obvious drawback to stand-alone card indexes, as well as stand-alone databases, is the "stovepipe" effect where silos of information exist that cannot be shared or utilized in a coordinated manner. The clue to determining the identity of a fraud suspect may exist in a Vice Squad card file. The key to the identity of a serial murder may reside in a street check in a prostitution stroll of a "bad date."

In Figure 5.2, a portion of a sample front page of a police occurrence report is shown. The distinct details that need to go into the report are name, address, date, time, and location. Perhaps the most important piece of information on the report is the "file number" which is unique to each report. For example, there can be many occurrences where a victim name and address can be the same — such as in the case of a retail store with continual shoplifting complaints. While unlikely, the occurrences may even have the same date and time. What is used to distinguish one occurrence from another is the unique file number. In a law enforcement database, the file number is often used as a primary key.

5.3   Basic Database Elements

Database concepts can be illustrated using the occurrence report as an example. All law enforcement agencies use pre-printed forms for completion by

CRIME	FILE		ANYTOWN POLICE	File	**97-363**
INFO			OCCURRENCE REPORT	Number	

PAGE ———————— OF ——

SECTION 1 – OCCURRENCE INFORMATION □

1. LOCATION				TEAM AREA	2.DATE OF	TIME
456 Elm Street				District	OCCURRENCE FROM:	1254
					TO :	
3. OFFENCE / OCCURRENCE				CODE	4. DATE	
Theft					INVESTIGATE	
					97-05-14	1320
				UCR CODE		

PERSONS CODE:	V – VICTIM	R - REPORTEE	P – PARENT/GUARDIAN

#	SURNAME OR BUSINESS NAME	Given 1	Given 2		LANGUAGE ASSISTANCE	STATEMENT YES □
	Buddah	Susan	Phyllis		No □	NO □
V	RACE	SEX	D.O.B.	AGE	HEIGHT	WEIGHT	HAIR	EYE	UTI
	Caucasian	F	27-11-01		5'2	110 □	grey	blu □	ALCH □ DRUG □
	RES. ADDRESS (NO. DIR. NAME, TYPE, APT/STE, CITY)					ZIP CODE		RES. PHONE	
	456 Elm Street							555-8798	
	BUS. ADDRESS					BUS. PHONE		OCCUPATION Retired	
	Reporting Officer Name					PIN		Distirct	
	Weibe					1160		3	

Figure 5.2 Sample occurrence report.

an investigator or, perhaps, by the victim of the crime. The occurrence report depicted in Figure 5.2 asks for important details such as the location, crime type, time, and reporting officer. Using this example, a computer database can be described through the following elements:

Character — This consists of a single alphabetical, numeric, or other symbol. A character is made up of a byte, which is a sequence of eight binary digits or bits. The word "bit" is a contraction for "binary digit" and has one of two values: a zero (0) or a one (1), or by the physical states of on or off. The term "digital" derives its meaning from the binary conditions (base of 2) that exist at the bit level — and, of course, is a contrast to an analog value, which is continuously flowing over a range.

Field — Each box in an occurrence report is called a field. In a database, fields may be designated numerical (file numbers) or alphanumeric (a name). A grouping of the characters in a victim's last name forms the surname field. The victim is an entity (an object, person, place, or event). Associated with entities are attributes. For example, a person has characteristics which are reflected in fields such as date of birth (D.O.B.) or address.

Records — When all (or as many as possible) of the fields to an occurrence have been completed, the grouping of fields is known as a record. An occurrence report narrative is an example of a variable-length record since the size is unknown. For example, there could be many suspects or witnesses, with an unknown number of text narratives associated with the record.

File — Groupings of related records are known as files. For example, occurrences can be assembled into an occurrence file containing the information from all of the police contacts. In early computerized systems, because of storage and processing limitations, only the tombstone information would be entered into a computer program. In effect, the card file was the only thing automated and the retrieval of narrative information still required the investigator to find the paper report.

Database — The term "database" can refer to some, or all, of the following:

- A collection of data or information that is stored and indexed on a computer
- The software that is used to organize, store, and retrieve the information or data
- A combination of data, organizing software, and commercially purchased or custom written codes and procedures that allows the user to obtain information to assist in operational or managerial decision making

The job of organizing the many files that are derived from the information collection and administrative needs is the work of the database and its management system.

There are several models of information storage structures. When mainframe computers first appeared in the late 1960s and early 1970s, the applications were typically written in Cobol and utilized hierarchical and network models. Today, the most widely used structure is the relational model, which was used in many early PC database programs such as DBase II. Modern PC systems that use the relational model include Access and Foxpro. Larger implementations (client server, web-based) of a relational model are found today in products from IBM, Oracle, Informix, Sybase, and Microsoft. All have similarities in that they store and retrieve data, manage indexing, and perform housekeeping and management tasks.

File Number	Surname	Given 1	Given 2	Person Code	Reporting Officer	District Location
00-1	Sausage	Samuel	Raymond	V	974	3
00-2	Gadon	Nancy	Samantha	W	1498	6

| 00-73304 | Aguilar | Robert | Jose | W | 1876 | 2 |
| 00-73305 | Chen | Tien | Voung | R | 1499 | 1 |

Figure 5.3 A sample occurrence table.

Badge Number	Surname	Given 1	Given 2	District Assignment
1134	Falconi	Jean	Elizabeth	Retired
1135	Manning	Lauren	Emily	3
1136	Inkster	Phillip	Dawson	Retired

| 1498 | McQuiggin | Kevin | Arthur | 6 |
| 1499 | McConnell | Keiron | Darrin | 5 |

Figure 5.4 A sample employee table.

5.4   The Relational Database

The vast majority of DBMS systems are based on the relational model, which is intuitive to understand and very powerful. In illustrating the concepts, it is helpful to look back at the earlier card files and the occurrence report examples. A relational DBMS is table based. Figure 5.3 depicts a portion of the elements or fields recorded in the police occurrence report, and Figure 5.4 shows a portion of a police personnel officer table.

These examples do not need to be carefully studied and are used to illustrate the first characteristic of a relational model: all data are stored in

Surname	Given 1	District Assignment
Falconi	Jean	Retired
Inkster	Phillip	Retired

Figure 5.5 A new table of retired officers.

tables which have rows and columns — similar to a spreadsheet. The second characteristic is everything you can do to a table or series of tables results in another table. This can be shown by taking the Employee Table and asking for a listing of all the retired officers. Another table would result as shown in Figure 5.5.

5.5 Queries

A search of a table for a group or a single record can be achieved through a query. For a relational database, the standard language used to ask a question is SQL or Structured Query Language (also pronounced "sequel"). Applications such as a CAD, RMS, or a mapping program will be written in a traditional programming language such as Cobol, Fortran, C, C++, or Visual Basic. SQL is text based and will be inserted into the program.

Relational databases are rooted in matrix algebra and concepts such as sets, unions, and intersections. A SQL query can become very long and complex, but can be described simply as:

Select
Column (s)
FROM tables (s)
<WHERE condition>
<GROUP BY condition
<HAVING grouped characteristics>

A SQL statement that would generate the table shown previously in Figure 5.5 could be:

Select Surname, Given 1, District_Assignment from Employee_Table where District_Assignment = "Retired"

A more complex query could arise if a manager wanted to know how many officers were assigned to District 5 and took report calls in District 1. A portion of the SQL command could be worded as:

Select District_Assignment from Employee_Table, District_Location from Occurrence_Table where Badge_Number = Reporting_Officer

In the query, the portion that states "*Badge_number = Reporting_Officer*" links the records from the two tables. The application software can then manipulate the resulting tables or the new tables can be subjected to additional SQL commands.

In most applications, a user interface is provided that constructs or builds the SQL query to the DBMS. One intuitive method is to query with a form. Selected parameters are filled in on a form and the application will build the SQL statement. There are many examples on the Internet of these intuitive interfaces, including the database front-ends described in Chapters 1 and 2 which allow a person to query who is in jail.

5.6 Data Warehouses, Data Marts

A data warehouse is a term used to describe a system that manages a large amount of data. Often, the data are contributed from a number of internal and external sources including legacy systems. The data are kept separate from an organization's transaction database so that detailed queries and intensive searches do not affect response times for online transaction applications. The key difference between a data warehouse and a traditional transaction-oriented database is the storage schema. A data warehouse stores information so that retrieval and analysis are supported. The key purpose is to support analysis and decision making, not responsiveness.

For smaller subsets of data, the term "data mart" is applied. While the distinction between large and small is not always clear, a data mart can be more readily implemented by focusing on a subset of data.

In Practice: Data Warehousing in L.A. County

The Consolidated Criminal History Reporting System (CCHRS) serves 10,000 users in Los Angeles County. It is capable of providing a complete criminal history on a defendant in less than 2½ seconds from a data warehouse of over 200 million records. Ad hoc searches are permitted so that investigators can access suspect profiles in minutes rather than wading through paper files that may be stored at many locations. There are automatic warnings given if a defendant has warrants, a communicable disease, is dangerous, or requires special handling. Criminal histories are immediately updated whenever there is a new arrest, new case filing, or a significant change in a pending matter. In addition, high-resolution color photographs of mug shots and tattoos are available and can be used to assemble photo line-ups.

The application allows users to build a query using a highly intuitive "search within" capability. Suppose you are looking for the following: Burglary Suspect who is taller than 5'10" and is Asian and has a tattoo of a rose and a dragon. The actual SQL statement may be complex but the user can retrieve the relevant record from the database through an intuitive query process such as:

1. Find all Asian males who are taller than 5'10": 5032 names returned
2. Search within the 5032 names, find the suspects with a rose tattoo: 43 names returned
3. Search within the 43 names returned, find the suspects with a dragon tattoo: 3 names returned

Source: Chotnier, Kenneth, Presentation on Consolidated Criminal History Reporting System, IACP Law Enforcement Managers Conference, May 28, 1998.

5.7 Data Mining

The term *data mining* refers to the retrieval and statistical analysis of information in an unstructured format. Patterns and trends are sought out using statistical algorithms such as regression analysis. Data mining is quite similar to traditional crime analysis. An analyst might look for patterns in crime behavior that suggest a certain suspect may strike next in a specific geographical location. This type of knowledge then can be used to concentrate special task force or directed patrol efforts.

Data mining lends itself to being used by a broader range of knowledge workers in the law enforcement organization. A goal should be to remove the intermediary (analyst) and provide the tools to the officers who have the best understanding of what information is needed. A detective investigating a special type of robbery may wish to correlate locations of offenses against a geographical database of group home locations and their curfew times.

5.8 Data Dictionary (Meta Data)

A data dictionary provides a standard for how information is recorded and accessed. The term *meta data* is used to denote data about data. As an illustration, even if two law enforcement agencies used the exact same paper occurrence report, if different data dictionaries and file structures exist, it can be difficult to merge or access information across the two file structures. The specifications in a data dictionary are exacting and also assist in minimizing errors. For example, the dictionary can check if a data value for a field, such as age, is within specified parameters (greater or equal to 0, less than 120).

In Practice: NLETS Data Dictionary

Fields in a data dictionary must be described with exact precision. Eye color in the NLETS system is specified as:

Eye Color: The subfield contains a three-character alphabetical code from the following table to show the subject's eye color. (The codes listed below are included in the NCIC Code Manual, Part 4, Section 9.)

Eye Color	Code
Black	BLK
Blue	BLU
Brown	BRO
Gray	GRY
Green	GRN
Hazel	HAZ
Maroon	MAR
Multicolored	MUL
Pink	PNK
Unknown	XXX

Source: NLETS Interstate Criminal History Transmission Specification, Release 1.01, December 1998.

5.9   Specialized Applications

There are many crime-solving and crime-targeting tools that rely on the processing power of computers. Computers are able to manage large amounts of data, as well as able to display the results in a presentable form. Several applications will be described, and most utilize the ability to capture and store information in digital formats. The computer can make lightning-fast comparisons and display intuitively the successful queries. DNA and AFIS databanks are examples of data storage schemas that do not utilize tables and text data.

5.10   Crime Mapping and Database Applications

Crime maps play a large role in the research, analysis, and presentation of information. Map applications can be considered in a category all their own,

Table 5.1   Uses of Mapping

Use of Mapping	Percent
Inform officers and investigators of crime incident locations	94
Make resource allocation decisions	56
Evaluate interventions	49
Inform residents about crime activity and changes in their community	47
Identify repeat calls-for-service locations	44

and there are many books that describe the process and benefits well. Fundamentally, maps are a means of displaying information assembled from a database query. While the same information can be presented in table format, the use of a graphical presentation tool such as a "hot spot" map will enhance the comprehending of trends and relationships. The visual display a map provides results in information being more rapidly synthesized and understood. Crime analysts can look for hidden patterns through the layering of data. A map that shows overnight robberies can be used to brief senior commanders who in turn can use it to facilitate their questioning of district commanders. The maps become powerful control and accountability tools.

A computer-generated crime map is usually produced with a Geographical Information System (GIS) application such as MapInfo or ArcView. The software produces maps by merging information from a crime database and a geographical street file database. In the batch matching process, crime locations are geo-coded into x–y coordinates through a process using either street centerlines (every address in a block is encoded) or parcels (every piece of land that is bought or sold is encoded). A comparison is then made with the street file coordinates previously loaded into the GIS application. In a 1999 National Institute of Justice survey of law enforcement agencies on the usefulness of maps, uses were reported as shown in Table 5.1.

In Practice: ComStat and the New York Police Department

In 1994, Police Commissioner William Bratton and his senior officers pioneered the use of ComStat (computerized crime mapping) to assist in developing crime reduction strategies. Twice a week, large maps of precincts and crime occurrences were displayed. The sessions were designed to improve accountability while at the same time provide precinct commanders with local discretion and resources to manage their crime problems. Variations of ComStat have been implemented in many other agencies such as Broward County (POWERTRAC) and Los Angeles (RAPIDCOM). In his book *Turnaround*, Bratton outlined the purpose of ComStat and how it related to stopping crime:

Where are the crimes occurring? Put them on a map. What are the times by day of the week, by time of day. Here are the crimes, you've got them on a map. Let's coordinate the efforts between detectives and plainclothes and get there fast so we can catch the crooks. What are we going to do once we get there (decoys, buy and bust, warrant or quality of life enforcement)? Is it working? Were the tactics effective? Was crime going down?

Source: Bratton, William, *Turnaround, How America's Top Cop Reversed the Crime Epidemic*, Random House, New York, 1998.

5.11   DNA Databases

The Combined DNA Index System (CODIS) is a secure network and software application that was developed by the FBI and the U.S. Department of Justice. It has become the world standard for recording databank DNA profile-matching information and ensures reliable and accurate transmission of match information. CODIS specifies 13 genetic markers so that database fields are standardized. It can assist in cases that have no suspect, link serial crimes occurring among different jurisdictions, and can help identify and prosecute repeat offenders. Local statutes authorize law enforcement agencies to collect DNA samples from persons convicted of serious crimes such as sexual offenses, child abuse, homicide, and attempted homicide. In the U.S., unsolved DNA cases can be transmitted electronically to the FBI for a national database search.

In Practice: DNA Databanks Proliferate

The September 13, 1999 issue of *Time* magazine profiled the efforts of defense lawyers to free wrongfully convicted persons using DNA evidence. The story also described the status of state databases, and almost all U.S. states and many countries have built up DNA databases. Virginia's DNA bank, for example, currently has 190,000 samples, which have produced about 60 matches so far. Virginia is adding samples at the rate of 8000 a month. The FBI CODIS (combined DNA index system) system has been used by agencies to search profiles from other jurisdictions. While investigating a series of rapes in Sarasota, local investigators compared their DNA sample to records stored in the CODIS database. The system returned a match of a suspect who had served time in Virginia 6 years earlier for burglary. The suspect was arrested and convicted.

Source: Cohen, Adam, DNA, Putting bad guys away too, *Time*, September 13, 1999.

5.12   Automated Fingerprint Identification System (AFIS)

For decades, the turn-of-the-century Henry System was used to manually classify prints. Scores of technicians would pore over paper cards and inspect and classify prints rolled using ink. Numerical values would be assigned to a set of prints based on the patterns of loops, arches, and whorls. Federal agencies such as the FBI and the RCMP became central repositories for the ten print cards taken by local law enforcement. In fact, the FBI built an extensive conveyor belt system to facilitate the movement and processing of the fingerprint cards.

In the 1980s, the FBI relied on a hybrid manual and automated system to catalog and search prints. Providing results to local agencies became characterized by long delays and this was seen as unacceptable. In the first half of 1998, over 5000 fugitives were inadvertently released because their 10 fingerprint searches were not returned in time. The delays were especially frustrating for local law enforcement agencies. Many of them had completely automated their searches by implementing commercially automated fingerprint identification systems (AFIS) and some of the systems even eliminated the need for ink and used biometric (livescan) print readers.

The FBI conceived Integrated AFIS (IAFIS) to clear the logjam of national fingerprint queries. The new system inputs a gray-scale fingerprint, crops the image to 512×512 pixels, and employs a process of binarization to determine the thin ridges and extract the minutiae. IAFIS will need to be able to query a database of over 32 million digitized fingerprint cards, each comprising prints from all 10 fingers and containing 750 kilobytes of data after compression.

5.13   Facial Image Database Applications

AFIS has become a commonplace use of the techniques that are involved with digitizing an image, assigning the image a value, and using the value as a basis for searching, comparing, and matching. A newer application is facial recognition software, which can compare a facial image taken from a video camera, and use it to produce matches from a mug shot database. Most facial recognition applications use calculations that are based on the distance of certain identifiable facial characteristics from the eyes, and their nature. The accuracy of the results depends greatly on the quality of the input and database images. Facial recognition applications can be implemented as a back office tool and can be used to assemble photo lineups. In addition, they can be integrated with a closed circuit television (CCTV) system for real-time image searching.

In Practice: Surveillance Cameras in Newham, England

The East London borough of Newham installed FaceIt software from Visionics Corporation in 1998. In conjunction with control room hardware and software, the software is used to automatically scan the faces of people walking through a network of 250 CCTV cameras. The results are searched against a watch list of known criminals, stored in a police database within the control room. An alert is sounded if a match is found. There are claims that the system is responsible for an overall reduction of crime in the area.

Source: Visionics Corporation Website: www.visionics.com.

5.14   National and International Databases

National databases such as NCIC and CPIC have been in place for decades. Their ability to query millions of stored records and return an answer within seconds is one of the greatest enhancements for law enforcement in the 20th century. NCIC was brought online in 1967. Over 80,000 agencies are served and there are approximately 750,000 users entering 2 million transactions per day. Over 20 million records are stored and 17 information databases can be queried with a response time taking usually less than 2 seconds.

NCIC 2000 now has 20 databases containing over 40 million records. The databases include wanted persons, stolen vehicles, deported felons, gang and terrorist members, and missing persons. Other features include:

- Improved name search capabilities
- New and expanded fields
- The ability to search fingerprints
- Delayed inquiry (search automatically performed again after 5 days)
- Linking of information in different files (if a hit is made on a vehicle query, a hit would be made on the wanted persons file)
- New databases (convicted persons on supervised release, convicted sexual offender)
- The ability to send and receive images (mugshot, fingerprints)
- Online validations
- Mobile imaging unit (a laptop in a car can take a print and send it to NCIC)
- Graphical user interface

In Canada, a similar initiative is the CPIC renewal project, which was allocated funding of $115 million in 1999.

5.15   The Information Sharing Problem

There are close to 18,000 separate law enforcement agencies in North America. They serve populations ranging from under 100 to many million, and geographical areas that range from a few acres to an entire country. Most agencies operate within jurisdictional boundaries that limit their authority and service. While law enforcement agencies must legally respect these boundaries, criminals do not. For example, there are many metropolitan areas that are served by a single, regional police agency. More typically, these metropolitan areas are served by many small agencies. These agencies currently do not tend to share information. Paper files could be shared but the logistics and expense prevent this from occurring on a widespread basis.

It is the criminal element that benefits the most from this state of affairs. Following an attempted sexual assault, a person may be stopped on one side of a street, and an officer in Agency A would make a records query for previous encounters with the police. The person may be suspected, but never charged in stalking and sex crimes occurring in Agency B's jurisdiction, which begins on the other side of the same street. The information in Agency B's records database is likely inaccessible by officers working in adjoining agencies such as Agency A.

On March 3, 1999, Philadelphia Police Commissioner John Timoney testified before the U.S. House of Representatives' Committee on Government Reform and Oversight. He made several remarks on decentralizing management control to local commanders and presented examples of how the use of computerized crime maps can help local commanders set strategic and tactical enforcement targets. On the subject of multi-jurisdictional crime, Timoney stated:

> In order to fight crime effectively, police commanders have to identify crime patterns. Unfortunately, as you saw from the maps, these patterns often cross boundaries because criminals, for reasons best known to themselves, appear to have no respect for jurisdictional boundaries. This is not serious when the boundaries are between the districts of the Philadelphia Police Department. But it becomes more difficult when the criminals decide to ignore the Philadelphia city limits and to extend their activities to other townships, counties, or even states.

Commissioner Timoney outlined the problems the Philadelphia Police have encountered in trying to exchange information with the 100 other law enforcement agencies operating in the region. Using the example of mapping stolen vehicle incidents, he commented:

Each department collects this information in its own way and each has its own independent computer systems to maintain and analyze it. These systems cannot talk to each other because they each operate according to their own set of data and technical standards. As a result, exchanging information between these departments, while it can, of course, be done, is a laborious and expensive undertaking that is worth doing only in very special circumstances. If, on the other hand, all these departments were to share common data and technical standards, the exchange of crime information could be performed automatically — that is, electronically. That would make the preparation of regional maps of the kind that you have just seen — but regional ones that showed the whole story including cross-jurisdictional crime patterns — a matter of routine. How much more effective we would all be!

The presentation concluded with a plea for the federal government to take a greater role in encouraging information sharing in law enforcement.

That is why I believe that the federal government has an important role to play here. Enabling police departments across the country to exchange crime information electronically is too important a goal to be left to voluntary action at local levels. I know that the Department of Justice is thinking about how best to approach this subject. But I believe that the time for thinking is past; it is now time for action. If the federal government is serious about helping local communities to fight crime more effectively, this is an area in which it can and should take a strong lead. It should commission the development of common data and technical standards for the criminal justice system and take positive steps to encourage local agencies to endorse and adopt them.

5.16   Regional Information Sharing Projects

One of the most important improvements that can be made to make local law enforcement more efficient is information sharing. Even though electronic information is possible, the following barriers still exist:

- Political and partnership impediments
- Turf battles
- Lack of networking capabilities
- Incompatible data and application architectures
- Privacy issues

Data warehousing has been one type of architecture used as a means of bridging the jurisdictional gaps. There have been other systems developed that also address information sharing, and many are based on newer and commercially available development tools. In addition, the ubiquitous connectivity provided by the Internet has led to new and inexpensive networking approaches.

Case Study 1: NEGIS

The Northeast Gang Information System (NEGIS) was launched in 1996 with a purpose of pooling information on gangs that migrated from metropolitan New York to Vermont, Rhode Island, New Hampshire, and Maine. In the new territories, the gang members looked for fresh recruits and new markets. Local law enforcement agencies had little knowledge of who the gang members were, and where they were coming from. In a 1999 study conducted by the Police Executive Research Forum, it was stated:

> The greatest obstacle keeping law enforcement agencies from effectively tracking and arresting gang members is the lack of regional police agency networks that offer 24-hour-a-day, 7-day-a-week access to information databases. Law enforcement investigators and analysts need such systems so they can quickly access a broad, integrated database of information on gangs, gang members, gang intelligence, gang member history, and their alleged offenses. Before NEGIS, criminal information databases offered an index or "pointer" system, notifying an inquiring officer about other agencies with information on a specific subject. However, no system offered a true pooling of information. In that regard, NEGIS was a first.

NEGIS uses the functionality available in the GroupWare program, Lotus Notes, for e-mail and database templates. The major internal databases are:

Criminal Intelligence Database — This is the main function of NEGIS and contains information on specific gangs, gang members, and criminal activities.

Leads Database — This database serves as an automated bulletin board for posting general questions, issues, and trends not related to actual investigations.

Law Enforcement Directory — This database lists the specialized skills of investigators working NEGIS member agencies.

Reference Library — Court decisions, news reports, and public domain information are collected in this database.

The Massachusetts State Police host the system. Consideration was given to using a secure Internet interface but there was a concern over relying on a commercial provider who may have unreliable service. The original networking configuration was based on dial-up connections that linked the central hub server to servers in Rhode Island, New York State, Connecticut, and Vermont. Users within the state of Vermont connected using the state WAN.

Case Study 2: RISS

The Regional Information Sharing Systems (RISS) center is funded by the Bureau of Justice Assistance, U.S. Department of Justice. RISS supports investigative efforts that span multiple jurisdictions such as drug trafficking, organized crime, gang activity, and violent crimes. It ties together six multi-state regional databases using a secure Intranet architecture. The four components are:

> Secure Intranet — This provides electronic mail to the users, and also browser access to the six separate databases. Access is obtained using a regular Internet Service Provider (ISP) connection. The authentication of users is achieved through firewalls and smart card readers and information is encrypted.
>
> Intelligence Database Pointer System (RISSNET) — A facility is available that connects all six databases. If a search is performed using the pointer system, a search is conducted of all six databases.
>
> RISS National Gang Database (RISSGang) — This is a specific application designed to track information on gang members and activities. Images are also available.
>
> RISS Investigative Leads Bulletin Board (RISSLeads) — This is a collaborative product similar in structure to a USENET bulleting board. Information can be posted on a specific case or other law enforcement problem.

Case Study 3: ARJIS

San Diego County is served by the Automated Regional Justice Information System (ARJIS). The Intranet is statewide and the databases contain information on crime cases, arrests, citations, field interviews, traffic accidents, fraudulent documents, and stolen property. Information is used for criminal investigations, statistical information, and crime analysis. Access to ARJIS is through the trusted network, ARJISNet, and the client software is a standard browser. In 2000, a network of 1500 computers in San Diego County was supported and 7000 authorized users generated over 40,000 transactions per day.

Investigators can also request notification of information concerning an individual, location, or vehicle. The mobility of criminals within the county was the driving force for the creation of ARJIS. It is governed by a management committee, which has representation from the many member agencies. In addition, there are technical and user committees.

Some specific applications of note are Cal-Photo, which is a mug shot database, and Cal-Gang, which is a relational database that combines information from multiple sources on gang-related activities, members, associates, and organizations. Link analysis tools are also built into Cal-Gang. Its predecessor was the GREAT system, and the economics of Intranet technology have allowed 80 users to be put on the system for the same money it used to take to connect one user. The new system cost $800,000 and developing the system using legacy technology would have cost $2.5 million.

Case Study 4: PRIME-BC

The U.S. NCIC network was originally based on the Bi-Sync protocol and the migration to TCP/IP, which is the language of the Internet, started in the late 1990s. The Canadian CPIC application resides on the National Police Services Network (NPSN) which is already a TCP/IP network. Since all Canadian agencies require CPIC connectivity, they already have private NPSN connections. Members of the Vancouver Police Department and the RCMP developed a private Intranet for the Greater Vancouver area using publicly available freeware such as the FreeBSD operating system, Apache server, Sendmail e-mail program, and the MySQL relational database.

Applications that were developed included:

- Private e-mail
- Newsgroups/bulletin boards with keyword search capabilities
- Home pages — VPD robbery, parole info, hate crime
- Databases

The information stored in the legacy Vancouver Police database was imported to the Intranet and search tools were refined. For example, end users could now search for a range of descriptors such as height or weight. Previously, a special SQL query had to be written by IT staff. In addition, the information in the database was now available to every agency directly, whereas previously a phone call had to be made.

The bulletin board system generated an early success when an investigator from the city of Burnaby read a posting about a bank robber caught in the city of Richmond, a bordering community. The detective concluded from looking at the suspect's picture and comparing it to a bank surveillance photo that the same suspect had robbed both banks. A photo lineup conducted with the victimized bank teller confirmed the identification and charges were laid. The benefits of the new information-sharing tool were made even more obvious when it was noted that the investigators in both jurisdictions worked for the same law enforcement agency, the RCMP. They worked in separate detachments and the existing information sharing tool, PIRS, contained only limited text fields. PIRS was developed in the early 1980s.

Case Study 5: RACKETS

A major information sharing problem that is common to all large urban areas in the U.S is that criminal communities are organized by geography, but the investigating agencies are organized by specialty. For example, investigative agencies are divided among crime types (Drug Enforcement Agency, Immigration and Naturalization Service, and Bureau of Alcohol, Tobacco, and Firearms), but criminals operate in particular neighborhoods. As an example, a major roundup by the FBI of suspects in a building could take place on the same day as the DEA was planning to execute search warrants.

The commonality that these investigative bodies share is that the cases eventually end up in the U.S. Attorney's Office (USAO). In fact, the USAO, South District of New York (SDNY), began prosecuting large numbers of racketeering cases and found that there were numerous links to investigations from multiple agencies — both open and closed. This prompted them to develop a database of cases so that the interconnections in cases could be identified (hence the name RACKETS). Key data fields included:

- Addresses of defendants, victims, and witnesses
- Crime locations
- Areas and topics of cooperation of federal witnesses

The system was developed using:

- Microsoft Access as the database
- ArcView as the mapping program
- Geographic Data Technologies' Dynamap 2000 for the geographical base files. These files contain information on streets, rivers, parks, and schools.

RACKETS allows prosecutors to view most of the relationships and intersections at the click of a button and has greatly assisted the USAO SDNY in building solid, comprehensive cases. It has also proven valuable in assisting in homicide, forfeiture, and police corruption cases.

Case Study 6: HITS

The Washington State Attorney General's Office administers the Homicide Investigation Tracking System (HITS) which is a database application used to store data from individual violent crime cases, which are voluntarily submitted by police and sheriff agencies in the Pacific Northwest. In addition, the massive amount of data that is accumulated in serial crime cases is entered.

HITS accumulates information on the salient characteristics of murders, attempted murders, suspected murders, missing persons, and violent crimes. The four major databases are a person file, a vehicle file, an address file, and a summary file. These are linked to a murder file, a crime data file, a vice database, a department of corrections database, and a tip sheet database that manages the large amounts of incoming information that arise in a serial crime case.

The development of the system began in 1987 and was spurred by the investigations into serial killer Ted Bundy's crimes, and the Green River killer, who is suspected of killing more than 49 people. This Green River killer task force at one point accumulated 8000 pieces of information every day. Whereas the Ted Bundy investigation had 3500 suspects, the Green River killer investigation had 58,000. HITS currently contains data from over 6400 murders and over 7200 sexual assaults, and each year over 800 requests for assistance or information are made.

Using HITS, a query can be entered and an answer is obtained in seconds. In jurisdictions where violent crime information is not accumulated on a regional and automated basis, finding out the same answer could take thousands of hours of investigator time. In a conference discussion, Dr. Robert Keppel, the lead developer of HITS, remarked, "In serial murder cases and serial rape cases, [investigators] ought to be thinking about the fact that the name of the killer or rapist [being sought] is recorded somewhere in the investigative files." He further stated, "As an investigator that looks into serial offenses like robberies and rapes, you are always looking for somebody's case that may have more suspect information than yours."

A notable success story involved the time period from 1990 to 1996, and it was determined through HITS that 39 serial rapists (3 or more rapes) were active in the region. Further analysis of these cases led to the identification, location, and/or conviction of 22 of these suspects.

5.17 End-of-Chapter Comments

In all organizations, a DBMS has a key role in allowing users to access and process the vast amounts of information that are collected. DBMS products support the archival, retrieval, and mining of many data types including text, images, and numerical values. With the recognition that information sharing over a regional basis is very important, secure network access is also needed so that a remote user can submit and extract information. Internet-based systems using virtual private networking to address security are fast gaining acceptance as a means of connecting law enforcement agencies and officers.

References

ARJIS Website: www.arjis.org.

Bratton, William, *Turnaround, How America's Top Cop Reversed the Crime Epidemic*, Random House, New York, 1998.

Chotnier, Kenneth, Consolidated Criminal History Reporting System, Presentation at the IACP LEIM Conference, May 1998.

Chu, Jim, Multijurisdictional Sharing over an Intranet, Presentation at the IACP LEIM Conference, May 1999.

Cohen, Adam, DNA, Putting bad guys away too, *Time*, September 13, 1999.

Dussault, Raymond, GangNet: a new tool in the war on gangs, *Government Technology*, January 1998.

Glazer, Elizabeth, Harnessing information in a prosecutor's office, *National Institute of Justice Journal*, October 2000.

Harris, Keith, Mapping Crime, Principles and Practice, National Institute of Justice, 1999.

ImageWare Software Inc. Website: www.iwsinc.com.

Karchmer, Clifford, Northeast Gang Information System: Description of the System and Lessons Learned, Police Executive Research Forum, October 1999, Website: www.nlectc.org.

Mamalian, Cynthia and LaVigne, Nancy, The Use of Computerized Crime Mapping by Law Enforcement: Survey Results, National Institute of Justice, January 1999.

NLETS Interstate Criminal History Transmission Specification, Release 1.01, December 1998.

RISSNET Pamphlet, Bureau of Justice Assistance, U.S. Department of Justice.

Scigliano, Eric, The tide of prints, *Technology Review*, January/February 1999.

Technology Solutions for Public Safety Conference Report, U.S. National Institute of Justice Office of Science and Technology, NCJ 162532, April 1996.

Timoney, John F., Testimony at House of Representatives: Committee on Government Reform and Oversight, March 3, 1999, Website:
http://www.house.gov/reform/hearings/federalism/timoney.htm.

Visionics Corporation Website: www.visionics.com.

Washington State Attorney General HITS Website: www.wa.gov/ago/hits.

Computer-Aided Dispatch

6

6.1 Introduction to CAD

A functional area that saw early automation was the call center, which serves as the communications link between calls for assistance from the public and public safety responders. In the late 1970s, computer-aided dispatch (CAD) systems began to appear that automated much of the workflow associated with the receipt of calls for service from the public, and the command and control of police, fire, and emergency medical responders.

Initial installations saw the three emergency services implementing separate CAD systems. A growing trend is to implement a shared tri-service CAD, and an example of this is an ambulance crew that requires police and fire assistance. An integrated CAD could automatically create a police and fire call using the ambulance call information. The dispatcher only needs to add comments on the nature of the assistance request and perhaps verify the priority level of the response.

CAD systems have been used widely in many non-public safety organizations, such as transportation and shipping companies. For these private businesses, a CAD has provided them with competitive advantages by making more efficient, primary value activities such as inbound and outbound logistics. For example, a taxi company utilizing a CAD can move to entirely voiceless dispatches, and even handle requests for service through IVR prompts, thus negating the need for a live customer service agent. Currently, driver safety and the fair distribution of calls are important issues. In the future, a geographical positioning system (GPS) could be integrated and the overall travel mileage spent on pickups can be reduced as the closest cab can be sent to a caller's location.

For public safety purposes, a CAD system must perform to a mission critical level of stability and reliability, within a dynamic and often high volume environment. It is no understatement in emphasizing that CAD systems form a vital and integral part of the response to many situations, many with life or death implications. The major operational benefits are in the areas of:

- Timely information — Call details are presented quickly, graphically, and in a consistent and intuitive display format, so that confusion for dispatchers is minimized.

- Officer safety — Field units are continually monitored including call status and unit status. If an officer is on a "street check" or a call assignment for too long without an update, the CAD system can alert the dispatcher to contact a member for a status based on a "time out" feature.
- Decision support — Pre-established defaults in the system can guide a dispatcher and also prompt further actions. The availability of online information access improves the call center's ability to determine call priorities and appropriate unit responses.

6.2   Manual Processes and Workflow

The concepts behind a CAD can be illustrated by first understanding the manual workflows that a CAD can replace. There are many benefits in having a CAD system, yet many agencies, both small and large, still rely on paper "call tickets" to manually process calls and dispatches. In larger centers, the business process of responding to emergency and non-emergency requests for service often involves two components or positions. The job position descriptions are:

Call taker — This individual works with telephony equipment integrated to the PSTN. The call taker speaks to emergency and non-emergency complainants (members of the public) and records the relevant information for the dispatcher. Seldom does the call taker speak with field units over the radio.

Dispatcher — This individual primarily speaks with field units over the radio network. The dispatcher reads the information recorded by call takers and conveys the information, usually by voice radio, to field units. If mobile data terminals are available, dispatches may be made silently with an electronic message. Usually, dispatchers do not speak with 911 callers. In centers without a CAD deployment, all of the information is handwritten. Calls from the public are recorded on log sheets or on paper cards. Time stamps are used to note times such as when a call is received and when a dispatch is made. Also recorded by hand are details such as who is calling, what the caller is reporting, and dispatch and incident status information. A physical transport system (runners or conveyor belts) is often used as a means for passing information between a call taker and a dispatcher (Figure 6.1).

Dispatchers may utilize small card slots and place magnetic cars on a metallic map to keep track of which units are doing what. The assignment of work is a very subjective process and often depends on dispatcher judgment. This can be problematic with new or overburdened staff. The obvious drawbacks with manual paper systems are:

Figure 6.1 The Vancouver Police Call Center in 1975. Call information is written onto cards and placed on a four-track conveyor belt that takes the card to one of four dispatch stations located at the ends of the conveyor belt. In 1988, the conveyer belt was replaced by a CAD system.

- Information dissemination bottlenecks (time delays)
- Inaccuracies arising from handwritten notes
- The lack of an automated information retrieval process
- Inconsistencies in the applications of policies and procedures

In Practice: Houston Police before CAD

Prior to implementing a CAD, the Houston Police Dispatch Center used two rooms with call takers on the third floor and dispatchers on the second floor. Calls were written on message slips and addresses were verified using a microfiche index of the city. A continuous-loop conveyer belt would transport message slips between floors. The weak point was the transport belt, which often lost slips along the way, or would simply break down. The status of units was tracked using switches, lights, cards, and logs. Once the call slips were processed, they were filed into shoeboxes that made data retrieval and analysis so time consuming that it was rarely done.

Source: Kennedy, David, Computer-Aided Police Dispatching in Houston, Texas, Case Program C16-90-985.0, Kennedy School of Government, 1990.

Figure 6.2 The Herkimer County, NY dispatch center. This photo was taken on opening day, August 14, 1999.

If the volume of calls is low, such as in smaller centers, one individual will perform both call taking and dispatch tasks. An example of this model is in the Herkimer County, (NY) PSAP and dispatch center shown in Figure 6.2. Herkimer County's center has three combined call taker/dispatcher work areas.

In very small centers (one or two staff), problems can arise when multiple calls arise or if a major protracted incident arises. These provide strong reasons to consolidate or partner so that a larger pool of staff is available. Further factors driving the consolidation of smaller centers are:

- Economies of scale — Technology systems are expensive and complex. Having more agencies partner in a center (including police, fire, and ambulance) allows for the sharing of the substantial initial fixed costs of an automated system.
- Training — In a paper-based smaller center, casual employees can be used for shifts with only a requirement to be familiar with the agency procedures. Sworn officers could be placed in the center with very little training required. With automation, all employees must be trained and certified in the automated systems or they simply will not be able to dispatch. These additional training needs mean that it is expensive to deploy casual employees that fill in for only a few shifts a month.
- Proficiency through practice — Automated systems require practice, and this becomes very apparent during major incidents where dispatcher speed becomes a critical contributor to an effective response.

Figure 6.3 Call taking stations in Salt Lake City Police headquarters. The dispatch stations have hydraulic lifts for ergonomic reasons.

Figure 6.4 Dispatch stations in Salt Lake City Police headquarters are located in a separate room, next door to the call taking room.

Again, casual employees will not be able to perform as quickly as staff who use the automated systems on a regular basis.

Figures 6.3 and 6.4 show the separate call taking and dispatch rooms in the Salt Lake City Police Dispatch Center.

6.3 CAD Architecture

The architecture of a CAD requires hardware and software. The key physical components in a dispatch or call taking workstation are:

- Computer workstation with one to three display monitors (dependent on mapping capabilities being available)
- Printers
- Local area network (in the case of multiple workstations)
- Radio microphone or headset used to speak with field units over the radio system
- Radio control equipment
- PSTN equipment (ANI/ALI displays for centers with E-911, telephone headsets)
- Call check recorders to log the most recent call activity on radio or 911 telephone circuits (used to verify garbled messages or information from excited callers)
- Ergonomic chairs and desks (dispatching is especially stressful and shifts tend to be long)

The CAD software application is installed on a server or host. Depending on the system design, the processing is heavily dependent on the central processor, or designed using distributed (client/server) architecture. Early CAD systems were based on mainframe and minicomputer operating systems such as MVS and VMS. More recent systems are built using the UNIX or Windows NT operating systems. A dispatcher can use a combination of the computer keyboard, hot keys, and the mouse to indicate commands to the CAD system.

6.4 CAD Functionality

Most CAD systems allow the dispatchers to arrange their display screens so that information is laid out using floating windows (Figure 6.5). This makes the system easier to use and also provides an intuitive display structure for decision support data. Other basic screens and functions include:

Call entry and display — A mask is drawn on a computer screen that asks for details such as location, type of call, and caller's name. In older systems, the call taker must refer to a list and enter the correct call code and priority. In newer systems, the complete call list can be accessed through drop-down menus (pick-lists or look-up functions).

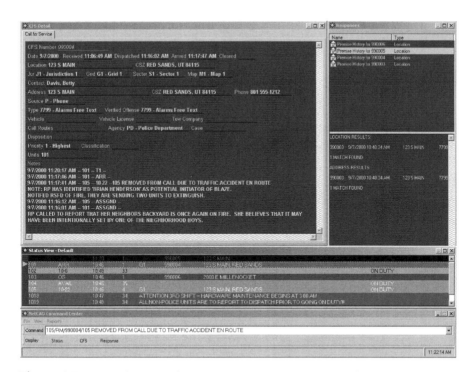

Figure 6.5 A sample screen from NetCAD™, a CAD product from MEGG Associates Inc. (Used with permission.)

Address and jurisdiction verification — A geographical address file (geofile) is maintained so that the location of a call can be cross-referenced and verified against block numbers, map reference areas, census tracts, and cross streets. The call taker then can verify that the incoming call is valid for the jurisdiction being served. If the address is misspelled, similar street names can be displayed using an algorithm such as Soundex. In addition, common names, abbreviations, and common misspellings (park names, public gathering points, etc.) can be entered in the geofile and the CAD system will automatically provide the correct address.

Call pathing — Greater consistency in the area of caller interrogation and information gathering can be achieved through the incorporation of pre-specified questions into the CAD. Questions and directions are displayed through drop-down menus and decision boxes. The call taker is guided through a path of questions to ask. The follow-questions are predicated on answers to previous questions. This can be very helpful in ensuring the necessary information elements are included in calls. CAD systems used for medical call taking may use a call pathing protocol such as ProQA, which specifies questions to ask, and bases subsequent questions on the response from the person reporting the medical problem.

Database lookups — The CAD system will automatically query the call address with an internal database and will advise the call taker or dispatcher if there are relevant call histories or hazard warnings. Other online databases can incorporate city service directories, personnel lists, and telephone lists.

Duplicate searches — When a call for service occurs in a populated area, such as a traffic accident on a busy highway in rush hour, many calls can be received on the same incident. A CAD can alert a call taker if more than one call is entered at or near the same location. Having all calls available online allows the call taker to verify that the incident is already known. A call taker can quickly scan the first call's details and make a determination on whether the current caller has new or additional information.

Call status — All incidents can be reviewed and the calls waiting for a dispatch can be highlighted based on their priority. Calls that were closed off can be retrieved in the event there is a question about what happened or if there is new information to add to the call.

Recommended unit — The CAD can look at the location of the call and recommend a unit based on criteria such as type of required response (Code 3 etc.), what type of call it is, and available sector units. The order in which the CAD system recommends units can be pre-specified in the system. For example, the recommendation can be based on sector assignments or even proximity based on AVL data. This reduces the ability of field units and dispatchers to "call shop." Some CAD systems provide sophisticated algorithms that take into account unit locations and suggest the unit for dispatch with the shortest travel time.

Calls in progress — All units that have been assigned calls will be displayed using a priority ranking system. Units that have been assigned calls will have a timer running. If the unit has not changed status or has failed to provide a situation report within a pre-established call-in period, the dispatcher will be alerted.

Unit status — The CAD will assist dispatchers and supervisors in managing the assignment of work and maximizing the time of the field units. The CAD screen will keep current status information such as:

- Which units are on active calls (and the types of calls they are on)
- What a specific unit's progress is on a call (enroute, on scene, completing reports)
- Which units are available for assignment

- Which units are occupied on other matters but can still be dispatched to a call (headquarters, completing administrative reports, meeting with supervisors, etc.)
- Which units are on duty but out of service (court, lunch workout, occupied with an arrest)

Mapping — A call can be entered and the dispatcher may utilize the mapping subsystem, which displays streets and other geographical features. The exact location of the call can be plotted and a close-up of the location will be displayed. The dispatcher can use the map to guide the responding units. Also overlaid on the mapping subsystem can be calls waiting for a dispatch, unit locations, and even active units if there is an automatic vehicle location AVL/GPS device in the police vehicle. If the map is integrated with operational databases, dispatchers can simply point to a field unit or incident on the map and status information will appear on the screen.

Media and public reports — The CAD system can automatically remove personal information such as a reportee's name and address from a call and provide an edited copy of the call that can be distributed to the public or the media. For incidents such as traffic accidents, CAD systems have been integrated into Websites that show maps and the location of accidents. In addition, some database lookup functions may be ported to a Website and this enables the public to examine call patterns in a given area.

Electronic messaging — CAD systems facilitate the exchange of messages between dispatchers and field units (if they are equipped with mobile data devices). These messages were, in fact, early forms of e-mail and often were used to provide a secure communications channel due to a lack of security (unauthorized listeners) on analog voice radio channels. Furthermore, the data capabilities can serve as a backup in the event the voice radio system becomes overloaded or non-functional.

In Practice: Electronic Messaging — Rodney King and an Early E-mail Lesson

An often repeated adage about e-mail is "don't write it unless you are prepared to have it published." In 1991, many years before e-mail was widely used, the Rodney King incident in Los Angeles saliently illustrated this fact. Across the U.S., the videotaped footage of Mr. King's beating enraged the public. The protests heated up even more when transcripts of the officers' messages sent over their Mobile Data Terminals were released. Messages with racist overtones were passed from unit to unit and they led the public to believe that racial slurs and excessive force were normal conversation items for the officers that policed their communities.

Voice recognition — As the technology with voice recognition by computers matures, more CAD systems will have the capability of responding verbally to system prompts. The CAD can pop up requested function or information screens. Another benefit to dispatchers is that the voice recognition software could be used to recognize radio responses from field units. This could provide automatic status updates as a unit responds by voice to a call.

6.5　CAD and Management Information Systems

The management reports from a CAD can assist in matching resources to the time of day calls are received and the day of the week. Management decision can be made with information such as:

- Response times — Average times before an incident is dispatched, plus the travel time taken for calls, will provide an overall response time. This information can also be separated by the priority of calls and the type.
- Workload — This provides information on the calls per service area (patrol district) and distribution of the many calls over the time of day and day of week.
- Units fielded — The CAD can record how many units were deployed per service area and over what times of the day.
- Officer activity — Managers, supervisors, and the units themselves will access history logs that show calls handled and other activities.
- Call analysis — Call center and field operation planners can analyze what times the calls are coming in and what types of calls are being received. If the addresses are verified using a geographical database (geofile), then x–y coordinates can be retrieved and calls can be imported into maps.
- Ad hoc queries — CAD systems allow for the export of raw data. The tables of data can then be manipulated using standard database programs (Access, Foxpro) or spreadsheets (Excel, Lotus).

6.6　Interfaces

CAD systems can be integrated to many other systems. This enables the CAD to serve as a portal for all real-time information needs. Figure 6.6 diagrams this. Examples of interfaces are in the following sections.

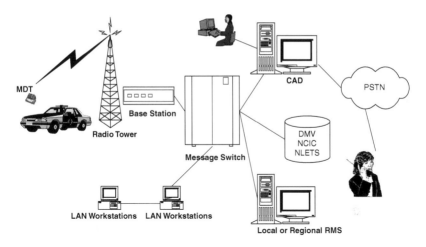

Figure 6.6 The call center, CAD, and mobile data.

6.6.1 E-911

Automatic number information (ANI) and automatic location information (ALI) are database services that may be implemented on the Public Service Telephone Network (PSTN) with a 911 service. If this is present, the "enhanced" prefix is added to 911 (E-911). If this is integrated to the CAD, the telephone subscriber information automatically populates the call taker's screen, saving call entry time and improving accuracy.

6.6.2 Message Switch

A CAD system will allow for multiple external systems to be accessed using one or more message switch configurations. The CAD message switch may need to support connectivity using multiple protocols (SNA 3270, BISYCN, ASYNC, TCP/IP, NETBIOS, etc.) and multiple host sessions. Once implemented, local, state/provincial, and federal databases can be queried such as NCIC, NLETS, CPIC, and state and provincial motor vehicle records. The query itself and the results received can be recorded in the CAD call or unit activity history log.

6.6.3 Mobile Data

During the late 1970s, the first applications of mobile data technology involved the placement of mobile data terminals (MDT) in vehicles. This allowed call information to be displayed on terminals and screens mounted by the front dashboard. CAD systems not only received information (messages) from the MDTs, but also acted as the message switch for the MDT to access local and national databases. The early terminals had smaller screens and operated on private RF networks using proprietary protocols such as Motorola's MMP or MDC.

The displays were small and could display only short text messages. Newer implementations of mobile data utilize laptop Pentium computers with modems accessing public data services such as CDPD, ARDIS, and RAM. If MDTs are integrated with the CAD, the message switch has to be able to support wireless data protocols. In addition, the switch must be able to differentiate messages intended for broadcast to all units, or to specific units based on their call status. For example, only units responding to a particular call should receive call supplements.

6.6.4   Voice Radio System

The CAD system can be linked to a trunked radio system and can show which units have "pushed to talk" (PTT). The radio identification number can be mapped to the unit number that is assigned the radio. If an emergency button on a radio is activated, the radio number and the unit number can be displayed prominently.

6.6.5   Commercial Paging

A CAD system can be linked to paging systems that would advise users that a call has started (such as volunteer firefighters), and can also alert investigators that wish to be notified for specific types of calls.

6.6.6   RMS

An end-to-end integration of the many information gathering and retrieval processes present in law enforcement means that the CAD, as the front-end system, needs to be able to pass information to the mobile reporting and RMS systems. Using the example of a complainant's name on a call, the number of times this is written down in a manual process can be four or more times. For example:

1. Call taker — Takes information on call.
2. Officer in the field — Writes the name of the caller in a notebook.
3. Officer in the field — Transfers the caller's name to a paper report.
4. Data entry section – Takes the officer's report and enters the name into the records section card file or computer index.

This duplication leads to wasted time and also affects the accuracy of the information as it is passed on through the stages of the information processing assembly line. An integrated CAD enables "one-time data entry." Many

Figure 6.7 NetCAD™ from MEGG Associates Inc. can run on a TCP/IP network and can connect to the Internet. A dispatcher can view images from standard Webcams.

agencies see the need to pass CAD call information electronically to a mobile reporting and RMS application. This is now considered a mainstream requirement — especially as older data terminals are being replaced with fully functional ruggedized laptop workstations mounted in police vehicles.

6.6.7 The Internet

NetCAD™ is an example of a CAD system that can be used over a TCP/IP network. This means that a CAD session can be implemented over an Internet connection and connections are possible to the other environments supported by the Internet. This can include standard e-mail messaging, as well as viewing images from Webcams (see Figure 6.7). Firewall and other network protection measures are essential to prevent unauthorized access to message switches and databases.

6.7 Community Policing and CAD

The first CAD implementations in the 1970s had a primary focus on improving response times. Their use, along with mobile data terminals, became the culmination point, and perhaps last gasp of the "response driven" era of policing. In the 20th century, law enforcement brought in the technology devices of the telephone, the automobile, the mobile radio, and finally the computer in the car. Many community policing experts have argued that these technologies distanced the police from the community. Chapter 2 provided perspectives on this subject.

6.8   Costs

Purchasing a CAD system from a vendor can involve the expenditure of several hundred to several million dollars. Factors that will drive costs include:

Number of users — A one-workstation CAD can be purchased for under $1000.

Call volume — Large centers require more workstations to support.

Level of sophistication required — Mapping, integrated AVL, and other advanced features add to the cost.

Level of customization — If the software needs to be altered, then development and support costs rise.

Level of reliability and redundancy — The CAD may have to have failover and hot-backup provisions.

Interfaces — Unusual or one-time interfaces will add to the costs.

Support — Agencies without in-house IT support will need more support from the vendor.

Additional non-vendor costs include:

- Workstation costs and support
- Network administration and costs (wireline, wireless)
- Help desk
- Training

6.9   End-of-Chapter Comments

CAD systems have proved their worth in public safety, and no agency can argue that a CAD system is not required. Call takers can enter call information, and accuracy and speed are improved over manual systems. A CAD will assist dispatchers and supervisors in the real-time management of field units. These officers are paid by the hour and the time savings can be considered a financial offset against the costs of a CAD. In addition, officer safety is enhanced by the availability of online databases including hazard warnings and special instructions. Finally, a CAD is required as a front-end to mobile computing and RMS applications. In a fully integrated environment, even more time savings and greater quality in investigations are achievable.

References

Kennedy, David, Computer-Aided Police Dispatching in Houston, Texas, Case Program C16-90-985.0, Kennedy School of Government, 1990.

Computer-Aided Dispatch, PSWN Website: www.pswn.gov.

Records Management
Systems

7

7.1 Introduction

Television and movie images of policing will portray the main police characters constantly encountering exciting situations, or relaxing with coffee, doughnuts, and the camaraderie of their sidekicks. In reality, a large portion of a police officer's time is spent on the drudgery of paperwork, and this unappealing part of the job is seen as a necessary evil to many. Obviously, regulatory and administrative reasons exist for the extensive record-keeping functions. These include:

- Documenting crimes or occurrences for investigators, insurance companies, and other interested agencies
- Passing information from one unit to another within an agency, or to another law enforcement agency
- Recording police actions should subsequent questions arise
- Establishing how officers are spending their time
- Enabling the statistical reporting of crime occurrences to senior governments
- Maintaining the status of investigations
- Providing documentation for prosecutions

However, the more important reasons for "paperwork," which are often forgotten, are that information:

- Helps solve crimes and problems
- Assists in optimizing the deployment of resources

Administrators and operational leaders must recognize the importance of information and place a greater focus on the usage of the information repositories, not just its collection. The adage, "information to be useful must be shared," is violated continually in the many organizations that have built silos of information. Examples are a drug unit that establishes a stand-alone database on a single PC that cannot be accessed by the robbery squad. A less direct, but perhaps a more important example is the traffic citation database that cannot be "mined" by an investigator looking for a suspect vehicle.

The focal point for the automated entry, storage, and retrieval of information is a records management system (RMS). A properly designed and implemented RMS will allow investigators, crime analysts, and managers to make use of the information that other officers spend so much time and effort collecting and recording. A modern RMS with electronic document and text management tools, and that is integrated to CAD and mobile reporting, can reduce the tremendous amounts of time allocated to the record-keeping process. Moreover, the RMS can increase the quality of the information gathered and ensure the timely distribution and use of information. A sound IT strategy in this area has been shown to save money and produce better information products.

7.2   Filing Systems and the Public Library Analogy

Information archival systems are the foundation of public libraries. The systems that we are all familiar with, such as the Dewey decimal system, can be used to provide an analogy to the evolution of law enforcement RMS systems.

The basic filing process used in law enforcement is the case or file number. Under this unique identifier (a primary key in database terminology), all related documents can be stored. With paper reports, the file number will point to an actual file folder that holds many documents. These folders are stored on shelves in a filing room and take up large amounts of space. In the 26,000-officer London Metropolitan Police Service (New Scotland Yard), 9 miles of shelf space are used.

Key attributes of a report, such as the names of the victim or suspect and the location, may be recorded separately onto a card file (described in Chapter 5, Section 5.2). This card file usually stores the names associated with the file in alphabetical order. When the investigator wishes to access a case, the name of the person involved can be looked up on the card index and the file number will be on the card.

In the case of suspects who have regular contacts with the police, several cards and case numbers will be in the index. Similarly, in a public library, searching for the author name of "O.W. Wilson" will provide Dewey decimal numbers for the works that the library possesses. This will allow a patron to locate the exact shelf where the books are located. An obvious limitation of the card system is the index "key" chosen. By using the "name" field as the primary key, an investigator would be unable to search a vehicle license plate, or an address, and find all of the related incidents.

The first stage of automating a paper card index was to replicate the index systems on a computer. Older RMS systems followed the paper index structures

Figure 7.1 A document imaging workstation in the Aurora (CO) Police Department records section.

and allowed a user to search for a name, which then pointed to a paper file folder. Again, the user would have to either physically inspect the original paper reports or ask a records clerk to forward a copy. Depending on the sophistication of the RMS, all or some of the other information on a hand-written paper report could be data entered by a clerk. This, of course, is duplicate data entry, and problems of accuracy, cost, and backlogs make the feasibility of keyboarding all of the handwritten text quite unappealing.

There are many agencies that have officers in the field telephone a report center and dictate a narrative to a typist. This reduces the quality of the written narratives, and it is expensive to have staff on standby for telephone calls.

Similarly, in the library world, computerized indexes replaced card files in libraries, and users within the facility, as well as remote users, could browse the catalog. Entering the name "O.W. Wilson" will return a list of all of the library's holdings and the screen could even include the "copy status" information. The RCMP Police Records Information Retrieval System (PIRS) is still in wide use today and is an example of an index-based system.

Some agencies that cannot afford the expense of entering every single typed or written word into their RMS will document-image all or a portion of their reports (Figure 7.1). This, essentially, is similar to taking a picture of a piece of paper. The reports become readily available without the need to retrieve a paper file. Unfortunately, search capabilities are limited, as the text in a scanned image cannot be indexed, searched, or copied.

Unless all information is entered into a RMS as digital text, which is not the practice in most agencies today, it is not possible to search key words. For example, an investigator may have a new case where a pedophile lured a child into a secluded area on the pretense of searching for a lost pet animal. The investigator would want to be able to quickly search the RMS for the keyword "lost" combined with various pet types (bunny rabbit, bunny, puppy, doggie, kitty, kitten, etc.). This should return lists of potentially related cases where, hopefully, there is more suspect information if not actual suspect names.

In a public library, searching for a keyword will only provide related works that include the keyword in the publication abstract. This search will not go through every written word in every book in the library. In both the library and police settings, the ideal situation is for all of this text to be captured in digital format. For example, an ideal library search will not only outline O.W. Wilson's many works, but also allow instant access to his writings, and the writings of others who mention his name.

There are copyright issues that somewhat constrain this capability in public libraries. Arguably, another institution will, or has already, supplanted libraries as the most accessed repository of information. The Internet permits keyword searches and will retrieve Web pages with related content. A modern RMS should permit similar keyword searches so that investigators can get the relevant information in a timely manner.

7.3   Information Gathering Features in a Modern RMS

Data should be easily entered into a RMS. The data entry system should prompt the user for mandatory fields such as time, location, crime code, etc. Field reporting must be a major priority so that reports will not become backlogged for data entry. Moreover, integration to a field reporting subsystem results in lower costs (no duplicate data entry) and is more accurate. Data entry clerks may guess at bad handwriting, and may have to send an entire report back to an officer with a question on the desired word. Other benefits are that supervisors can review reports immediately after they are written, and all work becomes available immediately after it is completed (timeliness).

7.4   Report Structure

The RMS should organize the different reports in a structure that is consistent with their varied use. Some types of reports are given in the following sections.

7.4.1 Occurrence Reports

These reports provide information on reported crimes and certain occurrence types (sudden deaths, industrial accidents, thefts, assaults, robberies, etc.). They provide a picture of what happened, when it happened, and how it happened. Full narratives are provided including initial investigator observations. Chapter 5 has a sample front page to an occurrence report.

7.4.2 Street Check or Field Interview Reports

Officers use this report to document suspicious activity that is not criminal. For example, a person found loitering in a certain area late at night could be responsible for overnight burglaries. A narrative is completed of the incident and the report will link people to people, people to vehicles, and people to events. Determining the identity of an unknown suspect can be made through the linkages that are established.

7.4.3 Traffic Citations and Accidents

Traffic incidents involve property damage and injuries and deaths. Recording the types of accidents and the locations will allow an analyst to determine enforcement priorities. In addition, recording the citation details provides a wealth of linkages involving people and vehicles. Many witnesses have difficulty describing a suspect, but are able to provide vehicle descriptions or license plates. The RMS system should permit searches based on a partial license plate number.

7.4.4 Sex Offender Registries

Certain parolees and persons convicted of sex crimes are required to report on a regular basis to the police agency serving the area that they live in. Tracking these individuals and being able to assemble lists of their addresses over several years can be very useful.

7.4.5 Booking Reports

When a suspect is lodged in a custodial facility, detailed information on the suspect's physical appearance, addresses, next of kin, and medical problems is gathered. Indications on whether a suspect is a parolee or probationer at the time of arrest can be captured.

7.4.6 Criminal History Information

All law enforcement agencies are required to maintain a database of their arrests. This information is forwarded to federal and state agencies including the Records of Arrest and Prosecution (RAP) sheets (CREMDES in Canada).

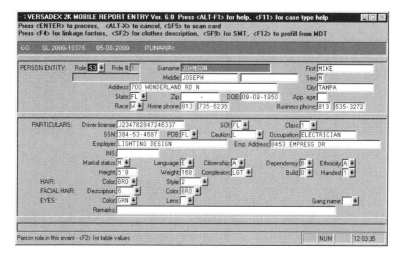

Figure 7.2 A data entry screen from Versadex 2k™ mobile reporting system. (Used with permission from Versaterm Inc.)

7.4.7 Investigation Reports

These provide a more detailed description of crimes and will extensively document the investigator activities, and suspect activities and actions. Opinions and conclusions of the investigator may form part of this report and enable others to look at a suspect's actions and make a judgment on whether the suspect is likely involved in other unsolved crimes.

7.4.8 Evidence Reports

Forensic investigators and scenes-of-crime technicians will gather detailed notes on physical evidence found and the subsequent collection and analysis processes.

7.4.9 Property Reports

Suspects may have a predisposition for favoring certain types of property (jewelry, weapons, etc.). Having the ability to analyze this can be useful when a crime trend is identified.

7.4.10 Statements

Information obtained from suspects, witnesses, and victims can be extremely valuable. A comment about a personal attribute such as, "I saw George reading his horoscope. He does it every day," could be turned into a key suspect descriptor in the case of a psychological profile. Figures 7.2 and 7.3 offer examples of electronic report screens in a RMS.

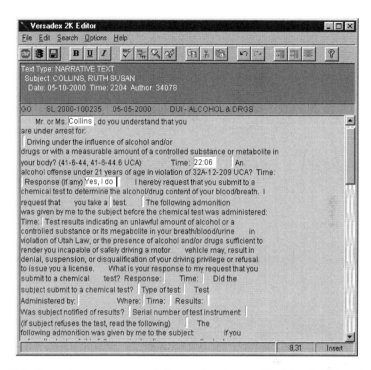

Figure 7.3 Narrative text entry. Information is pre-filled in the Versadex 2k™ screen editor. (Used with permission from Versaterm Inc.)

7.5   Information Usage in Modern RMS

There are many limitations associated with paper processes. The problems are compounded in larger organizations that break down the work and allocate portions to disparate units. In Hammer and Champy's book, *Reengineering the Corporation,* the authors note that:

1. You need to step back at times and examine the processes that are in place. Often, they evolve and become very complex.
2. If the work is broken into many pieces, nobody can see the whole process and the work will bog down.
3. Too many handoffs create too many points of failure.

Many larger agencies experience problems such as information backlogs, lost reports, and inefficient retrieval processes. These problems encourage special units to build their own information systems, which perpetuate the "information silo" effect.

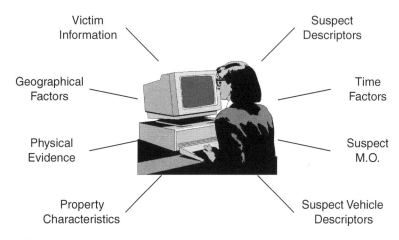

Figure 7.4 Information data types.

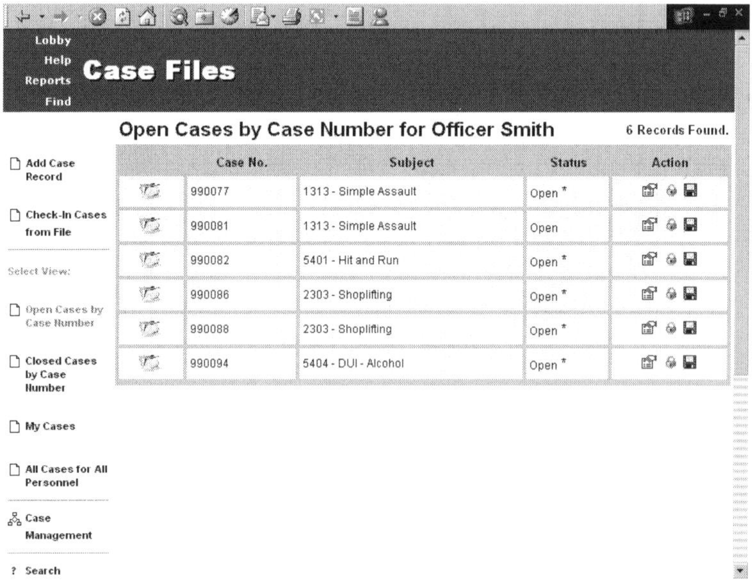

Figure 7.5 Workflow Management Screen NetRMS™. (Used with permission from MEGG Associates Inc.)

A modern RMS can move an organization into the realm of electronic document management. It can ensure that the right information gets to the right people at the right time. Figure 7.4 illustrates the major data types that an investigator needs to access. A RMS system must properly index these categories.

7.6   Workflow Management

A final important function that a modern RMS performs is in the area of incident handling. A workflow management system can increase the accuracy of the work produced (Figure 7.5). Equally important, it can help reduce cycle time — the time it takes a call to be concluded, a report filed, and a case assigned for a follow-up. It must be remembered that the tasks associated with attending calls, interviewing victims and witnesses, searching for suspects, completing reports, reading reports and statements, and looking for clues are all primary value activities (refer to Table 1.2, Law Enforcement Primary Value Activities). IT-based workflow management practices can reduce the costs of these operational activities through:

- Officers tied up on calls for fewer hours
- Reductions in the time it takes to begin and conclude an investigation
- Quicker responses to the public on case status and progression
- Resources being deployed on cases that have the best solvability factors

The goals of a workflow management system are to eliminate multiple data entry points and to coordinate information gathering and usage. A comparison can be drawn with an internal memo sent by e-mail. The e-mail can be copied to several co-workers with a "read receipt" generated for a subordinate that is assigned an action item. Perhaps several months later, a keyword search can be conducted for the subject and the original e-mail will be found.

Workflow in a RMS does rely on the principles of e-mail but the functions are far more sophisticated. Major characteristics are:

- Direct input of information into the RMS using laptops (wireless data) in the field and workstations in the office
- Multimedia files (image and sound files) can be attached to reports
- Quality control edits allowed (changing names to correspond with a master name index file)
- Use of intelligent forms that prompt officers for information (text templates)
- Automatic duplication and routing (multiple e-mails) of information to operational units based on their demands for information (such as keyword- or incident type-based)
- Cases routed to supervisors for final assessments or quality control
- Automatic evaluation of documents for further processing and analysis (special study incidents)
- Solvability factors calculated

- Case assignments prioritized based on type of case, solvability score, and other agency specific rules (differentiated case management), and supervisor allows overrides
- A tracking mechanism provided for reviewing the status of cases by incident and by assigned officer (diary or "assignment due" dates)
- Alerts and messages provided to supervisors if a report (piece of work) is late
- Major case management capabilities so that tips and leads from other officers can be appended to a central file number and an alert (e-mail message) generated for the primary investigator
- Major or sensitive cases prevented from being accessed unless special or pre-set permissions are granted
- Audit trails provided of who accessed what files, and when they were accessed

In Practice: The New Scotland Yard and Nine Miles of Shelf Space

In 1999, New Scotland Yard selected a collaborative Intranet-based solution to manage its records and open case files. The existing document retrieval process involved an officer having to contact a central inquiry office, open 9 A.M. to 5 P.M. Monday to Friday, unless a major incident required immediate access. The Livelink system was purchased from Open Text Inc. and provides online access, through an Intranet, to over 600,000 case files, which occupy more than 9 miles of shelf space. New Scotland Yard hopes to extend its information base into a collaborative knowledge network and forecasts savings of $2.4 million over the next 5 years. According to Alan Oakley, Chief Registrar and Department Record Officer, the new system will "provide officers and support staff with a much faster, more efficient method of tracking down case papers, which can often contain information that will help in new investigations. The search system will enable more precise search results, ultimately enabling officers to investigate crimes more efficiently."

Source: Knowledge net helps Scotland Yard nab criminals, *Knowledge Management World*, 9(3), April 2000.

7.7   End-of-Chapter Comments

In actual practice, very few agencies have reached their desired objective of implementing a fully electronic, end-to-end workflow process. The larger the organization, the more challenging is this task. Mobile reporting, with a wireless data network, is a key component, and Case Study 4 in Chapter 8 provides a description of fully integrated and electronic operations environment in the London, Ontario Police Service.

References

Gottlieb, Steven, Arenberg, Sheldon, and Singh, Raj, Crime Analysis, *From First Report to Final Arrest,* Alpha Publishing, 1999.

Gurton, Annie, Best practice, *IBM Police, Justice and Identification,* 2000.

Hammer, Michael and Champy, James, *Reengineering the Corporation: A Manifesto for Business Revolution,* Rev. Ed., Harper Business, New York, 1997.

Knowledge net helps Scotland Yard nab criminals, *Knowledge Management World,* 9(3), April 2000.

Mobile Computing

8

8.1 Introduction

The previous chapters have outlined the various technology building blocks used in law enforcement, and mobile computing can be viewed as the nexus for the many technology tools already described. While the concept behind a computer in a car has been a reality since the late 1970s, the capabilities of the end computing devices have led to ever-increasing uses. The term "a gun, a badge, and a laptop" has been used to describe what a newly hired police recruit is issued. Now that palm-based computing devices and other hand-helds are becoming more mainstream, even the "laptop" reference may soon be dated.

8.2 Community Policing and the Mobile Worker

While technology has yielded many benefits for law enforcement, there are detractors who pointed out that the automobile, the radio, and the computer in the car have led to the police being further distanced from the community. This characterized the professional policing era. With the current focus on community policing, new ways of looking at technology have led to police leaders realizing that frontline officers can remain in the community longer through mobile computing. The challenge is to provide the tools and information resources to officers in the field so that they can function just as effectively as if they were in the office.

8.3 The Communicating Information Continuum

The context of where mobile computing falls in the communications and information continuum can be illustrated by first looking at the electronic devices that have been available in the past, and then looking at what is used today. This discussion is intended to provide a picture of the information and communications needs that exist in law enforcement and the fact that many tools must be deployed in order to meet these diverse and situational needs. Table 8.1 lists the tools used in law enforcement and compares their utility with three information-sharing parameters.

Table 8.1 Communicating Information

	Parameters		
	1. Timely	2. Mission Critical	3. Access to All Information
Call box	No	No	Not good
Mobile radio	Yes	Yes	Not good
Cellular phone	Yes	No	Not good
MDT	Maybe	No	Better
MWS	Maybe	No	Very good
PDA	Yes	No (presently)	Very good

1. Timely — A call needs to be dispatched immediately or information must be relayed from unit to unit without delay. There is a requirement that the officer be contacted right away. An example of this is an in-progress robbery where field units must be directed to respond to the call as soon as possible.
2. Mission critical — This is defined as a situation where an emergency situation is occurring and many police officers need to be dispatched immediately and coordinated. An example of this is a foot pursuit of a suspect where many units will respond and will need coordination.
3. Access to all information — In the office, a collection of information exists that the mobile worker will need. There are limitations to current technologies that prevent the officer in the field from seeing or hearing everything that another officer sitting in the office can access.

The devices listed in Table 8.1 are still in everyday use, with the exception of the call box. The latest versions of these devices all contain microprocessors and essentially are computing devices. Consistent with the conventions used in this book, a MDT (mobile data terminal) refers to a "dumb" data terminal permanently mounted in a vehicle with a small monochrome display (see Figure 8.1). The MWS (mobile workstation) refers to a laptop computer (mobile data computer or MDC) usually with a color screen (see Figures 8.2 and 8.4). The PDA (personal digital assistant) is a handheld computing device. In addition, it is helpful to think of the user interaction with the device. A user will listen and talk with a portable radio, and will type and look at a laptop computer.

Table 8.1 can be further illustrated through examining a situation where field units are asked to help an officer in a foot pursuit. The mobile radio obviously can be used to contact immediately many units to assist with the pursuit (timely — yes). If the officers only possessed a cellular phone (which is a radio operating on the public network), they could still be alerted quite quickly to assist (timely — yes).

While the call is in progress, the pursuing officer, if equipped with a portable radio, can provide updates on the direction of travel and the suspect description (mission critical — yes). The responding officers can base their containment locations on the directions of the pursing officer. Officers that have cellular phones, but that do not have radios, cannot actively assist (mission critical — no) since cellular phone conversations are between two people and are not broadcast.

Officers that do not have portable radios or cellular phones but have MDTs and MWSs in their vehicles would only be alerted to the situation if they were in their vehicles (timely — maybe). Obviously, the fast pace of communications in a foot pursuit makes the MDT and the MWS ineffective in the chase (mission critical — no). Officers cannot drive and look at a computer screen and if they left the car, they would be without communications.

The suspect is later captured and refuses to say why he ran away or what his name is. The officer, using a portable radio, verbally relays to the dispatcher a possible name for the suspect. A "warrant hit" is retrieved for the name query and the dispatcher broadcasts over the air that the warrant entry states the suspect is "5'10", dark curly hair, Caucasian, born in 1976," and lists the aliases used by the suspect. An officer listens to the description on the radio but he is still uncertain if the right suspect has been apprehended (access to all information — not good).

A digital mugshot image is available to the dispatcher through the CAD and RMS interface, along with the physical description. The digital image is not available to the officer with the radio (access to all information — not good). However, a second officer drives up to the scene with a MDT in his vehicle and runs the same name query. The warrant details and a lengthy report showing the suspect's detailed description are now available for careful review (access to all information — better).

A third officer drives to the scene with a newly installed MWS. This officer has performed the same name query and, in addition to the warrant details, she also has the mugshot image of the suspect on her MWS screen (access to all information — very good). The original pursuing officer shows the suspect his mugshot on the MWS. The suspect, realizing he has been outsmarted by technology, acknowledges his true identity.

The perfect mobile device would have a "yes" answer for all three parameters. While this device does not exist today, in the future the Personal Digital Assistant will likely merge functionality with a portable radio to provide a single robust information tool that can be used for all operational settings. Already, pagers have been merged with computers (Research In Motion, Motorola) and phones have been Web enabled. Today, getting the right information at the right time to mobile police officers requires multiple mobile computing devices.

Figure 8.1 Motorola 9031 MDT used by the Vancouver Police Department. These operated on a private 4800-bps radio channel.

8.4 Mobile Data Terminals

Older mobile devices (Figure 8.1) had to function with limited memory and processing power. They were also known as Status Messaging Terminals and had limited lines for information display. Proprietary operating systems and software (often burned into read-only memory or ROM) were utilized and special interfaces were required to obtain information from CAD systems. The terminals made use of pre-programmed keys such as "in service" and "on scene," and pre-programmed masks were used for motor vehicle and database queries.

8.5 Mobile Workstations

A MWS (also referred to as mobile data computer or MDC) is a PC-based device usually running Windows as an operating system. Law enforcement agencies utilize both standard laptop computers as well as rugged computers. Standard laptops are more suited for use in agencies where there is personal issue, or where laptops are fix mounted in vehicles. While standard laptops have a more limited life span, the cost of one rugged laptop can equal three standard laptops. The New York State Patrol uses a standard Dell laptop (see Figure 11.3).

8.6 MWS Products

There are many variations of mobile computing devices. Due to the rapidly evolving marketplace, many hardware devices that are described here have, or will become, obsolete very quickly.

8.6.1   Rugged Clamshell Notebook

Most rugged computers have a "clamshell" construction style and are designed and built with extreme usage conditions in mind. Special features include shock-resistant motherboards, vibration-resistant connectors, gel-mounted hard drives, and environmentally sealed heavy-duty enclosures made from magnesium or other alloys. The outer case also acts as a heat sink, since fans are not a viable cooling option. An airtight vacuum prevents condensation. Many screen options are available including touch screens. The keyboards are permanently attached and may be backlit.

Most manufacturers of rugged computers are committed to the same form factor while improving the functionality of the internal electronics. This is an important consideration when mounting and docking requirements are considered, since it is expensive to change mounts and consoles. Computers in police vehicles have to withstand vibration, sudden shocks, dust, and liquids. One standard that rugged notebook manufacturers should exceed is MIL-STD-810E for vibration and shock.

Examples of rugged notebook products include:

- Panasonic CF-25 (Figure 8.2), CF-27, and CF-28
- PC Mobile by Cycomm Mobile Solutions
- Microslate MSL 3000P
- Itronix X-C 6250

In Practice: Chicago Police and Personal Digital Terminals

In 1997, the Chicago Police Department spent $7.5 million on 1500 Personal Digital Terminals (PDTs) which primarily were Badger computers with a Motorola 405I+ modem (manufactured by Texlogix Industries). By 1998, officers were making over 40,000 person and vehicle queries per day, and for the year, approximately 23,000 warrant arrests were made and 28,000 stolen vehicles were recovered. In addition, voice radio traffic decreased significantly. The devices are integrated to the new CAD system. The devices have batteries with a 4-hour specified useful battery life and internal modems. The PDTs relied on an upgraded radio infrastructure and all 26 cell sites were connected to the CAD system using a 176-mile fiber optic network.

Source: Ryczek, Martin and Glasser, Richard, Revisiting Chicago's digital revolution, *The Police Chief*, October 2000.

8.6.2   Rugged-Handled Tablet Computers

These computing devices are built to withstand extreme operating conditions. Most are tablet-style computers with display sizes of between 8 and

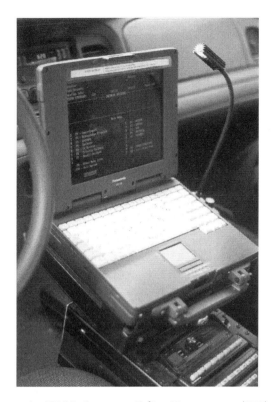

Figure 8.2 Panasonic CF-25, Syracuse Police Department (NY).

10 inches. They are pen based and the keyboards can be optional. Displays are touchscreen and small pens are used instead of a mouse. Tablet computers first appeared in 1993 and were the predecessor to the PDAs. They are primarily used for out-of-vehicle applications although fixed mounts are available. Few agencies still use tablet computers and they have been replaced by PDAs. Products in this category include:

- Fujistsu Stylistic ST 2300 (Figure 8.3)
- Motorola FORTE
- Hammerhead P-233 by Walkabout Computers

8.6.3   Personal Digital Assistants

The mobile computing device of the future, if not the present, is the wireless-enabled PDA. The equipment costs are low, as the devices are available through consumer retailing channels. They are lightweight and their transportability makes them ideal for foot, bicycle, and motorcycle patrol officers. GPS and

Figure 8.3 Fujistu tablet computer, Miami Police Department (FL).

Automatic Person Location (APL) integration allows for the locations of the officers to be pinpointed. Further integration is enabled through intelligent gateway servers, HTML-based software, and TCP/IP transmission protocols. This permits access to the Internet, e-mail, and other public sources of information in addition to the in-house public safety systems. More rugged devices with cellular phone capabilities are starting to appear. Products include:

- iPAQ by Compaq
- PDQ Palmtop by Qualcomm
- Palm VII from Palm Computing
- RIM 950 from Research In Motion

In Practice: The First Law Enforcement Uses of Wireless PDAs

In September 2000, officers in Rolling Meadowlands, IL and Highland Park, TX began to experiment with a wireless-enabled Palm VII computer. The device enables access to local, state, and federal databases as well as e-mail. Administrators in the Highland Park Police envisioned that the Palm Pilots could be used by motorcycle, foot, and bicycle officers. Early concerns, though, were the durability of the device and the small user "keyboard."

Source: Pocketcop: an officer's ticket to freedom from the car, *Law Enforcement News*, September 15, 2000.

Figure 8.4 Litton MobileVu mounted in a SUV patrol vehicle, Castle Rock Police (CO).

8.6.4 Modular Computers

Modular units are generally two- or three-piece computers with the display, keyboard, and processing unit all mounted separately and permanently. Placing the CPU in the glove box or the trunk increases the mounting options in the vehicle. This may be very important in the case of smaller patrol vehicles. Because the computer is never removed from the vehicle, the power draw is always from the vehicle's batteries. Brighter displays have been incorporated that draw power to a level that cannot be supported by internal batteries. A modular unit may have 1000 NITS displays compared with 250 NITS for a laptop that needs power occasionally from internal batteries. Leading products include:

- MW-520 by Motorola
- MobileVu from Litton Data Systems (Figure 8.4)

8.6.5 Combination Clamshell and Modular Computers

In August 2000, Panasonic released its Permanent Display-Removable Computer (PDRC) line. This combines a 1000 NIT display with a portable Toughbook 34 computer. The vendor claims the product is the "best of both worlds" and provides users with readable displays (very important in regions with lots of sunlight) and the freedom of movement associated through carrying a laptop.

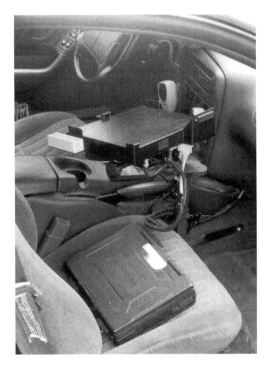

Figure 8.5 Colorado State Patrol, MWS mount in a Camaro.

8.7   Printers

Rugged vehicle printers rely on dot matrix or thermal printing technology. Thermal printouts require special paper and the output will fade over time — especially if direct sunlight or extreme heat conditions exist. An advantage of dot matrix is that several copies of a print job can be made using multi-layered carbonized paper, and this is ideal for traffic citations.

8.8   Mounting and Consoles

The mounting systems for law enforcement have to accommodate a number of operational needs because of the adverse and extreme operating conditions. Especially important is safety. The mounts must be strong enough to not break in an accident (Figure 8.5). They must be able to hold the laptop outside the airbag deployment zone, and vehicle manufacturers publish their air space zones. If both safety conditions are not met, projectiles could be launched at officers in the car or bystanders.

8.8.1   Functionality and Ergonomics

The MWS keyboard has to be accessible to the officer so that short messages can be typed, and the display must be in a place where officers driving to an in-progress call can read supplemental call information sent by the CAD. Ideally, the display will be viewable in sunny conditions. A very good screen for all conditions is a transflective monochrome display. However, the newer information requirements (pictures, mugshots) require color-active matrix displays. For lengthy typing requirements, the MWS has to be removable so that it can be placed on a level surface directly in front of an officer. Obviously, a fixed, mounted MWS with a screen in the middle of a dashboard is not a good platform for lengthy keyboarding. Swivel and positioning capabilities improve the ergonomics.

8.8.2   Durability

The mounts and workstations must withstand the strains of high speed and sudden vehicle movements. Notebook laptops generally sit in docking stations mounted on the consoles which also hold the siren, light controllers, and the voice radio status head. Removable computers are secured with a lock and key. The docking frame must hold the MWS tightly and also connect it to vehicle-mounted systems such as a power supply, external wireless modems or boosters, and printers. The constant locking and unlocking can take its toll on small pin connectors. The docking station ideally has a sliding mechanism to connect the vehicle systems after the MWS is locked into place.

8.9   COPS MORE and Mobile Computing

Since 1994, close to $1 billion in federal COPS MORE grants in the U.S. have been handed out for technology projects. Of this, 33% was used for mobile computing. The usage has literally exploded, as newer inexpensive rugged computers with high levels of functionality become available. Moreover, these laptops are integrated with commercial data services such as CDPD, which offers low costs and low capital risks — as compared with building a private data radio system.

8.10   Definitions of Mobile Computing

In the literal sense, any device utilizing a microprocessor without the need to connect to wireline infrastructure can be considered a mobile computing device. In addition to the legacy MDT, the list expands to include commercial products such as the cellular phone, PCS, pager, and wireless-enabled PDA.

Figure 8.6 An early adopter of handheld MDTs was the Huntington Beach (CA) Police Department, which used the Motorola KDT 840. The device has 64K of RAM and 64K of ROM, and messages are displayed on a 4-line by 40-character liquid crystal display. The MDT uses a private RF system (Motorola DataTAC operating at 4800 bps) to connect to the CLETS and NCIC databases.

Similar to digital phones, the newer generation of mobile radios can be considered a mobile computing device as they are microprocessor controlled and use keypads.

The initial deployment of MDTs (Figure 8.6) was geared to offsetting the operational demand on dispatchers and the congestion on voice radio systems. Field officers queried state, provincial, and federal databases, and device-to-device messaging was permitted. The early MDTs used proprietary operating systems and control software. They offered the advantages of security (MDT messages are difficult to monitor) and speed (officers are not faced with information request bottlenecks at the dispatcher position).

In the mid-1990s, computers using standard Windows operating systems began to replace the MDTs. These devices were initially used to emulate the functionality of a MDT, and initial rollouts often were unable to deliver connectivity to report writing and records systems. Many vendors promoted mobile data solutions and the uses proliferated, driven by needs such as congestion on voice radio channels and the availability of federal funds in the U.S. (COPS MORE grants).

Since 1995, the processing power and reliability of Windows computers have increased. This coupled with the increased availability of commercial wireless services has allowed law enforcement agencies to move closer to the vision of the "office in the car." Clearly, the desired goal is to allow the officer to connect with all of the information services, not just the subsystems that took the workload from the voice-radio channels.

In Practice: Los Angeles Police and MDTs

The LAPD has used silent dispatch and MDTs for more than 15 years. Congestion on voice-radio channels was one of the main reasons for the acquisition of mobile data terminals. The LAPD considers MDTs primary, not secondary dispatch tools. Units receive dispatch information and send status updates without any voice interaction with a dispatcher. The CAD system records the acknowledgments and records the confirmation of the dispatch. The current technology platforms support 73 dispatch consoles, 22 area Command Center consoles, 1419 MDTs, and 10,000 mobile/hand-held voice radios.

In 1998, the LAPD issued 435,607 file numbers. Associated to these individual cases were over 1 million handwritten reports. The process is extremely labor intensive and requires officers to spend their time in offices rather than in their patrol areas. A field data capture project is underway with the objectives of:

- Reducing the time required to generate reports, both in the field and in the station.
- Improve the quality of information gathered by the initial reporting process and increase the efficiency of detectives.
- Eliminate the unnecessary trips to the station to hand in or complete reports that could have been handled in the field.

Source: City of Los Angles, Los Angeles Police Department 90-Day MDC Vendor Selection Study, Request for Information: Mobile Data Computer System, Version 1.0, January 19, 2000.

8.11 Mobile Computing: Method or Product?

It has been argued by one vendor that mobile computing is not a separate stand-alone product. To the officer on the street, the laptop needs to become a window to all of the systems that hold the information required. The mobile data application must be an extension of the CAD and RMS. In the fully integrated environment, mobile computing becomes a method of delivery and integration, rather than a separate application. If this is achieved, then significant officer time savings, along with improved investigative capabilities, are possible.

Today, only a handful of agencies have implemented such an end-to-end solution. It must be emphasized, though, that agencies that have embarked on an incremental technology approach should be commended. These are the agencies that undergo funding, technical, and operational hurdles with the mission to deliver crime-fighting tools to front-line public safety personnel. The managers and technology champions in these agencies know that there are financial and operational payoffs.

The challenge today is that there are numerous "pieces to the puzzle" that have to be put into place for a fully integrated environment. These pieces require extensive planning and significant efforts are needed from managerial, technology, and end-user personnel. The agencies that have started the long and difficult journey, and have taken the business risk associated with complex technologies, are far ahead of the many agencies that have nothing. Furthermore, the size of the agency and the enforcement environment are major factors to weigh in the prioritization of technology projects. The following four case studies describe differing levels of integration and progress.

Case Study 1: Colorado State Patrol

In 1999, the Colorado State Patrol began the first phase of rolling out 500 MWS units. The project goal was to automate the accident reporting and field citation processes. In terms of productivity, troopers are experiencing a 35% increase in productivity on accident reports. The old work process involved troopers making notes in their notebooks and then handwriting reports. The information would then be sent to data entry personnel who would enter the details into a mainframe. With mobile computing, data are collected on laptops and are sent directly into the mainframe. Not only has accuracy improved dramatically, but also the Colorado Department of Transportation now has faster access to accident information. On the citation side, the state Department of Revenue has improved its fine collection process, as they now have access to the front end of the collection process. Early estimates are that $1 million per annum savings in officer and records personnel time is possible.

The equipment selected for use includes Pentax thermal printers, ID Technologies barcode scanners, 3Com digital cameras, and Panasonic Toughbook rugged notebook computers (Figure 8.7). Gamber-Johnson mounting

Figure 8.7 Colorado state trooper and a Panasonic CF27 MWS mounted in a Chevrolet Camaro.

structures were used. In the field, one laptop was retrieved from a high-performance Chevrolet Camaro that was totaled by a state trooper in a rollover accident. Another laptop had its surface damaged by acid from a hazardous materials spill. Both emerged in working order. The wireless data network selected was CDPD. For remote areas, the use of satellite data is being explored. Current interfaces include access to the Colorado Crime Information Center, which permits queries such as wants and warrant queries, criminal histories, and vehicle information. Car-to-car messaging is also supported, and digital images can be attached to a message. Interfaces to CAD and RMS are in the works.

Case Study 2: Valley Emergency Communication Center, Utah

The Valley Emergency Communication Center (VECC) serves a population of more than 1 million and handles 3500 911 calls and 1700 dispatches per day. Several police and fire departments in the Murray and Salt Lake County areas have partnered on a large multi-jurisdictional integrated public safety communications network. VECC selected CDPD because of the large coverage areas, system redundancy, and encryption options. In addition, because CDPD is based on TCP/IP protocols, network versatility was enhanced.

On the hardware side, VECC purchased two IBM AS/400 servers to handle the anticipated 700 users. Toshiba Model 110 laptops and Sierra

CDPD modems were selected. Following a procurement process, HTE Inc. was selected as the CAD vendor and Software Corporation of America (SCA) was selected for its mobile data software. The products were integrated and the mobile computers featured in-vehicle paging, text-to-voice capabilities, and in-vehicle mapping. Field officers can access NLETS and NCIC.

Case Study 3: The Coos Bay (OR) Police Department

Coos Bay Police Department in Oregon has a complement of 30 officers serving a population of 15,500. The patrol officers were caught in a "catch-22" situation every time they hit the streets. To do their best job as field officers, they had to leave the streets for hours on end as they traveled to the police station, logged into the station mainframe, and accessed the databases. These trips reduced the available time for patrol and, consequently, impacted negatively on the department's community policing efforts. In addition, the dispatch center felt overloaded with the volume of information requests. A PacketCluster Patrol system provided by Cerulean Technolgy Inc. was implemented in 1998. Based on Microsoft BackOffice technologies and the NT operating system, the system transfers data in a compressed format utilizing the existing conventional UHF radio network. Coos Bay does not have CDPD coverage.

Officers are able to query remote county databases as well as access the station mainframe. The new functionality was described as being similar to "extension cords to headquarters," and information previously accessible only in the office was now accessible in the field. Information retrieval time was slashed by 99%. Next on the horizon are mug shot imaging and fingerprint recognition.

Case Study 4: The London, Ontario Police Service

The London Police Service in the province of Ontario has a complement of 430 sworn officers and 165 civilian staff. It serves a population of 345,900 and covers 422 square kilometers. In 1992, a four-phase technology procurement project was initiated for:

1. CAD
2. RMS
3. A voice and data radio network
4. Mobile workstations in all patrol vehicles

In 1993, an RFP led to Versaterm Systems being selected as the principal vendor for the CAD, RMS, and MWS projects. Ericsson EDACS was selected as the voice and data radio vendor. In 1993, CAD was live, and in 1994, RMS went live.

For the MWS project, London adopted the theme: "Enter data once, as close to the source as possible, then use the data after that." Driving this were the business needs of the force and the need for timely and accurate information. The London Police wanted all officer statements and witness statements to be accessible as digital text. Options they explored included expanding their data entry pool and setting up a telephone resource center for voice dictation of reports. In 1995, they conducted a pilot project by equipping five cruisers with laptop computers so that direct "from the street" data entry was possible. The pilot proved to them that:

- Officers can use computers to enter reports. In fact, many prefer it.
- The time to complete a report is less than using paper.
- Officers would use a MWS extensively out of the cruiser.
- Statements could be "locked" and electronically signed and these digital statements have been accepted by the courts.
- RMS integration was very critical.

By November 1996, all 85 cruisers had laptops, and in-car mobile report entry replaced pen and paper. Initially, a "sneaker-net" process was used and officers would bring in diskettes at the end of their shifts. In 1997, a 20-channel Ericsson EDACS system was brought online with all channels capable of voice and data traffic. Versaterm Systems worked on this implementation and was able to minimize data transmission requirements using Nettech (now Broadbeam) middleware. The usable wireless bandwidth was 9600 bps. MDT functions were now available and car-to-car and car-to-RMS messaging became possible. More importantly, CAD integration was achieved.

In a typical scenario, a 911 call would be entered on CAD. The officer would receive the call in the MWS MDT window. Status keys would be used to respond to the call. While en route, the officer could query names and license plates. When the officer arrived at the call, an "on scene" hot key could be pressed. Once the call was resolved, the reporting process would begin. The officer could use the CAD call information to pre-fill a report screen on the MWS. There is no need to re-type the location, complainant names, or time and dates. The officer could then add additional information, including UCR codes selected from drop-down menus as well as narratives and statements, and send the complete occurrence report to the RMS. In November 1998, mug shot images were made available in the car.

Major efficiencies were made possible because:

- A laptop report did not take more time than paper and pen.
- All of the investigations were now online (digital text).
- Text searching was possible (word search in narratives and statements).
- The RMS had additional tools such as tip/lead management.
- Mangers and supervisors could easily monitor investigations.
- Prosecution reports could be easily assembled from the online reports.
- Data retrieval needs were virtually eliminated. London was able to reduce data entry personnel by 33%.
- Information was speedily entered into the system. Previously, reports could take days before they were available in the RMS for others to view.

In October 2000, the London Police Service received the ITX award, which is sponsored by agencies that include: *CIO Canada Magazine,* the Conference Board of Canada, and the *Globe and Mail* newspaper. The award recognizes the top IT initiative in Canada, and both government and private industry submissions are evaluated.

8.12   End-of-Chapter Comments

The first wireless computing devices that were used in law enforcement in the late 1970s were specialized devices that were sold in niche markets. Law enforcement was one of the few select clients that were able to afford the RF infrastructure that was required to support the wireless transfer of data. Today, the proliferation of commercial services such as CDPD has resulted in an explosive rise in wireless data usage. In many respects, law enforcement is now lagging behind the consumer and commercial users. The benefits of wireless information are clear in our information-everywhere society.

Law enforcement managers should take advantage of the changing economics. The competition and demand in the consumer markets are driving the functionality of the devices up and the costs down. Moreover, IT professionals must monitor closely the features in new information devices. The cellular phones that are morphing into pocket computer devices will have important uses in law enforcement, especially now that officers in a community policing model see less of their vehicle dashboards and more of the streets. There can be little argument that information available "anytime, anywhere" allows police agencies to improve officer productivity and improves on the service they provide to the public.

References

Amoroso, Eldon, Information Technology in the London Police, PowerPoint Presentation, 1997.

City of Los Angles, Los Angeles Police Department 90-Day MDC Vendor Selection Study, Request for Information: Mobile Data Computer System, Version 1.0, January 19, 2000.

Colorado State Patrol, Slashing costs, *Field Force Automation*, May 2000.

Hedgepeth, Kevin, A cutting-edge mobile communications solution, *The Police Chief*, January 1999.

Loomis, Warren, Mobile Data: Method or Product? Versaterm Systems Whitepaper, Website: www.versaterm.com.

Ryczek, Martin and Glasser, Richard, Revisiting Chicago's digital revolution, *The Police Chief*, October 2000.

Utah public safety thrives on mobile data, *Radio Resource Magazine*, November–December, 1997.

Valley Emergency Communications Center Website: www.vecc9-1-1.com.

IT Infrastructure

Chapters 9, 10, and 11 describe wireline and wireless technological infrastructure. Without question, an agency's IT infrastructure will have a major influence on the level and quality of services that can be provided.

A voice radio system is the most important IT infrastructure component. New radio systems are complex and require special cooling, security, and networking configurations. The cabinets shown above contain components of a Com-Net Ericsson EDACS digital trunked radio system that is housed in the E-Comm building. The cabinets contain dispatch console interface cards, digital voice interpolation units, audio processing cards, and network interface modules.

Wireline Infrastructure

9

9.1 Introduction to Infrastructure

In this book, a wide variety of IT applications were described and all required an IT infrastructure. The personal computer, which can be easily purchased and deployed as a stand-alone workstation, is not the critical piece. What is important are the linkages the computing devices have to each other, and IT infrastructure is focused now on the ability to communicate. In the information age, data communications around the world can occur almost instantaneously.

Infrastructure acquisition, planning, and design can be a complex area since the business needs, and the hardware that can meet these needs, are quickly changing. In the late 1980s, mainframe and minicomputers were deployed in the law enforcement market. Today, microprocessor-based servers, networked to thin client PCs, are a leading technology. In the near future, the accessing of information and applications may be based on low-end "network computers" that utilize a browser and applications delivered over an Intranet, Extranet, Internet, or combination of the three.

This chapter will survey the major wireline infrastructure components that provide the platform for software applications to run on. Chapters 10 and 11 will cover the same infrastructure issues, in a wireless context. Many aspects will be described in this chapter as a written "tour" of a modern law enforcement facility.

Warning: The next three chapters form the most technical part of the book and readers without a background in computer systems may find parts tedious. There are many concepts and terms that will be covered and most already fill books on their own. The intent is not to replicate what a reader would learn from a book on computer or network architecture. Instead, an overview and context is provided so that a high-level understanding of networks and their use in law enforcement is obtained. The chapter concludes with two leading-edge law enforcement wireline computing case studies.

9.2 Elements of Communications

Communications can be described as a three way-process:

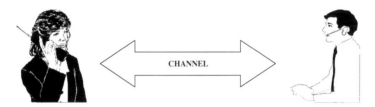

Figure 9.1 Channels permit communications.

1. A device (node) that allows a person (entity) to send a message
2. A channel or communications medium which carries the message
3. A device (node) that allows a person (entity) to receive a message

The radios and mobile data terminals (MDT) used in law enforcement are essential tools that are based on wireline and wireless networks. The network may be local or wide area. While the technology can be very complex, the end goal is simple. There is a need for efficient channels that relay information from one entity to another (the sender to the receiver) (Figure 9.1). A paper occurrence report delivered by the internal mail system or the post office is an example of an older, manual communications channel. Modern networking systems create electronic channels that connect nodes such as:

- Telephones (wireline and wireless)
- Radios
- Fax machines
- Desktop computers
- Mobile computers
- Computer terminals
- Personal digital assistants
- Pagers
- Video receivers

The everyday occurrence of a person (the sender) calling 911 (the receiver) relies on elaborate and constantly evolving communications channels. The following paragraphs use terms applicable to a 911 call center, and the uses of wireline and wireless channels are explained in Table 9.1.

The voice call made through the local loop to the PSTN is routed through a digital cross-connect switch into our PSAP where the agent answers using the CTI device. The details are passed to the CAD with the ANI/ALI pre-filling the GUI incident mask. This CAD information is routed through the Ethernet LAN to the dispatcher.

Table 9.1 Messages and Channels

Message	Channel
911 Call by citizen	The public switched telephone network (PSTN) is accessed through an analog copper line (local loop) connection. The call is connected to a computer that recognizes the location through comparing the address to a database, and identifies the correct primary service answering point (PSAP). A 911 call taker in the PSAP answers the call using a computer telephony integration (CTI) device which is a computer that displays the phone number and location of the telephone, and integrates telephone functions. This information is pushed into a CAD system on a separate local area network (LAN).
Call entered into a computer-aided dispatch (CAD) system	The CAD is a personal computer with a graphical user interface (GUI). Colored text boxes with drop-down menus are filled out with the caller information. The LAN routes call information from the call taker to the dispatcher.
Unit dispatched	A land mobile radio (LMR) system is used to voice dispatch a unit that is listening on a pre-arranged talk group. A digital trunked radio uses a number of frequencies and the voice is digitized before it is laid over a carrier wave and transmitted from a base station. A wireless data network, in this case the commercial Cellular Digital Packet Data (CDPD) network, is used to send the entire CAD record and updates to a laptop computer or mobile work station (MWS) mounted in the vehicle.
Unit makes a tag query from a MWS	A license plate query is typed into a MWS and the data are sent over the wireless CDPD connection to a dedicated computer functioning as a forwarding device (message switch). The query is then transported over an external wide area network (WAN) which breaks down the data into frames or packets. These are sent through to the frame relay National Law Enforcement Telecommunications Network (NLETS). In this case, the NCIC national database is accessed and the answer to the query returns via the same path.
The dispatcher views a map on a screen and observes that the unit has arrived	The MWS is interfaced to a global positioning system (GPS) radio receiver that detects the GPS satellite signaling information. The location information is sent to the CAD system over the CDPD connection. The CAD system integrates a mapping program that visually displays the location coordinates.
The 911 caller answers the door and speaks to the officers	A spoken voice conversation between two human beings takes place.

The next step of a dispatcher sending a patrol unit to the 911 incident requires the use of a wireless communications channel.

The radio dispatcher reviews the CAD details and broadcasts these over the LMR system on the DVP trunked talk group. The full CAD record is relayed to the unit over a CDPD connection to a MWS equipped with a wireless modem. While en route, the MWS is used to check a license plate on NCIC. This query goes over the CDPD network to a message switch and over a frame relay WAN connection. The dispatcher records the arrival of the unit through the CAD mapping and GPS interface. The police officer arriving at the caller's address knocks on a door and speaks to the 911 caller.

9.3 Historical Electronic Communications Devices

By reviewing historical communications devices, a context is provided for understanding the modern communication needs in law enforcement. Moreover, since technology advances are so recent, many officers with over 20 years of experience will well remember some of the devices that are described.

9.3.1 The Telegraph

The first electronic communication device that was used on a widespread basis was the telegraph. Law enforcement use of this, and most other technologies, almost always followed the commercial adoption. The telegraph supplanted physical communication channels like the fabled Pony Express and allowed relatively quick communications for remote areas. While many other commercial and public entities were served, the obvious benefit for law enforcement was the ability to send information on crimes and criminals to remote locations. Law and order was enhanced through the use of the telegraph to summon help, and historians attribute the faster settlement of the western frontier regions to the telegraph.

The telegraph transmits information with dots and dashes. It requires a physical channel, or wire, to allow the transmission of the direct current impulses that formed Morse code. In addition, trained personnel were required at each end of the channel to encode and decode the messages. The initial telegraphs allowed for only one conversation on a line at time. Several inventors, including Thomas Edison, worked on a multiplex telegraph, which could accommodate several operators. Multiplexing (transmitting several signals over a single channel) did make more efficient use of the wires, which were often strung along railroad tracks. The telegraph companies wanted to invent a telegraph that did not require human intervention, and Baudot's printing telegraph allowed multiplexing and did not use Morse code. English inventor Donald Murray improved on Baudot's work and sold his patents to Western Union and Western Electric. These patents became the basis for the teletypewriter, also known by AT&T's brand name of "teletype" or TTY (Figure 9.2). Telex service was the basis for most remote electronic communications until displaced by the fax machine in the 1980s.

Figure 9.2 Teletype systems are still in wide use in Europe. These machines are in use in the London Metropolitan Police Service Command and Control Center.

A notable use of the telegraph was by the Chicago Police Department in 1870. Telegraph equipment was placed in private boxes and keys were issued to police officers and certain privileged citizens. The telegraph was joined to a device that looked like a clock with a bell on top. To operate the device, the user had to move a pointer to one of eleven choices on the face of the telegraph, and pull a handle. A message would then be sent to police headquarters with the following crime types: arson, thieves, forgers, riot, drunkard, murder, accident, violation of city ordinances, fighting, testline, and fire.

The first use of the teletypewriter in law enforcement appears to be by Connecticut agencies in 1927. In 1929, the Pennsylvania State Police adopted its use and, in 1930, the first interstate teletype connection went into service between New Jersey, New York, and Pennsylvania. These regional systems gradually expanded and, in 1963, most eastern U.S. states were interconnected through a network that extended from Maine to South Carolina and as far west as Ohio. The cooperation among states was limited, as standards were parochial. In 1965, representatives from the states agreed on the development of a nationwide interstate communications system, and the Law Enforcement Teletype System (LETS) began operation on May 2, 1966. The Arizona Highway Patrol headquarters had consented to housing and operating the network, and punched paper tape-switching equipment was installed in Phoenix. The system had a bandwidth of 100 words per minute, which decreased if more than one user started sending or receiving on one of the six lines.

In 1970, two small computers were installed to upgrade the capacity of the system, and the organization was incorporated as a non-profit corporation. In 1973, the system abandoned its teletypewriter roots and is now known as the National Law Enforcement Telecommunications System (NLETS).

9.3.2   The Telephone

In early 1876 the telephone was patented. This technology is based on circuit switching, which means that a physical connection must be established and maintained for communication to occur. The obvious major improvement over the telegraph was that more information could be transmitted over a channel (a telephone circuit) and there was no special training needed to operate a telephone. As the Public Switched Telephone Network (PSTN) emerged, there was no need to run from a residence to the street in search of the beat cop. People with phones used them to call for assistance from public safety agencies.

> **In Practice:** 19th Century Resistance to Technological Change in the Chicago Police Department
>
> The discovery and development of new methods of communication have contributed significantly to the changes made within the (Chicago) police department over the years. Early foot patrolmen walking a beat were really on their own: they could get help only by running back to their precinct station, which, as the city increased in size, could be quite a distance away. The Police Patrol and Signal Service, originated in 1881, alleviated some of these problems. Booths with direct telephone communication to the stations were set up around the city and officers and residents of the neighborhood were given keys to the enclosed sentry boxes. Patrol wagons waiting at the stations would be ready to respond to any calls. There was much initial opposition to this method because officers feared that they could now be held accountable for their time on duty. Eventually, the signal devices were accepted. The adoption of these sentry boxes marked the end of the extreme isolation of the patrolman and the beginning of a more centralized approach to police work.
>
> Source: A Brief History of the Chicago Police Department, Website: www.chipublib.org.

For the police officers deployed outside the police facility, telephone call boxes were deployed at set locations (see Figure 9.3). The call box often consisted of a cabin with a telephone, a shelf, and a pencil. At regular intervals, these call boxes would be used to contact the central police station, and the officer would note the various requests for service. The obvious limitation

Figure 9.3 A call box on display in the Vancouver Police Museum.

of this system was that certain calls were of a high priority and required immediate action. Even if a call for service was close by the beat officer, there was no way of knowing about it until the call box was in view. Some call boxes had flashing lights, which signaled that a call was waiting. For areas patrolled by vehicle, a common method used was for callers to phone designated facilities such as gas stations. A flag would then be raised and patrolling officers would stop and obtain the call details.

Many officers followed a set pattern of patrols, and citizens could still go out on the street to physically find the officer. However, criminals could also monitor set patrol times. Even though wireless radio appeared in the 1920s, many agencies relied on call boxes even up to the 1970s.

9.4 A Law Enforcement Facility

In reviewing IT infrastructure, a law enforcement building will likely have a mix of modern and legacy systems and devices. These fall in the general categories of:

- Telephones (Sections 9.5, 9.6, and 9.7)
- Computer architecture (Sections 9.8 and 9.9)
- Local and wide area networks (Sections 9.10 to 9.21)

Often, these systems are taken for granted, until they become unavailable. Users will become frustrated or angry that a vital work tool is taken away, even if it is for a short time period. The term "mission critical" has been used to describe the importance of certain technologies such as 911 telephone service. These infrastructure systems are used by law enforcement, with varying degrees of adoption due to cost, complexity, and operational need.

9.5 Telephone System Fundamentals

The PSTN is a circuit-switched network and was created for short voice conversations between two people. There are a limited number of physical copper lines that users will share (trunk lines), and phone companies route the calls (establish connections) through a local facility known as a switch or central office. Telephone switches first relied on human operators to connect callers, and, later, on mechanical switches. Modern switches are computers dedicated to routing messages along a path or network. In a specific building, a switch can control the distribution of telephone calls internally. Police agencies, similar to regular businesses, manage their voice communications through Private Branch Exchange (PBX) and Centrex systems.

The provision of public safety services has many linkages to the Public-Switched Telephone Network (PSTN). The developments around 911 and E-911 service are predicated on the majority of the community having PSTN access, and this is changing fast as the advent of cellular telephones has changed the utility of E-911 enhancements such as wireline Automatic Number Identification and Automatic Location Identification (ANI/ALI). There are now legislative initiatives that will require cellular companies to provide subscriber location information to a 911 PSAP.

Home users of the Internet commonly use a modem to connect a personal computer to a regular telephone line and through to a local Internet service provider (ISP). A remote computer in a community policing station can be connected through a modem to the central server over the PSTN. This type of access can be expensive if long distance charges are incurred. More importantly, there can be security problems if the access is not strictly controlled.

The term bandwith can be used to describe the difference between the lowest and highest frequency of the waves transmitted in analog mode (see Chapter 10). In networking, it more commonly is used to describe the capacity of the channel, expressed in megabits or gigabits per second. The PSTN is often referred to as a narrow-band network due its limited data-carrying capacity. During breaks in a telephone conversation, or in a fax transmission, the bandwidth is, in effect, wasted. More efficient use of bandwidth is achieved through packet switching networks such as frame switching (frame relay) or cell switching (asynchronous transfer mode or ATM) which will be covered later.

9.6 Emergency Calling Service (911 and E-911)

There will always exist a need for a voice channel between a caller and an emergency services call taker, since voice communication is the fastest way humans can relay information. In the future, for non-emergency situations, a crime victim may e-mail the police, or log onto a Web page to obtain assistance, rather than using a telephone connected through the PSTN. Perhaps even a voice over the Internet Protocol (VoIP) contact could be made.

Up until the late 1960s, the only way to receive emergency police, fire, or ambulance assistance was to dial the seven-digit emergency access number, or to call the operator who would transfer the call. The time delays resulted in many deaths that could have been avoided if a more timely response had been provided, and in 1967 a Federal Commission on Law Enforcement recommended a single national emergency service number be implemented. In 1968, AT&T introduced 9-1-1 as the three-digit number to reach the local switchboards of public safety agencies. These primary service answering points (PSAPs) originally consisted of manual equipment, and the operators receiving the calls would transfer calls manually to the appropriate agency, whether police, fire, or emergency medical.

The 911 service provided a big improvement, but many problems still arose in trying to identify the location from where a caller was phoning. The technology answer was enhanced 911 (E-911) which offered three new services: ANI, ALI, and selective routing. The first versions were implemented in 1971, and a more current version of E-911 was introduced in 1981.

When a subscriber dials 911, the following activities occur in the PSTN (refer also to Figure 9.4).

1. As each number is dialed, the central office starts narrowing the options of where to send the call.
2. When 911 is dialed, the call is sent through a cable connection to a dedicated switch that can identify the correct (usually closest) 911 call center (PSAP). The selection is determined through the entering of the address information into a database.
3. Once the correct PSAP is identified, another dedicated line is used to connect the call to the correct local office.
4. The local office is connected to the PSAP through a dedicated cable. Sent along with the call itself is the ANI information.

The original expectation of 911 systems was that faster call processing would result in more rapid response to crimes and, consequently, a higher probability of apprehending a suspect. Subsequent research into the "response time" focus of many police agencies showed that many callers

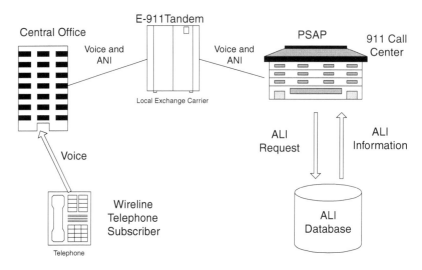

Figure 9.4 911 call routing.

waited many minutes before placing the call for help. Consequently, the advantages of the 911 system were diminished.

Another attraction of 911 is the greater sense of security that citizens have through their power to summon the police quickly. There are associated downsides and in his book, *Problem Oriented Policing,* Professor Herman Goldstein refers to 911 as a "tyrannical" force that places a preemptive demand on police resources. By the late 1960s, the telephone became the main determinant of how police resources would be used — not the policy decisions of police management or the community. Many agencies are vulnerable to having all of their resources consumed in responding to calls from the public for matters not always related to law enforcement or public safety (as discussed in Chapter 2).

9.7   The PSTN and Customer Services

There are many telephony systems that can be integrated into a law enforcement call center.

9.7.1   Centrex

The features from Centrex service are similar to what is provided in a Private Branch Exchange (PBX). Centrex is a brand name of a product offering from the local telephone company (telco) and is a leased service based at the telco switch. It provides more telephones than actual lines, and has features such as intercom, call forwarding, least-cost routing, toll restrictions, caller ID, and call hold. There is little capital outlay associated with Centrex service as the equipment is housed and maintained at the telco's central office. Generally, the business communications needs of a police department are handled through a Centrex in the same manner as if it were a private business. If a facility is prone to power failures or other problems, Centrex service can be more reliable as it is housed at disaster-hardened central offices. Over the long run, it will tend to cost more than a PBX but there is lower risk of obsolescence.

9.7.2   Private Branch Exchange (PBX)

PBX systems implement most of the features a Centrex can provide, and many more. They initially appear more costly, especially if purchased as opposed to a lease. In the long term, a PBX will make more sense for larger organizations. Moreover, they can be used for more than voice communications. A PBX is a powerful computer and has a processor and memory. Newer systems are fully digital and support high-speed data connections. Even more advanced are wireless PBXs which do not require a building to be wired with copper.

The telco charges a fee for each trunk line connection (or circuit) to the central office. Because not all telephones are in use at any one time, an organization can deploy more telephones than physical trunk lines. The PBX acts as a switch and sends a call from the trunk line to the correct telephone. These principles of trunking are similar to what is deployed in modern radio networks (see Chapter 10). Other functions that are provided through a PBX are:

- Voice mail, call waiting, call forwarding
- Allowing the use of telephone keypads as a data terminal (pay bills through banking)
- Automatic least-cost routing (which carrier to use for a long distance call)

In Practice: Centrex vs. PBX at E-Comm

The Centrex costs for the Vancouver region dispatch center (E-Comm) were estimated as being 50% of what the costs would be for a PBX system ($800,000 to $1.4 million). Disadvantages cited for Centrex service were:

- An inability to provide termination for emergency backup communications trunks such as satellite and cellular
- A complex rate plan which meant separate charges for changes to recorded announcements
- No intercom capabilities
- Limited flexibility in relation to system performance and configurations

An advantage of Centrex is that E-911 services are easier to implement. In the end, PBX won out despite the higher capital and administrative costs. E-Comm could control the technology advancement upgrades, and the service costs of Centrex would add up to more in the long run.

9.7.3 Automatic Call Distribution (ACD)

An automatic call distributor (ACD) routes incoming calls, such as 911 or non-emergency calls, to a workstation where an agent (call taker) has been idle the longest. If all agents are busy, calls are held and they are assigned on a first-in, first-out basis. In a 911 PSAP or any dispatch center, statistics or metrics can be recorded such as longest and average wait times, and number of calls abandoned. These are essential performance parameters that enable administrators to adjust staff deployment so that the number of call takers is correlated to the call levels over a 24-hour period.

9.7.4 Auto Attendant

An auto attendant feature is well known to many consumers who have touch-tone "dialed" a commercial enterprise. Pre-recorded messages are played and the system waits for a touch-tone response. It is used as a replacement for, and in conjunction with, live telephone answering. In law enforcement, the applications can include pre-recorded information such as the directory for employees, service hours and locations, and safety warnings and tips. In addition, the call tree can be structured to include multilingual options. In many respects, callers are more empowered through the control they exert on their menu choices. They could select a "faxback" option or reach an information menu choice.

In Practice: The Vancouver Police Auto Attendant

A study of the non-emergency calls made to the telephone report lines and to the police switchboard revealed that many callers thought their issue was a police matter, but it was not. In Vancouver, accidents not involving personal injury are not investigated. Another high rate of non-police calls is in the area of landlord tenant disputes, which are handled by a local regulatory agency. The auto attendant call tree was configured so that, first, the caller is instructed to hang up and phone 911 if there is crime in progress and/or just occurred, or there was a person injured or likely to be injured. Once it is verified that the situation is not an emergency, the caller is asked for a language preference. Several languages, including Spanish, Punjabi, Cantonese, and French, are included. Options include referrals for the most common non-police issues, the location and hours of the local crime prevention offices, and the ability to "zero out" at anytime to be placed in the ACD queue to await a live operator. The use of technology leads to improvements in the quality of service provided to the caller through:

- Reduced call wait times
- Fewer abandoned calls
- Faster and more efficient reporting procedures

9.7.5 Interactive Voice Recognition (IVR)

An interactive voice recognition system allows a caller to state certain words as a response to a recorded message. IVR is used by the telephone company to verify acceptance of collect phone calls. The computer employs speech recognition software to obtain the input. In addition, speech functionality may be used in subsystem components and applications. While simple phrases can be deciphered, the technology is at the functionality level where, generally, only one word responses, such as "yes" or "no," and the numbers 0 to 9 are reliably recognized from the variety of different speakers.

These technologies can be used to create an interface with an operational system such as a CAD. The status of an incident could then be retrieved for the caller based on IVR or auto attendant inputs. Another application is to utilize skills-based or caller-controlled routing. The ACD could take the ANI, the dialed number, or an IVR response and compare this to an online database. Selective routing decisions then could be made including queue jumping or re-prioritization.

9.7.6 Computer Telephone Integration (CTI)

CTI refers to how the telephone and the computer can be integrated over a single platform (Figure 9.5). In the past, voice and data systems were considered separate, and today they converge. CTI has seen many uses in commercial telemarketing and service call centers. Calls can be routed to a designated service representative, and caller information (based on ANI or ALI keys) can be "popped" onto the screen for the call taker to review before and during the interaction with the caller. An example could be the paths taken by a caller to an Auto Attendant. A non-emergency call taker would know that the caller first accessed the Spanish language call tree and listened to the motor vehicle accident recording before "zeroing out" to the live agent.

9.8 Terminals and Personal Computers

This chapter has provided a historical timeline for communications starting with the telegraph and concluding with telephone systems. As was just described with CTI, the convergence of telecommunications and computers has made the divisions of hardware uncertain. These distinctions were clearer with past implementations of computers, which were designed and implemented prior to the advent of open networks and client server computing.

Figure 9.5 A CAD terminal and a VESTA CTI terminal (flat panel display monitor on far right) in the Huntington Beach Police 911 center. The VESTA system allows call takers to answer incoming calls with a mouse and a keyboard. It launches designated applications that are based on the type of incoming call. Examples are speed dials, conference calls, TTY (communications for the hearing impaired), and IRR (instant recall recorder).

The mainframe in the water-cooled backroom has been supplanted by smaller and significantly more powerful computers. In any organization, there will be many personal computers in use as stand-alone devices. There may also be many terminals without processing power (dumb terminals) connected to a mainframe or server. At the most basic level, a police agency is similar to any business and will deploy PCs for personal productivity and administrative tasks, such as word processing and spreadsheets. For example, completing occurrence reports with a typewriter is far less productive than using a word processor.

9.9 Computer Architecture

The term "Moore's law" describes how the processing power of computers doubles approximately every 18 months. It came into widespread use after the introduction of the IBM PC in the early 1980s, which really heralded the advent of modern computing platforms. More recently, "Metcalfe's law" is used to describe the phenomenon of transmission capacity doubling approximately every 12 months.

In examining computer architectures, it is useful to recall the six basic computing processes first introduced in Chapter 1, Table 1.1. Using the example of a NCIC query of a vehicle license plate, the processes are:

1. Capture: A license plate number is typed.
2. Transmit: The information is transmitted to a computer housed in Washington.
3. Store: NCIC has a database of millions of data records with continual updates being made.
4. Retrieve: The NCIC system needs to be able to find quickly where a certain record is located and will determine whether a "hit" is made.
5. Manipulate: The algorithms used to find matches in a relational database have their roots in matrix algebra. The computer performs calculations so it can quickly narrow down where the right data are located.
6. Display: The computer presents the NCIC search results on a screen.

These six processes can be implemented in one of the following computing architectures.

1.   Host-Based Mainframe or Minicomputer

In this legacy model, which is still in wide use today, terminals are connected through private local lines, or telephone lines, to a mainframe or minicomputer that performs all of the processing and controls the peripheral devices such as terminals and printers. Batch processing (capture) using punched cards and terminals was originally employed. In the 1970s, the systems became online and real-time. Batch processing gave way to single transaction processing using "dumb" terminals, which had no processing capabilities. The terminals served merely as input/output devices.

Security and maintenance were simpler under a centralized mainframe approach as only one computer (the mainframe) was administered. The mainframe stored all of the data and software. The problem with this approach was that the central computer could be overloaded and not handle the user demands. Not only did it have to perform all of the data manipulation and storage processing, but it had to track the status and progress of work being done for every terminal and peripheral device connected to it. This meant substantial resources were devoted to controlling jobs, rather than performing the work itself. In the late 1970s, some intelligent terminals were developed that could handle some of the presentation demands but this made networking more complex. Mainframe applications were often written in Assembler, Cobol, and Fortran. Common operating systems included MVS (IBM) and VMS (Digital Equipment Corporation).

NLETS and the Canadian Police Information Center (CPIC) are examples of systems that run on a mainframe approach. NLETS runs on four Alpha computers. Most agencies use dumb terminals to connect over the frame relay network to NLETS. These older terminals have no processing power and display information in monochrome with a typical 25-line by 80-line character display. Because "dumb" terminals are not in production, these systems today will use a PC running a terminal emulation program.

2. *Personal Computing*

In the early 1980s, microcomputers were widely deployed and at first were not connected. The PC was ideal for solitary uses such as word processing, spreadsheets, and stand-alone databases using software such as DBase III. In addition, the PC was quite suitable for storing the record databases for small organizations. Users worked independently, and it was difficult to share data and applications. Because deploying individual PCs is not a true network architecture, access to external data resources such as NCIC were not possible unless specific PCs were configured for this access. This often gave rise to a two-terminal system where terminals connected to mainframes coexisted with PCs — often on the same desktop. Moving data back and forth between the two systems was not possible.

A PC had many benefits and, operationally, police personnel recognized that the large card files that cataloged information could easily be imported into an electronic database which would be supported on a PC. This resulted in many stand-alone systems, which are still in place today. Separate databases may be maintained by the burglary squad, the organized crime unit, the sexual offenses unit, and any other specialized unit that wants to start up a database. For smaller organizations, the entire criminal occurrence database may be stored on a single PC.

The problem with the first uses of PC technology is that information could not be shared. "Islands of information" cropped up and still exist today. Many investigators know that information recorded from one type of crime may be valuable for solving another type of crime. While the burglary detectives may not speak regularly with the sex crimes detectives, there is no reason why the two databases cannot be linked, if not be in one single database to begin with. In addition, one jurisdiction may have extremely valuable information that another jurisdiction could use to solve a case. LAN and WAN technology, and more recently Data Warehouse and Intranet-based tools, can be deployed to span the many "islands."

At first, the PCs had text-based interfaces that resembled a dumb terminal interface (DOS). Eventually, graphical user interfaces (GUIs) were developed that made the PCs easier to use (Windows). Commands could be accessed through intuitive menus using a mouse. The first dominant operating system was DOS, and applications were often written in Pascal, Basic, and later C. The dominant GUI operating system now used is Windows and graphical applications were developed using Visual Basic and C++. Even more modern applications are written using a browser interface and HTML or Java.

In Practice: The Stand-Alone PC

In late 1999, a colleague and I visited a 200-officer police department serving a city of 100,000 in New York State. On the dispatch desk was a PC configured as a NYSPIN (New York State Police Information Network) terminal which allowed the dispatcher to make NCIC and local state database queries. The radio system was the only technology device deployed in the police vehicles. The first police officer working in the dispatch center was on light duty due to an injury. He showed me a stand-alone PC on the desk with a Microsoft Access database set up to record call details. The routine went live the previous month and was written by a former patrol officer seconded to perform small programming projects. The database program recorded only a few fields such as the time and date, call location, type of call, and unit assigned. This application replaced the paper dispatch logs.

The agency had no automated records management system. The handwritten reports completed by officers were reviewed by records personnel and cards were typed up and inserted alphabetically in a card file to facilitate the retrieval of information. The facility had no LAN and PCs were used for solitary tasks such as word processing. The second police officer in the dispatch center was a keen young officer who was assigned temporarily to fill the dispatch position. She admitted it was a quiet day and passed the time by surfing the Internet over a dial-up connection.

3. Distributed Computing

The use of stand-alone PCs had many productive benefits, but these became inherently limited because of a fundamental necessity in organizations — people need to work together. Information, such as e-mails, databases, and documents, and peripherals, such as faxes and printers, need to be shared. In distributed computing, the PC was used to perform individual work and was linked to a LAN, which permitted the sharing of data, messages, documents, and peripherals. The distributed environment brought many administrative and technical complexities such as data location and synchronization, access and security controls, and telecommunication requirements.

Client–Server Computing

Distributed computing has many forms and a common architecture of the 1990s is client–server, which balances the processing load between the workstation and a more powerful computer known as the server. For example, a client may handle the presentation logic (GUI) and validate the data inputs while the server houses the network operating system, the network version of an application, and the data. In some cases, the application logic is split between both (fat client). Modern CAD and RMS applications are designed on client–server architecture.

Servers can be upgraded with multiple processors and storage devices such as RAIDs (redundant array of inexpensive storage devices). In addition, many types of clients and servers can be supported, and the network is more reliable as multiple servers and disk drives can be utilized to provide redundancy and more scalability. Popular network operating systems include Windows NT, Windows 2000, and Novel NetWare.

Network Computing

This newest type of architecture relies on a central processing model with an Internet-configured server instead of a mainframe. The server is accessed by diskless network personal computers (NC) that do not store any procedures or data locally (thin client). The NC relies on the download of applications from the source which are called applets (single-function applications) and are often written in Java, the first network-centric programming language. Network-centric systems have distributed and mainframe characteristics and have a heavy reliance on the network capacity (bandwidth). UNIX is a commonly used operating system, and it is still uncertain whether this architecture will dominate as client–server computing did in the 1990s.

9.10   Network Fundamentals

As stated, the first introduction of PC technology involved stand-alone computers and there clearly existed a need to connect these computers, to support people working together, and to allow them to share peripheral devices. Personal computers replaced mainframes as the preferred choice for processing information. What slowed this trend down was the difficulty in networking. This problem did not exist for the mainframe applications where the many dumb terminals simply connected to the minicomputer or the mainframe, thus sharing information through the central processor.

A LAN that connects personal computers can provide the functionality of a mainframe, with much more. If a mainframe crashes, everyone's work is halted. If a LAN crashes, some users can continue to work at their computers and share the data later on. This is contingent on the application design and its purpose. Perhaps most important, a LAN can do virtually anything a mainframe or minicomputer could do, at a much lower cost. Ethernet LANs have speeds of 10 Mbps and up. Fiber-Distributed Data Interface (FDDI) is similar to Ethernet and operates at 100 Mbps or greater. There are wireless LANs available that operate at slower speeds.

9.11 LAN Components

The major components found in a LAN are described in the following sections.

9.11.1 Workstations

An "intelligent" workstation is a personal computer (PC) with a central processing unit (CPU) and random access memory (RAM) that is used to store programs retrieved from a disk drive. An end user performs work on the software loaded into the workstation, or uses it as an access point for files on another computer referred to as the file server. The term "client" is used as a reference to the workstation. For example, a CAD system may be based on a client PC running software that draws input screens and processes location data for display on a computerized map. A function such as a database query will be sent to the "server" for processing over the LAN. A wireline-based workstation will contain a network interface card (NIC). This is the device in the PC where the physical LAN wiring is connected to, typically using a RJ-45 jack.

A "dumb" terminal has limited processing capability and memory. It must rely on the host for any processing. An IBM 3270 terminal, with its legendary green 25 by 80-character screen, is an example of a dumb terminal. Many are still in use and provide all the functionality that is needed. In a mobile setting, a legacy mobile data device (MDT) would be useless if it is not connected to a host and is considered a dumb terminal (see Figures 8.1, 8.6, and 11.1 for examples).

9.11.2 Host or Server

A "host" or "server" are terms used to describe the backroom computers that are used to provide processing and data from the disk drives. These machines are generally more powerful than workstations and are especially suited for sending, receiving, and accessing data. They may be a high-end PC, a mini-computer, or a mainframe. They need to be durable and support high-speed input and output. Typical functions are to provide application processing, printing services, and database management (DBMS) functions. The server will also run the LAN operating system. The most common operating systems are Windows NT, Windows 2000, and UNIX. In older systems, VMS and MVS are common operating systems.

In a CAD system, a location of a call may reveal a previous visit by the police and possibly involve hazardous conditions. A client would send a premise history query to the server, which would search its hard disk drives using a DBMS. The data from the DBMS are formatted and displayed in an intuitive manner for the dispatcher. For example, a hazardous address may be presented as a text box that blinks bright red.

9.11.3   Physical Media (Cable Connections)

A LAN must have connectivity, and wireline-based LANs offer substantially more bandwidth and lower costs than a wireless LAN. The main wireline physical cable connections are:

> Copper twisted pair — These are insulated copper wires that have a minimum number of twists per foot to reduce electrical interference (attenuation). Category 5 (Cat 5) cabling is the most widely used.
>
> Coaxial — The most common use of coaxial cable is for cable television. It consists of a woven copper braid that shields the center conductor from outside electrical currents. 10Base-2 refers to a type of coaxial cable used to connect computers. It has a maximum distance of 200 meters (607 feet) and is also called Ethernet or CheaperNet.
>
> Fiber — Fiber offers the highest bandwidth of any communications media and uses light rather than electricity. Fiber can span huge distances and at high speeds. It is free of interference and the light travels for miles without losing appreciable strength. Physically, it consists of a core of glass thread, surrounded by cladding that reflects light. At the sending end, the light source used is a LED. At the receiving end, a detector is used that converts light into electrical impulses. Fiber can handle many times the volume of conversations than copper wire cabling and is less susceptible to unauthorized eavesdropping.

9.12   Structured Wiring System

A modern law enforcement building will have wall outlets (similar to telephone jacks) in most office locations to provide the network connections (Figure 9.6). Behind the walls is a structured wiring system that provides a standardized way to wire a building for all types of networks. The main hubs link all internal networks and connect with outside lines provided by a telco. In a typical installation, unshielded copper twisted pair (UTP or CAT 5) distributes network connections to wall jacks. Vertical cables that connect floors are often fiber optic.

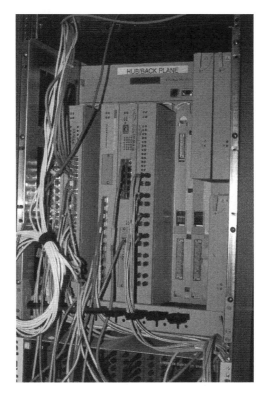

Figure 9.6 Structured wiring hub in the Vancouver Police Department.

9.13   A Law Enforcement Building — LAN and Backbone Networks

A LAN typically connects computers at a speed of 10 or 100 Mbps (Figure 9.7). The LAN is usually confined to one building or office location, and a high-speed backbone network connects LANs at one site, and out to other WANs and the Internet. In addition to cabling, other equipment used in a backbone network includes hubs, bridges, switches, routers, and gateways.

If a connection was made over the PSTN with a modem rated at 56 kbps, a severe data bottleneck would arise. Faster WAN channels are required and these communication lines are obtained from the telephone company, or from value-added networks such as Tymnet and Telenet. Services can also be obtained from satellite providers such as GTE and from the cable companies.

The WAN provides a path between LANs over which two or more LANs can share frames and packets. Workstations on one LAN can access data on

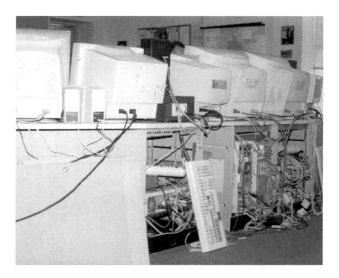

Figure 9.7 Many cables are needed to connect computers to a LAN. These computers and the cabling are deployed in the Denver Police 911 center to support police, fire, and emergency medical dispatch functions.

another LAN. For example, a driver's license query would require a local LAN to connect over a WAN to the LAN utilized by the state or provincial Department of Motor Vehicles. To establish these connections, a physical path is needed. Depending on geographical location, connections such as T service or ISDN may be available. More advanced network services include frame relay and asynchronous transfer mode (ATM).

In planning for future infrastructure, it should be assumed that bandwidth will be abundant and cheaper. Compare this with the first telegraph lines which were used by one operator at a time and were constructed with brittle copper wire and strung along railroad tracks. Fiber optic cables are being laid at the rate of thousands of miles per day along trenches and pipelines. Half of it is not even being used and awaits the future demand (dark fiber).

9.14 The OSI Reference Model and TCP/IP

Legacy mainframe applications use a "closed" network that locks in a customer to a proprietary network, environment, and specific manufacturer-supplied products. Examples are IBM's SNA and Digital Equipment's DNA. An open network is based on standards so that any manufacturer's products can be attached to it, and they are replacing proprietary networks. The marketplace has driven vendors to open their product platforms and provide the capability to connect devices from different manufacturers.

Networks are complex and by organizing the functions into layers, the design process is simplified. The layered approach enables the function and services of one layer to be independent and isolated from the other layers. In theory, a new technology implemented for one layer will not affect the others. The many aspects of networking are often described through the seven layers of the open systems interconnection (OSI) model. These layers roughly correspond to four TCP/IP layers.

In Practice: Lenexa (KS) Police and the OSI Model

During the 1999 IACP Law Enforcement Information Managers conference, The Lenexa Police presented information on their mobile data project. The OSI model was used to explain the integration of the laptop in the car to the RMS system deployed in the police station.

OSI	Station Host	Mobile in the Field
7. Application	Versaterm RMS	Versaterm mobile data terminal
6. Presentation	Windows NT Workstation 4	Windows 95
5. Session	Nettech Systems RFgate	Nettech Systems RFlink
4. Transport		
3. Network		
2. Data link	Eicon software	
1. Physical link	Eicon card	Antenna
	Lease line modem	RF modem
	RAM network	Serial cable, com port 1

Source: Rennie, Mark, Wireless Mobile Data, IACP LEIM Conference Presentation, May 1999.

9.15   Wide Area and Metropolitan Area Networks

Wide area (WAN) and metropolitan area (MAN) networking are a critical part of the law enforcement IT infrastructure. Internal facilities must be linked to state, provincial, and federal information resources. Connecting to regional criminal justice data warehouses also relies on WAN and MAN technology, which are often referred to as backbone networks.

9.16   Dialed Circuit Service

A dialed circuit service is a familiar type of WAN connection and is used by millions of home users to connect to a local Internet service provider for access to the Internet. A computer is equipped with a modem and the PSTN is accessed. Connection charges are usually free for local calls, and by-the-minute billing is incurred for long distance calls. This is identical to voice calls as there is no distinction between data or voice. The Northeast Gang Information System (NEGIS), launched in 1996, is an example of a regional law enforcement network that uses dial-up connections (see Case Study 1 in Chapter 5).

9.17   Dedicated Circuits

There are many options for connecting to networks outside a public safety facility. The first category is dedicated circuit services. As its name implies, the circuit is for the exclusive 24-hour by 7-day use of the customer, and lines are leased from common carriers such as the local telephone company. Because they are dedicated, implementations require careful planning and data transmission rates must be relatively stable. Charges are based on the type of line leased and vary with the amount of data transmitted.

9.17.1   Analog Telephone Circuits

At the most basic level, WAN connectivity can be made through a telephone connection using a modem. A private, dedicated telephone circuit can be leased (no dialup required), and these often have conditioning applied to them to reduce noise and distortion. This type of connection is often used to connect the components of older land mobile radio systems.

9.17.2   T-Carrier Services

Digital T services are fast replacing analog data circuits. A T-1 service can be constructed of copper lines but other media are more commonly used. They are leased in a manner similar to an analog circuit but use digital transmission. Speeds range from 1.544 Mbps for a T-1 line to speeds of 274 Mbps for a T-4 circuit.

9.17.3   Digital Subscriber Lines

A newer and high-in-demand form of digital PSTN connection is the digital subscriber line (DSL). This network connection utilizes unused frequencies on voice grade telephone lines to send digital data. The digital data coexist with analog voice signals.

In Practice: Communications Assistance for Law Enforcement Act (CALEA)

Passed in 1994, the CALEA law (also known as the Digital Telephony Bill) was designed to address the problems brought on by the newer digital networks replacing the old analog telephone equipment. This eroded the ability of law enforcement to carry out electronic surveillance orders as crucial evidence became very difficult if not impossible to obtain. The CALEA law required telecommunications companies to ensure law enforcement needs are met as they build out their digital telephony infrastructure. Nine capabilities were seen as required and the industry told the FCC that the requirements were over-reaching and unrealistic. Many interest groups have raised privacy concerns. Perhaps the biggest roadblock to implementation is cost. The industry estimates that each switch would cost $1 million to upgrade. There are upward of 700 wireless switches and 26,000 wireline switches.

Source: CALEA issues still unresolved, *Telecommunications*, March 1999.

9.17.4   Synchronous Optical Networks (SONET)

A SONET achieves point-to-point connections with fiber. Transmission speeds are known as optical carrier (OC) levels and reach speeds that surpass 1 gigabyte per second.

9.18   Circuit-Switched Services

Circuit-switched data services function similar to dialed telephone service. When a connection is purchased, the customer can request a circuit from the connection point to the end destination point. When the transfer of data is complete, the temporary circuit is terminated. ISDN is an example of a circuit-switched service. Basic rate service (BRI) provides a communication circuit with two 64-kbps channels (also called B channels), with an accompanying D channel which is used for control purposes. ISDN is commonly associated with switching but it can be used to provide dedicated connectivity.

9.19   Packet-Switched Services

Dialed, dedicated, and circuit connection methods share a commonality in that they rely on a physical circuit to be established between two communicating computers. Similar to a telephone call between two people, no other computer can use the circuit until the transmission is closed.

Packet-switched service allows multiple connections to exist simultaneously. Packets consist of individual packets of separate messages. Users connect to the network using packet assembly and disassembly devices that operate almost instantaneously. This is a more efficient use of the common carrier network capacity as most data communications consist of short bursts of data with intervening spaces that are often longer than the data transmissions. By interweaving many bursts of data, it maximizes the use of the shared communication network.

The first methods used to transport data used datagrams, which sent packets through the network with destination and sequence information. The sequence is important as some packets may arrive out of sequence due to different routing paths and the original message cannot be reassembled until all packets are received. The second method is a virtual circuit and the network establishes what appears to be one route for all packets. It appears to be one end-to-end circuit to the two computers.

9.19.1 X.25

X.25 is the oldest packet-switched network and it breaks up data into small packets that are transmitted through data paths to the end destination using datagrams, switched virtual circuits, and permanent virtual circuit services. It was designed for use over network infrastructures and physical media that are likely to induce high error rates and that do not have high capacity. The National Science Foundation Networks (NSFNet) and the Defense Advanced Research Project Network (DARPANet) were X.25 networks, and both of these evolved to what is now known as the Internet. X.25 is considered a legacy technology, and cannot support newer higher data capacity applications. Fiber networks are also in greater use today, and, consequently, there is a lower need for error-checking protocols.

9.19.2   Frame Relay

Frame relay is a faster packet-switching technology than X.25 due to the lower overhead of the error checking routines. The term "bandwidth on demand" can be applied as frame relay can create virtual circuits and can move large files such as images. Frame relay is used for private networks and the Internet, and, similar to ISDN, there are a number of incompatible standards. NLETS is an example of a frame relay network.

9.19.3   Asynchronous Transfer Mode (ATM)

ATM is built on SONET and is similar to frame relay. Each cell or packet is 48 bytes and has a 5-byte header. A cell is 53 bytes and a LAN terminal adapter will break up the message into ATM cells and reassemble the message at the destination. The multiplexing of cells in an ATM network provides good use of available bandwidth, and the fixed length of packets makes it more suitable for transferring multimedia (sound and video) files than frame relay. In addition, it can set priorities for different data types: high priority for voice and video, lower priority for e-mail. ATM is very scalable and can allocate cells on demand when traffic is high. Future speeds are in the gigabyte range.

In Practice: Oceanside, CA and ATM to the desktop

The city of Oceanside decided in 1998 to discard its separate voice and data networks and switch to a single ATM network. On August 30, 1999, the city opened its new Public Safety building, which housed the Police Department and the 911 call center. Over 400 PCs have direct ATM connections, which are used for voice, video, and data traffic. Selected PCs have desktop video conferencing and monitoring capabilities for areas outside the building and the indoor jail area.

Source: *Government Technology*, November 1999.

9.20   The Internet

The world's largest network is the Internet, and a connection is necessary for services such as e-mail and hosting a Website. Usually, these services are purchased from an ISP and charges are based on connection speeds, numbers of users supported, and data demands. The network options described previously can be used for Internet access, and agencies will often contract for T line service or better.

There are numerous other benefits to Internet access. For example, the proliferation of e-commerce has lead to a recognition that call centers need to be able to communicate over IP networks with clients. Examples of new types of interactions are:

- Chat (instant message)
- E-mail
- Web-touring and sychronization
- Click to call (a Website generates a call back from an agent over the PSTN or Internet)
- Video conferences
- Remote access to applications

Applications are promising for law enforcement in the area of non-emergency customer service. Customer information queries can be handled more productively — as compared with using IVR and auto attendant to distribute information. In addition, e-mail and browser forms offer the ability

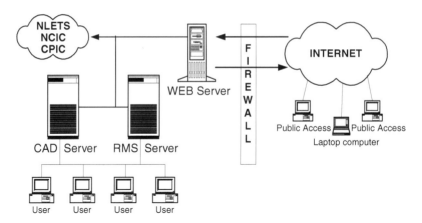

Figure 9.8 Firewalls and the Internet.

for victims and witnesses to crimes to handle their own data entry requirements. This could generate significant staff savings for an agency.

Chapter 2 provided examples of Internet access to database information contained on secure law enforcement networks. Firewalls need to be put into place to prevent unauthorized access (Figure 9.8). The NLETS security policy has the following regulations:

> The firewall selected should have a secure operating system that can protect its own internal code and files from intruder attack. No other non-security applications should be allowed on the firewall. The firewall must intercept all packets and permit only authorized communications to pass. Adequate authentication and packet screening controls must be present to reduce the chance of IP address spoofing. The firewall must have an application gateway component that intercepts traffic and authenticates users at the TCP/IP application level. As a good practice virus screening would be of value. The firewall is only a tool for security. States should have a plan in place on how to respond to security breaches and report all intrusions to the appropriate system administrator, such as the NLETS Executive Director. States are encouraged to keep the operating system changes current on their firewall.

In Practice: Carnivore — A Law Enforcement Wiretap Tool for the Internet

In July 1999, the FBI acknowledged that it has been using a wiretap application nicknamed Carnivore. The application plugs into an Internet Service Provider's equipment through a "sniffable" port on the ISP's hub or switch. Carnivore apparently can scan millions of e-mails every second. Alarmed privacy advocates have cited privacy concerns because of Carnivore's capacity to intercept and scan large volumes of e-mails. In response, the Federal government has introduced provisions to extend the same legislative protection of telephone calls to the new methods of communication. This includes the requirement for law enforcement officers to obtain court orders authorizing interceptions, similar to telephone wiretap practices.

Source: Johnston, Margaret, Wiretap laws to be updated for Internet Age, *Infoworld*, July 24, 2000.

9.21   Virtual Private Networks (VPN)

An emerging technology is the use of a virtual private network for connectivity between remote users using the Internet. The security architecture takes data, encrypts it, and sends it through the Internet using a series of secure paths or tunnels. The primary advantage of this is lower costs. The monthly charges to connect many remote users using leased lines can be exorbitant. With a VPN, the expensive fractional T1 office-to-office connections could be replaced with the less costly full T1 connection to the Internet. Privacy is ensured through encryption technologies such as DES and triple DES. Authentication can be provided by the use of digital signatures, which prevent unauthorized users from gaining network access. A disadvantage is that communications can travel at unreliable speeds because of Internet congestion factors.

The following two case studies illustrate practical examples of VPN technology. Both use a product from RSA Security Inc.

Case Study 1: The Kansas Bureau of Investigation VPN Network

The Kansas Bureau of Investigation implemented a VPN product from RSA Data Security Inc. Users must use a SecureID token, whether over the conventional frame relay network or the Internet-based VPN, to gain access to the system. The token is in the form of a key fob and has a constantly changing number (displayed on a LCD screen). It also knows the specific 6-digit value the key fob will display at a given time for every user. The server keeps track of the log-in information of a user and the password of a user. In addition, the server authenticates itself with a digital certificate, and the Public Key Infrastructure (PKI) server authenticates itself to the client machine. An exchange of encryption keys then occurs between the client and the server.

Initially, 4000 users had initial access to the VPN system with future growth predicted to be over 12,000. Access was provided to all systems (NCIC,

KCJIS), previously available only through expensive dedicated lines, which used the SNA protocol. The legacy network did not even have a log-on procedure. It operated at 4.8 kbps and permitted the transfer of ASCII (characters) text only.

Because criminal history information is accessed, the system had to receive a security approval from the FBI. In order to test the system security further, administrators invited course participants that were taking an Internet crime investigation course to attempt a break-in. The methods included physical attack (traditional hacking) as well as social engineering (pretending to be an authorized user and trying to fool a legitimate user into providing access information). The attempts were unsuccessful.

Case Study 2: The DISC System and Information Sharing over a VPN

In 1999, an Intranet database application known as DISC (Deter and Interrogate Sex Trade Customers) was developed in the Vancouver Police Department. The prostitution trade on the West Coast is well known for the "pimp circuit" that moves women between cities such as Calgary, Seattle, Portland, San Francisco, and Las Vegas. Vice detectives needed a way to share their databases and would mail floppy disks back and forth. The DISC Intranet was implemented over a TCP/IP network with access over a VPN. To enter the database, a local Internet connection was required and a SecureID token was needed. The VPN client software would prompt the user for the constantly changing SecureID LCD token number to authenticate the user's access. International information sharing became a reality using the VPN technology and by charging users just $200 for the security token.

9.22   End-of-Chapter Comments

In this chapter, there was a significant amount of time spent describing the PSTN and the IT applications available. This topic is important since 911 and non-emergency call center (PSAP) activities are a major focal point for police operations. In addition, improving the telephone systems will make the enterprise more efficient, and is an example of IT being applied to a support value activity (Figure 1.2). Many aspects of networking were described and old and new methods were compared. The concepts may appear complex, but a continued focus over time on current practices and terminology will lead to a gradual assimilation of what are the major planning and implementation considerations in computer and network architecture.

References

Alter, Stephen, *Information Systems, A Management Perspective*, 2nd Ed., Benjamin/Cummings, Menlo Park, CA, 1996.

CALEA issues still unresolved, *Telecommunications*, March 1999.

Dines, David, Web-enabled call centers: a challenge and an opportunity, *Telecommunications*, November 1999.

Fitzgerald, Gerald and Dennis, Alan, *Business Data Communications and Networking*, 6th Ed., John Wiley & Sons, New York, 1999.

Gallo, Michael and Hancock, William, *Networking Explained*, Digital Press, Boston, 1999.

Goldstein, Herman, *Problem Oriented Policing*, McGraw-Hill, New York, 1990.

Higgins, Kelly Jackson, No place like home: Kansas criminal data secured with PKI, *Network Computing*, June 1999.

Johnston, Margaret, Wiretap laws to be updated for Internet Age, *Infoworld*, July 24, 2000.

London Metropolitan Police Website: www.met.police.uk/police/mps/mps/history.

NLETS homepage: www.leo.gov.

PSWN, Commercial Wired Service Assessment, July 1999.

Rennie, Mark, Wireless Mobile Data, IACP LEIM Conference Presentation, Ft. Lauderdale, FL, May 1999.

Schaefer, Norma Jean, Securing the Kansas Criminal Justice Information System, IACP LEIM Conference Presentation, Denver, CO, May 2000.

Slomnicki, John, Communications: where did it start? *Dispatch Monthly Magazine*, Website: www.911dispatch.com/information/historycomm.html.

Tuomenosksa, Mark, Virtual private networks, the big payoff, *Telecommunications*, November 1998.

Vesta Homepage: www.peinc.com/products/vesta.htm.

Wireless Voice IT Infrastructure

10

10.1 Introduction

A mobile voice radio is the most important piece of equipment a law enforcement officer will use.

Having a functional voice radio system must be the highest IT priority for a law enforcement agency.

A radio is a vital tool in coordinating the police response to routine and priority calls from the public, as well as serving as an invaluable information resource (Figure 10.1). Moreover, the radio is critical to officer safety as it provides a means for cautioning field officers as they travel to calls, and allows the responders to call for assistance. If this is doubted, one only has to look at the local media headlines which appear on a regular basis throughout North America that dramatize how a radio failure led to a dangerous set of events. All radio vendors have anecdotes of how angry police managers, unions, or line officers have gone to the media to criticize their products, when often the root cause was an inadequate system design. These same headlines rarely appear when a server or a mobile computer system fails to operate.

For these reasons, land mobile radio (LMR) systems for public safety must be designed and constructed with an extremely high mission-critical level of reliability. There must be an assurance that messages are transmitted and received within the designated coverage areas. The systems must have redundancy built in so that failures do not result in the entire system becoming inoperable. This chapter will describe the underlying principles of wireless voice IT. These concepts are also commonly described by terms such as voice radio, or LMR systems. Chapter 11 will address wireless data IT.

Law enforcement officers are often involved in decision making about LMR systems for their agencies. With the recent focus on interoperable radio systems, police administrators may find themselves involved on a panel of user agency representatives, working with emergency medical and fire personnel. Understanding the basics of LMR technology, the trends, and recent developments will result in more informed and constructive input. Moreover, the entire context of radio and wireless voice acquisition planning has changed, with commercial cellular phone vendors now competing with traditional LMR suppliers.

Figure 10.1 In many deployment situations, the only practical communications and information device is the voice radio. In this picture, officers on horseback patrol the downtown London business district.

Convergence has blurred the lines between devices. A cellular phone is more comparable to a portable radio than to a wireline phone. For that matter, the newer generation digital cellular telephones and digital radios have more in common with a desktop PC than with their analog ancestors. The modern paradigm is that what used to move through the copper wire — such as voice and data on a telephone line — now increasingly moves through the air. What used to be moved over the air — such as television and commercial radio signals — will increasingly move through wires (cable TV).

10.2   A History of Law Enforcement Radio

The first reported example of a law enforcement application of wireless technology was in London, England in 1910 and involved a radiotelegraphy (Morse code) transmission from an ocean liner. Dr. Peter Crippen was suspected of murdering his wife and he fled the Scotland Yard investigators by boarding the SS *Montrose,* which was bound for Canada. An alert ship captain read newspapers accounts of the manhunt and used a wireless Marconi telegraph to report that Dr. Crippen was likely on board his vessel. The investigator in the case, Chief Inspector Walter Drew, pursued Dr. Crippen across the Atlantic on another ship and was able to make an arrest before the SS *Montrose* landed in Montreal.

In 1921, station WIL in St. Louis, MO made a voice radio transmission to a police car. In 1922, the Massachusetts State Constabulary began to communicate between its various posts by radio. Early systems were one way and a dispatcher had no way of knowing if a broadcast was received, unless an officer acknowledged by telephone. Over the next ten years, technological advancements were made to radio receivers in automobiles. In 1923, the London Metropolitan Police Service began to use a two-way radiotelegraphy system. Two vehicles were equipped with transmitters and receivers. In order to transmit, the vehicles had to be completely stopped.

In 1928, the Detroit Police Department began operating a one-way system for its police cars, and in the following year 22,598 police messages were broadcast. Radio-equipped cars were credited with 1,325 arrests, and an average response time of 1 minute, 42 seconds was claimed. By the end of 1930, 75 radio cars had been equipped and were credited with making more than 20,000 arrests.

In 1929, the Chicago Police installed one-way radio transmitters in five squad cars. Broadcasts were originally made over radio station WGN (owned by the *Chicago Tribune*) and in the following year, the Department installed its own broadcasting system. In 1930, the Winnipeg Police Service became the first Canadian agency to install radios in its vehicles. The transmissions were one way and officers confirmed the messages by responding directly or using call boxes. Battery limitations meant that the radios only operated for 12 hours per day.

In 1933, the first reported two-way LMR system was installed in East-chester Township, NY. This system allowed car-to-car and car-to-dispatcher communications. Around the same time, Bayonne, NJ acquired a two-way radio system. By the mid-1930s, many more police radio systems were installed. These initially operated in the 30- to 40-MHz region, and as more radio networks were installed, cooperative frequency usage plans led to VHF frequencies being used. In 1940, the Connecticut State Police in Hartford began to use a two-way FM radio system.

Each decade brought further improvements in voice transmissions systems. Solid-state circuitry replaced vacuum tubes in the 1960s, and these gave way to very large-scale integrated circuit chips in the early 1970s and microprocessors in the mid-1970s.

The microprocessor allowed for digital communications in land mobile radio systems, which opened the door for mobile data terminals. Today, there are multitudes of options available for law enforcement wireless voice communication. They range from private radio systems to the use of commercially available technologies such as cellular and PCs. The concept of "anytime, anywhere" is profoundly applicable to policing, as most service delivery points (a street corner, a drinking establishment, a freeway) are not in locations where a wireline link is an option.

In Practice: An Early "Through the Air" Communications Channel

In June 2000, officials with the Orissa Police Service, India recommended that the pigeon service they used for communications be disbanded. According to B.N. Das, Superintendent of Police, "The pigeon service made practical sense when we were superintendents two decades ago, as there were no VHF radios at that time, but now all police stations in Orissa are on the radio network, reducing the winged service to a museum piece." The three types of service the birds were trained for were:

- Static — The birds travel long distances with messages attached to their legs.
- Boomerang — The birds travel regularly, carrying messages between 2 points within a 60-mile radius.
- Mobile — The birds are carried by police officers patrolling remote areas, and are sent back to their home base to keep officers in touch with their colleagues.

When floods devastated much of coastal Orissa in 1982, the pigeons carried messages for help and returned with messages of hope. The pigeons became the only means of communication as the radio networks were disrupted by water.

Source: Das, Gopal, Pigeon service, once vital, is a remnant of India's past, Associated Press, *Seattle Times*, July 30, 2000.

10.3   Basic Principles of Radio

The term "radio" refers to the radiation and propagation of signals through space to convey information. Initiating an electromagnetic disturbance will cause waves to spread from the source to another point some distance away — very similar to a pebble causing ripples in a pond. These waves travel at about the speed of light (186,000 mph). Other variable characteristics are:

- Amplitude — the magnitude of the disturbance of a wave
- Frequency — the number of complete waves propagated past a fixed point in one second (cycles per second or hertz)
- Wavelength — the distance between one wave and the preceding or succeeding wave, measured in meters

There is an inverse relationship between a frequency and a wavelength. The higher the frequency of a wave, the shorter its wavelength will be, and both have a significant bearing on the type of electronic circuitry and technology needed for the transmission of the electromagnetic waves. Similar to light waves, as the distance from the source increases, the intensity of the radio signal decreases.

For a radio to work, four processes need to occur:

1. A transmitter receives some inputs and produces an electromagnetic disturbance.
2. An antenna radiates the disturbances through space as electromagnetic waves.
3. The waves enter a receiving antenna and produce electric currents in a receiving circuit.
4. The receiving circuit changes the electric currents into a form comprehendible by an operator.

One of the earliest applications of wireless information transfer was radiotelegraphy, which used breaks in wave transmission to produce the tones indicating Morse code dots and dashes. This eventually gave way to voice communications, which utilized continually flowing waves known as a carrier wave. By using a microphone to produce audio-frequency oscillations, the amplitude of the carrier wave would be modulated. This pattern of variation reflects the sound waves of the voice spoken into a microphone. At the receiving end, the process is reversed and the carrier wave signal is filtered leaving the audio information, which is passed through a loudspeaker. This process is known as modulation and demodulation, and the two basic approaches are amplitude modulation and frequency modulation (AM and FM). Table 10.1 lists the basic components of a radio system.

10.4 The Electromagnetic Spectrum

Radio waves generally travel in straight lines, like light waves, but certain characteristics of the atmosphere cause certain frequencies to behave in ways that can expand their use. Very low frequency waves tend to follow a path close to the earth's curvature. These are known as ground waves and have frequencies below 30 kHz. They can be received thousands of miles away but their information-carrying capacity is limited.

Higher frequency waves, which travel in straight lines, are known as direct waves. They are used in line-of-sight transmissions; very tall antennas, or a series of relay antennas that can see each other, are required. Because their transmission distance is limited, these tend to be used for local transmissions, and the frequencies can be reused in other geographical regions without interference.

Table 10.1   Components in a Radio System

Base stations	Hardware and software equipment is required to process the electromagnetic signals to or from mobile end-user radios. The power output of the station and the height, design, and size of an antenna are all important factors in determining signal propagation.
Repeaters	The transmission range of a radio signal is finite and a strategically located repeater can extend the transmissions. It receives a signal and retransmits it.
Control equipment	This equipment monitors the networks and allows the users to configure the system for optimal performance. In a digital system, hardware and software are required to encode and decode an analog transmission.
Interface equipment	This allows the radio system to link to other wire and wireline networks including the PSTN (telephone interconnect).
Dispatch consoles	For systems where a dispatcher has control, the patching of talk groups and channels may be required.
User equipment	The functionality of the "radio" itself is important. A portable handheld radio may have a power output of 0.3 watts, while a mobile radio may be rated at 5 watts or more.

Table 10.2   Public Safety Frequency Allocations

Public Safety Band Name	Spectrum Range (MHz)
Low VHF	25–50
High VHF	150–174
Low UHF	450–470
UHF TV sharing	470–512
800 MHz	806–869

To control the use of frequencies, every country has a regulatory body (FCC in the U.S., Industry Canada in Canada) to manage spectrum usage (Table 10.2). As a scarce and non-renewable natural resource, it has a high economic value. Additional spectrum cannot be created or discovered and the FCC has raised billions of dollars in spectrum auctions. Industry Canada is a more recent entrant to the auction process. Radio license (spectrum usage) regulations are stringent, and transmitting equipment cannot be moved, even in emergencies, without government agency approval.

In Practice: Testing of 800-MHz Systems

A combined communications system partnership was established in 1997 by the state of Colorado, the city of Aurora, and Douglas and Jefferson Counties. In examining technology options, issues such as reliability, support infrastructure, maintenance, and standards were considered. Extensive coverage testing was undertaken on VHF, 800-MHz analog, and 800-MHz digital systems. Test parameters included an examination of portable radio requirements and coverage for in-street, in-building, difficult or special areas (tunnels and large public facilities), and areas with high vegetation or forest growth. In every test, the system engineers found that 800-MHz digital technology provided the best audio quality and coverage.

Source: Borrego, Mike, Shared communications systems to help deliver critical public safety services, *The Police Chief*, May 2000.

10.5   Spectrum Bandwidth

The term "bandwidth" in modern data communications has been used to describe the throughput of a given network connection. In spectrum allocation, bandwidth refers to the range of frequencies that are assigned to a single channel. As a comparison, whereas wireless bandwidth is shared, wireline connections are generally not shared and therefore provide a wide available bandwidth.

The bandwidth allocated to public safety radio frequencies range from 12.5 to 30 kHz. As a comparison, television has a wide bandwidth of 6000 kHz with the video component consuming 4500 kHz. FM radio stations are spread 200 kHz apart. To conserve spectrum, regulatory bodies are loath to license new radio installations that are broadband (25 kHz). In the late 1990s, Industry Canada and the FCC have both undertaken a "redeployment" or "refarming" of the bands from 100 to 500 MHz. These deployment efforts will force radio systems to move to more spectrally efficient technology over the time frame from 2000 to 2010. In terms of data-carrying capacity, these narrow bands (a radio channel) typically transfer data in the 1200- to 9600-bps ranges. This translates into data rates as low as 250 characters per second compared to the 700,000 characters per second typically delivered over a wireline LAN.

Public safety users are accustomed to end user equipment that has "channel" settings. Depending on the age of the equipment, this can range from 1 to 16 settings on a radio knob, to tens of channels selected by ramping up and down a LCD display. End user systems will typically number their channels from Channel 1 on upward.

In a conventional system, a setting on a radio knob (a channel) corresponds to a frequency and a bandwidth licensed only in a certain geographical area, to a specified user. This geography factor means that the same amount of spectrum is available in every area, regardless of population density. Consequently, spectrum is most precious in populous urban metropolitan areas.

In Practice: Police Radio Traffic over the Air, Accessed over Wire

Many hobbyists track frequency allocations even to the point of providing call sign details. A listing of frequencies used in the Northeast U.S. can be found at www.netnerd-inc.com/joe. The Website also provides streaming of police audio. LAPD and Dallas are two law enforcement agencies that can be found at www.policescanner.com, and this provides an illustration of how a wireline Internet connection can provide access to voice radio traffic (radio broadcasts accessed over wire).

10.6 Spectrum Conservation

Many public safety agencies require more voice radio and data radio channels, but are unable to obtain them due to spectrum scarcity. Commercial demands for spectrum have proliferated and a public safety frequency allocation translates as a major investment by taxpayers (foregone auction revenue). Consequently, there are severe pressures to manage and conserve this precious resource, and significant research has gone into developing new technologies to conserve spectrum.

Multiplexing techniques (multiple signals over a single channel) such as code-division, time-division, and frequency-division multiple access (CDMA, TDMA, and FDMA) can be used to maximize throughputs on radio channels. Variations of CDMA are likely to become the standard for faster packet wireless networks that are also referred to as "third generation" or 3G wireless networks.

In looking at the information that is relayed by voice, it is readily apparent that the many non-mission-critical communications that occur over voice radio can and should be moved to a data radio platform. In fact, long-winded voice conversations to get non-mission-critical information (the call details of a non-priority incident) are an inefficient use of a radio channel. Having a mobile computer screen display the same information (a CAD dispatch ticket) requires far less radio channel use, in addition to potentially saving on dispatcher labor costs. Another example is a MDT being used by an officer to self-generate a CPIC or NCIC query, rather than having to ask a radio dispatcher to perform the query and read the results on the radio. Chapter 8 covers mobile computing and Chapter 11 addresses wireless data. Combining mobile computing and wireless data will reduce capacity demands on a voice LMR system and conserve an agency's allocated spectrum.

10.7 Providing Coverage (Making a Radio "Work")

A law enforcement officer carries many pieces of equipment on the issue gun belt. In addition to the sidearm, standard equipment includes a radio and a flashlight. If the flashlight works intermittently or has variable brightness, the officer concludes that it is broken, or it is of an inferior design and/or quality and is unsuitable for the demands of law enforcement. Many times, the same conclusion is reached in relation to a portable radio that "doesn't work." However, unlike the flashlight, the performance of the portable radio

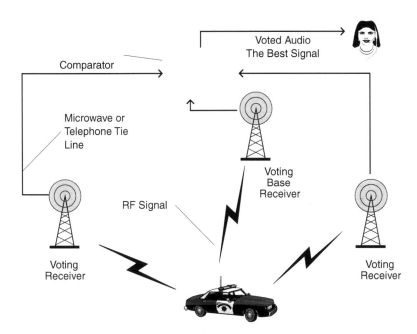

Figure 10.2 Receiver voting systems.

is highly dependent on the design and performance of the system and components that provide the overall radio system coverage. The following are some of the major technologies involved in propagating usable RF signals through the atmosphere. Receiving devices include portable radios, vehicle-mounted radios, data terminals, cellular phones, and pagers.

10.7.1   Receiver Voting Systems

Portable radios are less powerful transmitters than either base stations or vehicle radios. Their dependence on compact batteries as well as health and safety limits on radiation close to the body inherently limits the transmit power of portable radios. As a result, there is often an imbalance between the "talk-out" performance of a base station or repeater, and the "talk-back" or "talk-in" performance of portable radios. This imbalance can be overcome, in part, by the use of voting receiver networks (Figure 10.2), which place receivers strategically in areas where there is adequate signal from the system, but where portables are unable to talk back to the system. When a RF signal is received — often by more than one voting receiver — the detected signal is sent to a comparator by wireline or microwave links. The comparator, which is usually located in a dispatch center, determines which is the best signal, and it is this signal that the dispatcher hears (Figure 10.3). The two types of voting systems are:

Figure 10.3 Radio voting equipment in the L.A. County Sheriff's dispatch center.

1. Discrete signal-level system — The strongest signal is the "best."
2. Status tone system — The "best" signal is the one with the best signal-to-noise ratio.

10.7.2   Transmitter Steering

A transmitter steering system works with a receiver voting system. When the comparator determines which site has the best audio, the transmitter at that site only is turned on. Mobiles in this area then talk to each other through this site. The drawback with this system is that it does not cover the entire service area simultaneously.

10.7.3   Simulcasting

In a simulcast (SIMULtaneous broadCAST) system, audio is broadcast simultaneously over several transmitters on a single radio frequency. Areas where the signal areas from two or more sites are close in amplitude are referred to as overlap areas (Figure 10.4). Outside of an overlap area, where the signal from one site is significantly higher than the signal from any other site, a mobile radio will "capture" the signal from the dominant site.

Within an overlap area, the two signals being received by a mobile radio can interfere with each other if their phases are not synchronized, resulting in distortion of received audio. There are several techniques used to reduce the distortions, including synchronizing the frequencies and equalizing audio amplitude. The most current generations of simulcast systems utilize GPS technology to stabilize and synchronize base station transmit frequency and timing.

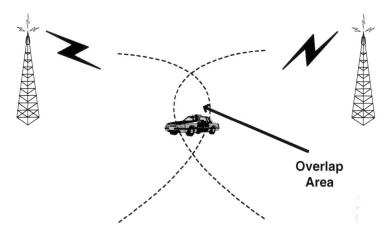

Figure 10.4 Simulcast overlap area.

A simulcast system is much more complex and demanding to maintain. The major advantages are that a wide area can be covered with a limited number of channels.

10.7.4 Multicasting

A multicast system is similar to a simulcast system with the difference being that a different RF channel is used at each site. While it can increase coverage with lower instances of co-channel interference, multiple frequencies are needed and, therefore, limited spectrum availability can be an impediment.

10.8 Coverage Impediments

The following factors will influence the coverage provided by a LMR system.

10.8.1 Propagation

The radio frequency signals that are generated by the LMR system need to propagate through the atmosphere with enough strength to reach the receiving device. The fields generated by a radio transmitter and received by a receiver are referred to in many ways. Generally, the power of a transmitter is referenced in watts. System losses and antenna gain are measured in decibels, and the effective radiated power is referred to in watts, or decibels relative to one watt. Received field strengths can be referred to in absolute terms, such as microvolts per meter, or in terms relative to a standard antenna and receiver (i.e., decibels relative to one milliwatt).

The strength of a signal received is dependent on:

- The transmit power
- Transmit system losses and gains
- Transmit antenna gain
- Transmit antenna pattern (both horizontal and vertical)
- The propagation of the signal over the path from the transmitter to the receiver
- The efficiency of the receive antenna and user device

A LMR system is typically constructed to cover a specific service area, such as the area within a municipal boundary. Within the intended coverage area, if too few radio towers are constructed, then the RF signal propagation will be insufficient to provide adequate and reliable coverage. The actual number of towers needed depends on the physical geographical characteristics and size of the area that is being served. For a LMR system, it is also particularly important to design the system so that the "talk-out" performance from base stations to the mobile and portable radios is balanced with the "talk-in" performance from the portables to the base stations.

In Practice: Wide Area LMR System Design

In 1998, I toured the Com-Net Ericsson RF Integrity group facilities in Lynchburg, VA. The engineers utilize the proprietary RAPTR software tool for designing and verifying coverage. Detailed terrain maps are imported and potential sites are then selected and assigned transmitter and receiver parameters. Path loss and coverage patterns can be plotted and statistical data are produced. We were shown the Greater Vancouver (E-Comm) digital trunked simulcast radio system, which was designed with RAPTR. A map of ten sites was displayed and the sites were placed with regard to identified "critical buildings" and other known "coverage challenged" areas. In actual practice, these desired sites were not always obtained. Site acquisition decisions had to also balance considerations such as:

- Geographical placement
- Be tall enough
- Not offend community interests and sensibilities
- Meet seismic requirements
- Not be fully loaded with existing users
- Not cost too much

In an unobstructed environment, RF signal propagation can be easily calculated. However, few points are unobstructed and factors such as the distance the signal has to travel, terrain, foliage, and buildings and other structures will all influence coverage.

There are many situational impediments that can affect both voice and data communications, but there is one major difference. A poor voice transmission, characterized by cracking and static, may still be usable because a human brain can listen, interpret, and decipher what the sender is transmitting. A data stream with the same problems may not be usable since the computer needs all of the data in the correct order in order to construct the message.

10.8.2 Fringe Areas

These are locations at the edge of a coverage zone where the signals may or may not be usable. A fringe area is comparable to a car driving in the countryside where the public radio station reception varies up and down. As the car moves farther from the city, the reception gradually dissipates to total static. In a fringe area, other factors that will affect signal propagation are:

Foliage — Leaves absorb RF signals, and an area that has good coverage in the winter when the trees are bare may have significantly reduced coverage in the spring and summer. Moreover, the effects are more pronounced in rural areas, which have more foliage, than in urban areas.

Specific Location — The penetration of RF signals is affected by buildings. As a user moves deeper into a building, or to the opposite side of a building from the nearest transmission tower, there are more surfaces for the signal to penetrate. Concrete and steel are materials that RF signals had difficulty penetrating, and they may produce shadow areas where coverage is limited.

Antenna Direction — In fringe areas, the direction the antenna is pointed has a significant effect on coverage, and small movements of the user device can align the antenna with the signal path.

Terrain — A coverage map often follows geographical variations such as with valleys and hills. Radio signals behave similar to light waves in that they travel in straight lines and can fill in behind an object. In a shadow, there is still some light. A radio signal may not be strong enough to "fill in" behind a hill or valley.

In Practice: Radio Problems in Kansas City, MO

During 1997 and 1998, Kansas City (MO) Firefighters were caught in burning buildings with radios that did not work. A police officer, shot in the leg by a suspect, tried to radio for help, but got only static. Kansas City awarded a $18.5 million contract for a 800-MHz digital-trunked system to a leading radio vendor but was warned by the vendor and its main competitor that its specifications were too weak to meet their service specifications. The original specifications called for a 33-dB signal loss to account for trees, tall buildings, and hills. The city went with a 21.5-dB loss factor. Building the system, as originally specified by a consultant, would have cost $26 million. The *Kansas City Star* editorial fumed: "A committee of midlevel bureaucrats, faced with a shortage of money, decided to build an insufficient system with insufficient funds, and didn't tell anyone about it." Kansas City needed to spend additional millions to retroactively fix the system. The final cost could exceed the original $26 million estimate.

Source: *Mobile Technology and Communications*, September 1998.

10.8.3   RF Dead Zones

Within a specific coverage area, there still will exist locations where coverage is non-existent or too marginal to be useable. No radio system will have 100% indoor and outdoor coverage and often coverage is defined as a percentage or probability of coverage. In LMR systems, 95% is an often-used standard for portable radio coverage. Examples of where the dead zones are likely to be located are:

   In-building — The deeper a user device moves within a building, the more materials and objects the radio signals have to pass through. Underground malls and train tunnels may not have any coverage unless specific enhancement devices are installed. Glass tends to allow signals to pass through but metallic glass does not. Moving to a basement boiler room means that numerous metal ducts, concrete walls, and other objects are in the way of the RF signals. Significant research has been conducted into in-building coverage, and loss profile ratings are available for categories of buildings. However, characterizing a building in terms of how much it attenuates a signal is very difficult. Typically, a general "building attenuation margin" is factored into the design in order to ensure that most buildings are covered.

   Terrain — As described with fringe areas, radio waves may not be strong enough to fill in behind particularly steep hills or valleys.

   Noise levels — In some areas, there may be strong RF signals but the ambient noise is so strong that the user device cannot function properly. Power lines, computers, arc welders, vehicle ignition systems, and neon signs are sources of noise. Atmospheric conditions and electrical storms also generate noise.

Figure 10.5 Model of L.A. County Sheriff's radio system microwave backbone.

Interference and reliability — Interference is a major factor in radio performance and usually is man-made with the exception of some atmospheric conditions such as lightning. Sources are vehicle ignition systems, neon lights, light dimmers, computers, and other types of RF transmission such as amateur radio, CB, public broadcast, and cellular.

10.9 Microwave

In earlier discussions, it was mentioned that a wireline connection, such as a conditioned telephone line, is used to tie together receivers in legacy voting LMR systems. Another connection method is a microwave, and as its name implies, the microwaves have very short wavelengths (Figure 10.5). Large amounts of data can be sent using multiplexing techniques. The problem inherent with microwaves is that because they are near the frequency of light waves, they exhibit similar characteristics such as reflection and refraction — which occur when microwaves pass through denser to thinner air levels. Propagation is mainly through line of sight, and factors such as earth bulge and diffraction are further considerations in calculating minimum tower heights. A parabolic antenna is used to radiate the energy so that it travels in a narrow beam.

In Practice: The E-Comm Radio Ring Architecture

The Vancouver regional radio system is built on ring architecture with a microwave backbone. All sites have two points leaving them and are built on post-disaster structures. Should a failure occur at any point on the ring, then the entire ring would reverse to maintain connectivity. Should a single site be completely disabled, then the ring would allow only that site to be removed from service. Communications integrity is still maintained between the balance of the sites by allowing communications in both directions from the hub site.

10.10   Satellite

Satellite transmissions are similar to microwaves except that instead of sending signals to a nearby line-of-sight microwave dish antenna, the signal is sent to an orbiting satellite. The satellite then sends the signal back to a ground station. Disadvantages with satellite transmissions are the propagation delay caused by the large distances the signals have to travel and the blockages caused by road overpasses and high rises. The most significant advantage is the ability to provide communications in remote areas that are not economically viable for regular radio or cellular coverage. The IRIDIUM satellite system failed financially but is being resuscitated. It was developed by a consortium headed by Motorola, and deployed 66 radio-linked satellites orbiting at a low altitude of 778 kilometers.

10.11   Wireless Digital Signals

All wireless signals (electromagnetic waves) are analog, but digital information can be placed on the carrier wave for transmission through the radio channel. Analog voice signals are digitized and compressed using a device known as a vocoder. Law enforcement operations are definitely made more effective and secure when criminals cannot monitor the digitally encoded transmissions. For example, there were no consumer market scanners available at the time this book was written that could be used to monitor transmissions encoded by the Improved Multi-Band Excitation (IMBE) vocoder. APCO Project 25 (see Section 10.13) has adopted the IMBE vocoder, produced by Digital Voice Systems Inc., as the public safety standard.

Digital communications are characterized by a defined number of symbols transmitted. In a binary system, only two symbols are possible and these symbols are called bits. The bit can only be one of two possible conditions: off and on, yes and no, 1 or 0, etc. The number of bits that can be transmitted per second is known as the baud rate (which is different than bps or bits per second). Many digital radio systems are multi-symbol — such as four-state — which allows for more information to be transmitted per second for a given channel bandwidth.

In a 1998 NIJ survey, 13% of law enforcement agencies reported using digital voice. While analog was far more prevalent, 55% of the agencies that are planning an upgrade indicated a preference for digital.

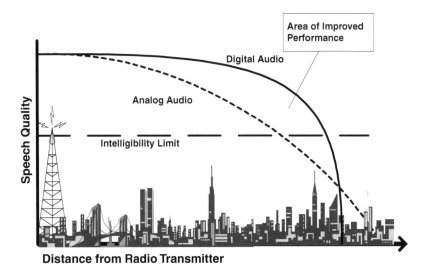

Figure 10.6 Digital propagation vs. analog.

In a digital world, the migration from analog seems very desirable and almost a non-issue. However, there are many challenges with digital. In a digital system, computers control all communications. A console may "hang" due to an operating system (Windows) problem and an operator may be unaware for several minutes that the console is not working. Other drawbacks are the higher costs, the difficulty of backward compatibility with analog, and reduced range in some circumstances. From an end user perspective, there is little warning if the edge of a coverage area is encountered. In analog, the signal will degrade to the point of incomprehension, whereas in digital, once the bit error rates exceed accepted tolerances, the reception will abruptly cease. This is shown in Figure 10.6.

The advantages of digital are:

- Clearer signal quality, especially in fringe areas
- Enhanced and more robust encryption options
- Greater spectral efficiency
- The ability to integrate voice and data over the same channel — a major advantage for statewide systems

10.12   Trunking

In addition to digital compression options, another technique used to conserve spectrum is trunking. In a conventional system, each user makes the decision when to share in the use of the frequency. At a busy moment, the user may break in during a pause or try to override another unit. If the channel is very busy, the user may switch to a "tactical" or "service" channel to obtain radio airtime.

In a trunked system, a microprocessor-controlled scheme coordinates the sharing of the channel capacity. A user keys a mike and waits for a "grant" tone (also known as a push-to-talk or PTT tone). This permits the user to have unimpeded access to a channel (frequency).

Trunking takes advantage of the fact that some channels are idle at a point in time when others are busy. For example, a large city may have units operating on a congested downtown radio channel (Channel 1). Units working on the slower residential radio channel (Channel 2) have excess capacity. Trunking will combine the capacities of both channels, and three or more talkgroups could be created. In effect, a third "virtual" talkgroup can be created from the excess channel capacity from Channel 2, and users from the congested Channel 1 could use this airtime.

Blocking factors can be calculated. For example, if Channel 1 in a conventional system were in use (loaded) 50% of the time, the grade of service (GoS) is 50%. In a five-channel trunked system with 50% loading on each channel, the user — because of the access to all of the channels — has a GoS (call blocked) of 12.5%. The downside to trunking is the call setup delay, which is the time needed by the network to return a radio tone (grant tone) indicating that the system is ready to receive a transmission. This delay is usually on the order of one quarter to one half second.

Since it is the system that assigns the radio channel, the term talkgroup denotes the radio setting that the users are operating on. Trunking allows for the creation of many more talkgroups than radio channels available. These system configurations are called fleet maps. Trunking also facilitates interoperability. Consoles (often touch screen) enable dynamic regrouping of talkgroups. For example, in an emergency situation involving users from different agencies that normally do not talk to each other, a pre-assigned talkgroup can be enabled that instantaneously patches users together in a seamless communications operating environment. Figure 10.7 displays a ComNet/Ericsson Maestro console controller which allows the operator to control up to 128 talkgroups. This can be compared with Figure 10.8, which shows a 6-channel radio console constructed in the early 1970s.

10.13   APCO Project 25

The Association of Public Communications Operators (APCO) is working on standards for digital-trunked radio systems. APCO Project 25 was initiated in 1989 and includes public safety, wireless industry, and regulatory agency representatives. Phase 1 of Project 25 is "narrowbanding" which involves taking a 25-kHz channel and splitting it into two digitized channels, each

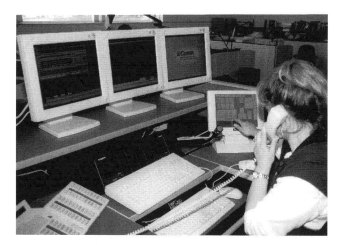

Figure 10.7 A Vancouver Police/E-Comm touch screen radio console controls 108 talkgroups and became operational in 1999.

Figure 10.8 A Vancouver Police analog conventional six-channel console is shown. It was used prior to the E-Comm system becoming operational.

12.5 kHz. Phase 2 of Project 25 will see a further doubling of spectral efficiency, moving to 6.25-kHz voice channels. Other major objectives of APCO Project 25 are to bring in standards on:

- Direct interoperability for seamless communications between agencies
- Enhanced user-friendly functionality (requires the least amount of mental and physical interaction by a user)

- The graceful migration from analog to digital technologies
- Multiple equipment sourcing to stimulate competition through an open system architecture

One example of a standard is the Project 25 common air interface standard, which selected Frequency Division Multiple Access (FDMA) as the channel access method. As stated, IMBE was selected as the vocoder standard for public safety.

In Practice: Project 25 and the Michigan State Police

The Michigan Public Safety Communications System is the first APCO Project 25 compliant statewide radio system. The Motorola 800 MHz ASTRO SmartZone digital-trunked communications system will comply with the APCO Project 25 standard for trunking, encryption, and Common Air Interface (CAI). It will provide radio communications for all seven State Police districts and local public safety responders serving the state's more than 10 million residents. The system is to be installed in four phases, with completion targeted for spring 2002. In addition to serving the State Police, the system provides radio communications for state conservation officers and park rangers, environmental officers, highway workers, and more. County and local law enforcement and firefighting agencies, ambulance services, and 9-1-1 dispatch centers also will be on the statewide system. Local and county agencies are expected to add 10,000 mobile and portable radios to the 3781 the State Police will have on the system. The system will cost $187,275,915 and Phase 1 is comprised of 26 towers. When completed, there will be approximately 180 new tower sites.

Source: Michigan State Police Website: www.mpscs.com.

10.14   Interoperability

In all jurisdictions, there is a need for public safety agencies to work together. This not only includes law enforcement agencies, who may be involved in cross-boundary crimes such as vehicle pursuits, but fire and emergency medical service responders as well. The need for all public safety personnel to interoperate is well illustrated in major incidents such as bombings, natural disasters, and transportation accidents.

In current analog systems, there are cumbersome ways to communicate with other agencies. One option is to enable all user radios to operate on pre-arranged regional frequencies. Another option is to issue multiple radios and have a person relay messages. The cost of new communications equipment and the recognition of the need to interoperate are the driving forces behind the creation of many regional communications centers and shared radio systems.

In Practice: Interoperability between Police, Fire, and Ambulance

Immediately after the bombing of the Alfred R. Murrah Building in Oklahoma City, radio communications were the principal means to coordinate the disaster response and concurrent criminal investigation. Radio communications between agencies quickly became a significant problem as there were not enough channels available to handle the public safety radio communications. The four primary VHF radio channels used by the Oklahoma City Police Department became instantly congested after the explosion as officers throughout the city felt the blast and reported the incident. One hundred and seventeen agencies, each with separate radio systems, responded to the incident. Because responding agencies could not communicate with each other, runners were used to relay messages. Fortunately, all police and fire agencies were equipped with MDTs, which operated on a dedicated 800-MHz channel. This became the only reliable means of communication with the command post at the scene.

Source: PSWN Program Symposium Compilation Report August 1997–April 1999, DOJ Website: www.usdoj.gov/pswn.

Digital interoperability requires the use of similar technologies and data standards. Unless a common standard is followed, digital radios cannot interoperate. While the standards have been identified in Project 25, it will still be several years before the manufacturers catch up and are able to provide reliable products.

In Practice: Littleton, CO

The public safety response to the Columbine High School shootings on April 22, 1999 was hampered by the lack of interoperability. The nine fire and police agencies that responded utilized radios on the following bands.

Subsequent to the shooting, a mobile command post vehicle was outfitted with a transportable radio interconnect system provided by JPS Communications Inc. Radios for all agencies are now mounted on a rack (see Figure 10.9) and they can be quickly programmed to specific transmit and receive frequencies.

Source: TRP-1000, Multiple Agency Radio Communications Interoperability System, JPS Communications Inc.

Figure 10.9 The radio interoperability system in Jefferson County, CO.

Agency	Spectrum Band
Jefferson County Sheriff's Office	VHF
Littleton Fire	VHF
West Metro Fire	800 MHz analog trunked
Denver Police	800 MHz analog trunked
Arapahoe Sheriff's Office	800 MHz analog
Douglas County Sheriff's Office	800 MHz digital
Lakewood Police	800 MHz analog
Littleton Police	800 MHz analog
Colorado State Patrol	VHF

10.15 Commercial Cellular Telephone

The adoption of cellular telephones has been at an explosive rate. Early cellular phones were analog. Newer digital PCS technologies allow for services such as paging, e-mail, and data transfer. The commercial service offerings are driven by consumer demand and coverage is provided in major metropolitan regions and along major roadways. Consequently, in locations where there is low consumer demand, such as rural areas, it is not commercially prudent for cellular companies to build out-coverage. Moreover, there is little inducement for them to provide coverage in difficult terrain or in-building coverage due to the costs. Many agencies utilize cellular services to supplement a private LMR system.

In Practice: Wireless E-911 and the FCC Mandate

In all 911 call centers, the percentage of cellular calls is increasing and is approaching 50%. Many mobile callers have difficulty in identifying where they are. In response, the FCC mandated on April 1, 1998 (Phase I) that wireless operators must be able to supply 911 call centers with the caller's location and a call back number. With Phase II, the location requirement moves beyond the cell/sector level and requires the location be narrowed to within 125 meters by October 2001. Initially, the progress of the wireless mandates was slow due to problems resolving cost-recovery mechanisms. On November 19, 1999, the FCC modified the E-911 rules and removed its original requirement that a cost recovery agreement be in place prior to wireless carriers providing Phase I and II services. APCO President Joe Hanna stated, "It's our belief the actions taken by the commission are of significant benefit to the 81 million wireless subscribers throughout the United States, as well as the 5000 PSAPs that deal with the emergency calls placed by these 81 million subscribers each day."

Source: FCC Website: www.fcc.gov/e911.

10.16   Commercial Radio

There are several wireless voice options for public safety agencies other than acquiring a private radio system.

10.16.1   Specialized Mobile Radio

In 1974, the FCC created the specialized mobile radio (SMR) industry by allocating spectrum in the 220-, 800-, and 900-MHz bands. The service is primarily for business users such as construction and transportation. Public safety users also can use SMR services, and the low cost makes SMR an attractive option.

In Practice: Black Hawk County, IA

Black Hawk County officials initially expected to spend about $4.2 million for their own radio network, but a decision to turn to a local SMR provider saved them about $2 million. After hearing proposals for a private system,

Black Hawk County's Enhanced 911 and Consolidated Public Safety Communications Center Board agreed to a leasing arrangement with a local SMR vendor, RACOM, for access to their EDACS network. The contract calls for 500 Ericsson mobile and portable radios.

Source: Public safety finds high value in new shared networks, *EDACS Open Mike*, Fall 1995.

10.16.2 Enhanced Specialized Mobile Radio

There are now advances to cellular telephone technologies that enable an enhanced specialized mobile radio (ESMR) provider to further compete with private LMR systems. "Push-to-talk" (PTT) radio service is accessed by "keying a mike" or a button on a user device which resembles a cellular telephone. The procedure is similar to the process used in a trunked LMR system. Depressing the PTT button will set in place a call setup process, and the network will return a grant tone and assign a radio channel. The radio call is handled without any interaction with the PSTN.

The leading U.S. ESMR operator is Nextel, which uses the proprietary Motorola iDEN technology. In Canada, the leading iDEN operator is Clearnet. Digital radio, paging, e-mail, and traditional cellular PSTN services are provided. There are also data transfer capabilities and all of this is combined in one handset. There are no standards for this new technology, and since the service is new, the coverage areas lag behind more established cellular networks.

In Practice: Adoption of ESMR in Law Enforcement

In a PSWN study, Grade of Service levels of 5% were calculated for the "direct connect" service. Most law enforcement users found the iDEN system reliable and coverage was relatively good. In 1999, a mid-sized Canadian city converted on a trial basis to a mobile radio system provided by a Canadian ESMR vendor. At the conclusion of the trial, it was determined that the system coverage and the quality of transmissions did not meet the performance levels needed by public safety responders. Users also complained about the quality of the user devices, which were initially designed for consumer uses. After the test, a RFP was issued for a private LMR system.

The iDEN protocol uses a proprietary vocoding technique and modulation process. In addition, congestion and setup time factors may be dependent on the loads placed by other users on the system — and this could be untimely in the event of a critical incident. Because of the potential for system congestion, public safety agencies still rely mainly on private LMR systems

Table 10.3   PSWN Survey Results on Commercial Wireless Usage

Wireless Service	Percent
Cellular	72
Paging	59
Satellite	9
PCS	5
SMR	4

for users that may encounter tactical or emergency situations. ESMR providers are reluctant to offer priority access to their networks.

10.17   Commercial Wireless Service Usage

In a study of the Washington, D.C. area, the PSWN found that 80% of the law enforcement agencies relied on commercial services to augment their regular radio infrastructure (Table 10.3). As expected, these agencies tended to use commercial services for non-tactical and non-emergency communications, or for mobile data.

10.18   Acquiring a Land Mobile Radio System

A LMR system project has many similarities with large traditional IT projects. Project planning, funding arrangements, and developing a RFP are some of the high level steps needed to bring a complex and often multimillion dollar project to fruition. In addition, many shared systems are being acquired today in the context of consolidating dispatch centers. In March 2000, the National Law Enforcement and Corrections Technology Center published a free guidebook, which covers public safety wireless technology, issues, planning, and management. It can be accessed at www.nlectc.org.

In Practice: Site Acquisitions and a Tale of Two Cities

A special requirement in a LMRS project, which is not encountered with other IT projects, is the need to acquire real estate for radio towers. Often, existing radio towers cannot meet the design needs of a new LMRS. Particularly controversial are towers constructed in residential areas. In July 2000, the city of Surrey, British Columbia became engulfed in an uproar over the proposed construction of two 250-foot towers in residential areas for the proposed Fire Department radio system. A media story on the development variance permit application ignited public sentiments, and angry residents began petition campaigns. The administrators of the radio project, because of the political sensitivity, decided at the last minute to withdraw the request for the tower located in Fraser Heights. Their modified proposal had Fraser Heights now being covered from an adjoining site, plus a mobile repeater mounted on a command vehicle would be driven into the area in the event of an incident.

The Surrey situation was ironic because in the same month, extensive media publicity was focused on Orange County, CA and the problems with their new radio system. Police officers had gone public with their complaints. Many examples of officer safety concerns were aired, including an incident involving a search for carjacking suspects. Officers with their guns drawn outside a warehouse didn't get a radio message that a SWAT team was coming out until after they emerged. In Orange County, the vendor asserted that a major reason for the coverage gaps was due to the public outcry over the proposed height of radio towers in Laguna Beach. Public pressure led to the tower heights being lowered for aesthetic reasons. While the Orange County media dramatized the police complaints, a technical debate was occurring simultaneously on the Usenet newsgroup, alt.radio.scanner. Several postings were made on the tower height issue, including an opinion that the site choices were not optimal, and that existing sites could have met the needs of the new system.

Source: Leonard, Jack, O.C. emergency radio upgrade halted for bugs, *L.A. Times*, Orange County Edition, June 24, 2000.

10.19   LMRS Vendors

The vendor with the most installations in the LMR market is Motorola. ComNet/Ericsson (formerly General Electric) and EF Johnson are also leading vendors. The technologies they use are generally proprietary single source standards, and customers have to purchase equipment from the same manufacturer. Commonalties do arise from the APCO 16 standard which covers channel access times, emergency call button requirements, and user equipment design. APCO 25 is attempting to move the manufacturers to common vocoder and common air interface standards for digital-trunked radio, so that equipment from different vendors will interoperate. Limited licensing agreements between vendors have resulted in compatibility between some of the Motorola and EF Johnson offerings.

10.20   End-of-Chapter Comments

Data devices will never replace voice radio completely (see Chapter 8, Section 8.3). Having a functional LMR system should be a high, if not the number one IT infrastructure priority. In most mission-critical public safety responses, talking to one another is the only effective and efficient form of communication.

Building a wide area radio system is a complicated task with inherent risks. If coverage is not present, or if equipment is faulty, project leaders in public safety must be prepared for extreme hostility from end users, including the fact that they will use the media to dramatize their complaints. No other IT project will generate this level of attention and this illustrates the importance of the voice radio. On the other hand, a proposed optimal design for a LMR system may face alterations because of public hostility over radio tower heights and placements.

References

Borrego, Mike, Shared communications systems to help deliver critical public safety services, *The Police Chief*, May 2000.

Brief History of the Chicago Police Department, Chicago Public Library Website: www.chipublib.org.

Coe, Lewis, *Wireless Radio: a Brief History*, McFarland, Jefferson, NC, 1986.

Das, Gopal, Pigeon service, once vital, is a remnant of India's past, Associated Press, *Seattle Times*, July 30, 2000.

Digital Voice Systems Inc. Website: www.dvsinc.com/papers/iambe.htm.

Dobson, Kenneth, How Detroit Police reinvented the wheel, *Detroit News* Website: www.detnews.com.

Evans, Alvis J., *Antennas Selection and Installation*, Master Publishing Inc., Richardson, TX, 1989.

History of the Winnipeg Police Service, Winnipeg Police Service Website: www.city.winnipeg.mb.ca/police/history/history3.htm.

Imel, Kathy and Hart, James, Understanding Wireless Communications in Public Safety, National Law Enforcement and Corrections Technology Center, NIJ, Rockville, MD, March 2000.

Leonard, Jack, O.C. emergency radio upgrade halted for bugs, *L.A. Times*, Orange County Edition, June 24, 2000.

Michigan State Police Website: www.mpscs.com.

The Notorious Case of Dr. Crippen, Metropolitan Police Service Website: www.met.police.uk/histroy/crippen.

PSWN Program Symposium Compilation Report August 1997–April 1999, DOJ Website: www.usdoj.gov/pswn.

Public Safety Wireless Network Homepage, www.pswn.gov.

Regional Mobile Radio System Conceptual Design Report, Version 1, Prepared for the City of Vancouver, Teleconsult Limited, 1996.

Singer, E., *Land Mobile Radio Systems*, 2nd Ed., Prentice-Hall, Englewood Cliffs, NJ, 1994.

Taylor, Mary, Epper, Robert, and Tolman, Thomas, State and Local Law Enforcement Wireless Communications and Interoperability: A Quantitative Analysis, National Institute of Justice, Research Report, NCJ 168961, January 1998.

TRP-1000, Multiple Agency Radio Communications Interoperability System, JPS Communications Inc.

Wireless Data IT Infrastructure

11

11.1 An Introduction to Wireless Data

Wireless data services are important, if not essential in today's operational environment. Many law enforcement administrators view the laptop computer in the car as a standard equipment item, similar to the siren, the light bar, and the radio. Even this viewpoint is changing as the new millennium brings handheld computers into the realm of everyday consumer use. An important service extension is the ability of the computing device to connect to systems and databases wirelessly. This chapter surveys private and commercial wireless data options.

In the NCIC 2000 planning process, four service levels of interaction were described for remote information retrieval:

1. Level one is the lowest level of service and allows for users to call the dispatcher with a request and have the answer returned over radio.
2. Level two allows the officer to run an inquiry from his/her vehicle.
3. Level three allows imaging to be sent to the dispatcher via a wireline transmission, but the information still cannot be relayed to the officer in the field.
4. Level four is the most sophisticated level of service and allows data and images to be sent directly to the officer in his/her vehicle.

Chapter 10 discussed how voice information was transmitted over the air — a level one service. The level three application becomes a function of the wireline connectivity of the dispatch center. In trying to achieve levels two and four, wireless data transfer must be available and this forms the subject of this chapter. It should be noted that images (mugshots, maps, video) and text are considered data. Moreover, sound clips can be considered data as well and convergence is once again a relevant concept. For example, a real-time wireless sound file transfer is, in fact, wireless voice traffic (digital radio or PCS).

11.2   Bandwidth Limitations

Wireless connectivity provides anytime, anywhere access to resources such as a law enforcement agency's LAN, local and federal databases, other public networks, the Internet, and NCIC/CPIC. The vision of a fully functioning mobile office is very appealing but is limited by two factors inherent in a wireless link:

1.   Data radio is subject to the same factors that degrade voice radio performance. This includes interference, congestion, and coverage limitations. Chapter 10 covered these factors in detail.
2.   Data throughput is limited. There are many claims regarding the maximum speed for current wireless services, such as 19,200 bps, but general speeds are in the 4800- to 9600-bps range. This causes problems for many applications because of the amount of data that needs to be passed back and forth. For example, a thin client application that has the server performing the screen presentation details would be bogged down on a wireless link.

These limiting factors mean that applications written for networked desktop computers cannot be deployed "as is" in most mobile data environments. Because a wireless connection is unreliable, perhaps caused by a patrol unit driving through a coverage gap, a database application would need to be able to lock and unlock records if the connection is dropped. In essence, the software needs to be designed to account for the unreliability. (*Note:* A further problem could be the user interface, as it is impracticable to use a standard mouse or pointing device on a laptop computer mounted in a vehicle. Function keys are more desirable.)

The general characteristics of radio, including coverage and congestion levels, must not be forgotten. For example, despite the significant promotional material highlighting the virtues of digital cellular and PCS data services, it should be noted that wireless data transmissions still rely on the analog carrier wave to carry information. In the case of digital data, the carrier wave is modulated with digital signals.

11.3   How Wireless Data Are Used

In the late 1970s, the first mobile computing devices were deployed in law enforcement. This was spurred by the invention of the microprocessor, which allowed computing devices to shrink in size so they could fit into the console area of a patrol car. The apparent first wide-scale deployment of wireless computers in vehicles was in the Vancouver Police Department in 1978. The

Figure 11.1 The Vancouver Police Department is apparently the first police agency in North America to deploy on a wide-scale basis computers in vehicles that had a wireless link. Twenty Motorola data terminals were installed in patrol vehicles in 1978.

Motorola data terminal had a "chicklet" style keyboard and a red LED display (see Figure 11.1). It was configured for Canadian Police Information Center (CPIC) access and allowed rudimentary car-to-car messaging. The wireless link relied on a single RF channel operating on a single-site radio transmitter with a 4800-bps transmission rate. The basic components of the data radio system were still in use up until 2001.

The advent of new commercially available technologies has resulted in many more options for wireless data transmission other than using a private LMR system. For public safety, APCO Project 34 has the objective of creating a wireless high speed standard that will allow for the ubiquitous implementation of a nationwide public safety data network that encompasses voice/data convergence.

In a 1999 survey of law enforcement agencies conducted by the Public Safety Wireless Network (PSWN), the following uses of wireless data were reported by agencies in the Washington, D.C., San Diego, and Pittsburgh regions as shown in Figure 11.2.

A wireless data network can augment the voice radio system and increase the utilization of available spectrum. As stated in Chapters 8 and 10, administrators must look at the information that a dispatcher currently relays by voice. Much of the non-mission-critical transmissions can be moved to the mobile data environment for officers to serve themselves using mobile computers. Furthermore, wireless data can serve as a backup to the voice network. If a commercial service is used, the independence of the network to the PSTN

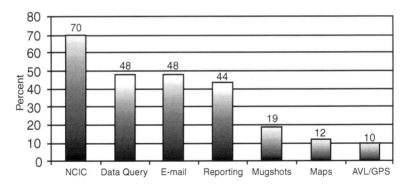

Figure 11.2 Wireless usage among surveyed law enforcement agencies.

and an agency's private radio network provides an additional level of communications redundancy.

In Practice: Tarranty County, CDPD Backs Up the Private Radio Network

In March 2000, twisters tore through the center of Forth Worth, TX. In addition to massive building damage, major parts of Tarranty County's telephone and power grid were knocked out. Very quickly, the 800-MHz voice radio system was overloaded. Fortunately, the Tarranty County Sheriff's Office was a Cellular Digital Packet Data (CDPD) user and had available 45 Itronix X-C 6250 mobile data computers, equipped with Sierra Wireless SB300 modems. These accessed a Cerulean PacketCluster message switch that connected to AT&T's CDPD network. Lieutenant Rob Durko noted that during the crisis, "the MDCs (mobile data computers) became the sheriff department's primary communications resource."

Source: Astler, Craig, Command and control in a Texas tornado, *Radio Resource Magazine*, November–December 2000, 52.

11.4   Components of a Wireless Data Network

There are three parts to a wireless data system that enable a computer to be deployed in a police cruiser or held in the hand of a law enforcement officer. These are user devices and applications, a wireless backbone, and software applications.

11.4.1   User Devices and Applications

Everyday, more powerful and ever-smaller mobile computing devices are appearing in the marketplace. Commercial users, who see major benefits to wireless connectivity, drive the demands. Law enforcement agencies can use the commercially available products as well as have their needs met by specialized vendors who design equipment to specifically meet the rigorous physical demands of public safety users. In addition, vendors are adapting existing applications to enable mobility. Chapter 8, Mobile Computing, describes both devices and applications in more detail.

11.4.2   Wireless Backbone

Mobile computers need connectivity to each other, and to local and wide area networks. Whether there are hundreds of devices deployed or just a few mobile computers installed, a backbone radio network is required.

11.4.3   Software Applications

As stated earlier, software in the wireless environment must be "mobile-aware." It must be specifically designed for unreliable wireless networks. Furthermore, there are special user data input and access conditions caused by the fixed mounting of computers in vehicles, or the need to use the device while standing on the street. There are law enforcement agencies that are utilizing voice recognition software. This technology will see more widespread deployment as processor speeds increase, and the systems are able to filter out background noises such as sirens and road traffic.

11.5   Private Land Mobile Radio System Data

It is very common for a LMR system to be used as the backbone for wireless data connectivity. A radio modem can link a computer to the wireline network, similar to how a telephone modem is used for desktop dial-up access to the Internet. The first implementations set aside dedicated broadband RF channels. There are now available trunked data and voice systems that transmit data in the "voids" that naturally occur in speech or on an idle radio channel. These trunked systems attempt to maximize spectrum and system utilization. Private radio products include Ericsson's EDACS and Motorola's DataTAC.

Wireless data are usually transmitted in packets and an early transmission scheme standard is X.25. Newer systems utilize TCP/IP. A system can have a number of base stations acting as receivers, and these are connected to a network processor that selects the first correct signal from a mobile unit. The network processor or communications controller is connected to a host computer or server to which it sends messages (queries), and it also notifies the host if a message was transmitted and not acknowledged by certain mobile units.

Figure 11.3 Dell laptop computer mounted in a New York State Patrol vehicle.

Advantages of a private system include the fact that the network is for the exclusive use of the owner and bandwidth is not shared. Using an existing voice LMR infrastructure can simplify the operations and administration, as only one system is maintained. From a user perspective, a police vehicle may not need a radio for voice and another radio for data.

In the 1998 NIJ study on wireless communication uses, 27% of the 1334 agencies surveyed indicated they use LMR system radio channels for data only. Of these, 67% utilize 800-MHz systems. Moreover, 30% of the agencies indicated a need for more data-only channels. Figure 11.3 shows a New York State Patrol vehicle with a standard Dell computer laptop running a wireless NYSPIN session. The data are transmitted over a private VHF data channel using a modem from DATARADIO (Figure 11.4).

In Practice: The Toronto Police Wireless Network

The Toronto Police acquired wireless data capabilities in their new Motorola 800-MHz LMR System. There are 14 base stations which are connected

Figure 11.4 Private RF data modem mounted in the trunk of the New York State Patrol vehicle.

through leased lines to two radio network controllers, each with a backup giving four radio control units. The network is connected to the LAN, which is controlled by Motorola's wireless network gateway. The gateway is fully fault tolerant and, in turn, connects to IBM's E-Net wireless gateway server software, which functions as a router into the police network.

Source: Toronto Police armed with wireless network, *Technology in Government*, May 1999.

11.6   Commercial Data Services

Older LMR systems were designed and built primarily for voice traffic. Adding on data traffic can strain the existing capacity and further investment would be required to upgrade the radio network. The greater impediment, though, is in trying to obtain more spectrum, and this is especially difficult in metropolitan regions. In addition, increased data uses may degrade current voice service. With the burgeoning options available for data, utilizing commercial services can offer a temporary or permanent solution.

Using commercial services to provide this wireless data capacity has further attractions, including:

- Faster implementations
- The opportunity to share technology upgrade costs with commercial users

Table 11.1   Build a Private Data System vs. Lease Commercial Data Services

Point of Comparison	Build a Data System	Lease a Commercial Data Service
System capacity	Level is a function of cost — number of sites and channels	Level is a function of cost — subject to negotiation and price
Uniformity of user equipment	Excellent	Excellent
Integrating consumer market user devices	Poor	Very good — depends on commercial service selected
Control over system performance (coverage, grade of service, availability)	Excellent	Fair — negotiable to a degree
Expansion flexibility	Excellent	Fair — negotiable to a degree
Capital costs	High	Low
Recurring costs	Low	High
Business constraints	Depends on spectrum availability	Depends on commercial service availability

- Lower risk of obsolescence
- Redundancy provided by the independence of the network from the voice system

Commercial data access charges are usually based on usage and monthly account fees. Financially, a comparison must be made between the net present value of the annualized costs of a commercial service and the infrastructure capital investment associated with the private LMR option (assuming spectrum is available). For example, large agencies that need hundreds of CDPD accounts may see a yearly bill that exceeds the cost of building a private LMR system for data, factoring in annual maintenance and administration costs. For small agencies that never could afford their own wireless data networks, commercial providers provide a beneficial and economical service. Table 11.1 compares the advantages of a private system vs. leasing services.

11.7   Circuit-Switched Cellular Telephone Networks

The advances with portable or laptop computer hardware and the parallel expansion of cellular telephone service have resulted in an obvious pairing. A laptop can be equipped with a PCMIA cellular modem and a data connection can be established over the cellular phone network. Unfortunately, the frequency and cellular site handoffs that occur can cause delays, which can seriously affect data transmissions. The cellular network was built for voice. Interference and momentary pauses are only a minor annoyance on a voice call. For automated procedures designed for reliable wireline environments, these RF problems can be fatal. A database program may lock a record from other users prior to an update, and a lengthy delay or a dropped connection can result in database synchronization problems.

The nature of a circuit-switched environment makes the costs of short data messages very high. For applications that utilize large file transfers, this technology is better than packet-based ones. Charges are based on connection times, similar to cellular voice phone billing since the connection is maintained regardless of whether data are being transferred. In law enforcement, the mobile messaging environment is characterized by many short messages, such as a call dispatch or a database query. The delays caused by setup times, plus the overhead costs, make packet-based networks more suitable and economical.

In Practice: Remote Access via GSM by the Dutch National Police Force

The coastal location of the Netherlands means that many important services are delivered by the Dutch National Police Force (KLPD) through their fleet of 30 police boats. A priority IT need is for officers to have the same computing applications that they use in the office to be available to officers working on the boats. These applications include file transfers, e-mail, and database queries. Early trials with wireless access involved satellite and packet data (RAM) services. In 1999, the KLPD implemented a mobile ISDN solution, which is an example of a circuit-switched mobile data connection. Remote computers use laptop computers equipped with Nokia Cardphone IIs to access the European GSM mobile phone network. Special communications software deploy "spoofing" techniques to handle dropped or lost connections. The GSM mobile switching center routes the data over a public ISDN connection to the KLPD servers.

Source: Blei, Jan, Mobile ISDN: Remote Access via GSM, World e-Police Conference Presentation, London, England, January 20, 2001.

11.8   Wireless Packet Data

The three national commercial radio networks designed for carrying packet data are:

1. ARDIS
2. BellSouth Wireless Data (known also as RAM and Mobitex)
3. Cellular Digital Packet Data (CDPD)

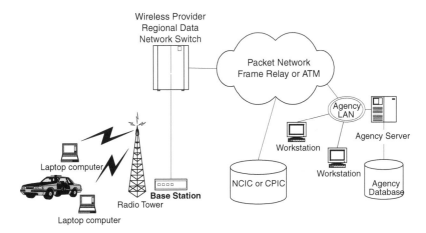

Figure 11.5. Wireless data integrated with wireline networks.

The coverage of these networks generally includes the major metropolitan areas, and in rural areas, some satellite services are offered in conjunction. CDPD is a newer service and is offered by many carriers across North America. All three operate on the "cellular" principle in that the nearest transmitter receives the data message from the low power, user-device transmitter. The information request is routed through a frame relay or ATM network to the host computer (Figure 11.5).

11.8.1   ARDIS

American Mobile's ARDIS (Advanced Radio Data Information Service) network was the first data-only service and was formed as a partnership between Motorola and IBM. It was originally intended for the 17,000 IBM field service technicians and was first deployed in the early 1980s. Since these technicians worked primarily indoors, the ARDIS system was designed and built with a focus on in-building coverage. The network uses the bands 816 to 821 MHz for the uplink of data, and the bands 851 and 866 MHz for the downlink.

There are over 1400 transmitter sites deployed in the U.S., and within a coverage contour, ARDIS guarantees a 90% probability of coverage. The signaling schemes used are known as MDC 4800 and RD-LAP 19.2 and incorporate error control algorithms that detect corrupted or missing packets. Their respective transmission speeds are 4800 or 19,200 bps.

11.8.2   BellSouth Wireless Data

BellSouth Wireless is the latest trade name for the RAM Mobile Data or Mobitex network. There are over 1000 base stations in North America although the technology has greater usage in Europe and other international locations. Ericsson controls the standard, and data speeds of 8000 bits per second are possible. BellSouth offers coverage to 90% of the top 200 to 300 metro areas in North America. It provides transparent roaming throughout North America as the network can recognize a registered radio modem in any coverage area.

In Practice: Lenexa, KS

The Lenexa (KS) Police Department has needs similar to all law enforcement agencies. They wanted images to be available in the field, compatibility with NCIC 2000, and full Records Management System access. They considered building their own RF network, sharing a private data network, or subscribing to a public data network. They also examined the feasibility of packet vs. circuit switched data. After careful consideration, they selected the BellSouth Mobitex service and purchased Motorola MRM 660 Data Modems for use with their AST laptop computers. Their RMS vendor is Versaterm (www.versaterm.com) and the complex integration between the RMS and the mobile computers is managed with a middleware product from Nettech Systems (www.broadbeam.com).

Source: Rennie, Mark, Wireless Mobile Data, IACP LEIM Conference Presentation, May 1999.

11.8.3 Cellular Digital Packet Data (CDPD)

CDPD emerged in 1993 and is now considered one of the more robust methods of wireless connectivity. As a newer technology, it builds on the principles used in ARDIS and RAM and is TCP/IP based. The service is built on the voice cellular network and, consequently, is unavailable in many rural areas. The higher protocol efficiencies achieved by CDPD allow speeds of 19,200 bps to be attained, although with application overheads speeds of 10,000 to 12,000 bps are more common. Roaming agreements among providers are in place and the availability is fast approaching the coverage zones provided by ARDIS and BellSouth. There are a number of equipment vendors for CDPD equipment. Modem manufacturers include Sierra Systems and Inet Technologies.

There are two CDPD network designs:

1. CDPD channel-hopping interleaves data messages over the unused cellular channels and in-between voice traffic pauses. Therefore, the congestion factors are dependent on the load imposed by voice users.
2. In a dedicated channel configuration, capacity on the cellular network is set aside for CDPD data only. However, public safety users would still have to compete with other CDPD customers.

In Practice: CDPD in Law Enforcement

At the 1999 IACP Law Enforcement Information Manager's Conference, officers from several Florida agencies discussed their use of CDPD. The Pembrooke Pines Police Department in Florida has deployed 144 laptops. Online chat, e-mail, and reporting are examples of applications used on the personal issue laptops which officers will carry home. Their CDPD costs are $49 per user per month and the main reason for adopting CDPD was the avoidance of the cost to build a private network. The Seminole County Sheriff's Offices use their laptops for field reports, messaging, and remote NCIC queries. Their field reports can be sent to supervisors who will review them and send them in for loading into the mainframe.

Source: CDPD Issues and Applications Presentation, IACP LEIM Conference, June 2, 1999.

11.9   Third Generation (3G) Wireless

The first generation of wireless was analog cellular. The second generation brought digital networks (PCS etc.) into widespread use. Third generation (3G) wireless networks could start to appear in North America in the 2003 to 2005 time frame (earlier in Europe and Asia) and will enable high-speed multimedia data and voice to be delivered. Implementation hurdles for commercial 3G providers include the need to upgrade networks, obtain frequencies (spectrum), and develop compelling applications and user devices. Mobile speeds will be in the range of 144,000 to 384,000 bps, and stationary speeds of 2,000,000 bps (2 Mbps) are possible.

Once the 3G services arrive, an explosion of mass-market consumer appliances (walkmans, PDAs, still and video cameras, laptops) will be available that can access the Internet. Law enforcement must keep abreast of these new devices. Currently, mobile data devices used in law enforcement involve expensive private data solutions and speciality market user devices.

As 3G devices become commonplace, new applications such as video court appearances from a police vehicle would be possible. Another possibility is that a witness to a crime in progress may be calling with a video-enabled "phone" and the 911 call center may be able to see, and relay to the responding officers, images of what the witness is seeing.

11.10   Geographical Positioning Systems (GPS)

A geographical positioning system (GPS) accesses a network of 24 satellites launched by the U.S. Department of Defense. The radio signals transmitted by the satellites are high frequency and have a specially encoded signal. A GPS receiver calculates a position through the triangulation (measuring the travel time) of radio signals from three of the satellites. In order to deliver Automatic Vehicle Location (AVL), a GPS receiver needs to be able to send its coordinates to a server which is running a mapping program. CAD systems often have integrated AVL functions that enable the closest unit to an emergency to be dispatched.

11.11 Middleware

Many vendors of law enforcement systems manage the wireless functionality by using third-party software, known as middleware. In Chapter 9, Section 9.14, the seven-layer OSI model was mentioned. For wireless data transmissions, layers 3, 4, and 5 (session, transport, and network) can be handled by the middleware application, which streamlines the wireless communications by:

- Reducing packet sizes
- Optimizing acknowledgments
- Enabling flexibility in the network connection to account for fringe areas or adverse conditions
- Handling temporary lost connections and re-sending issuing packets

As illustrated in Section 9.14, the Lenexa Police used a middleware product (RFlink) from Nettech Systems Incorporated to handle the session, transport, and network layers in their mobile computing project. Lenexa uses the RAM data network. The London, Ontario Police Service also uses Nettech middleware with their Ericsson EDACS private radio network, and this is illustrated in Figure 11.6.

11.12 End-of-Chapter Comments

This chapter provided an overview of wireless data. The concepts become relevant as major law enforcement applications, such as CAD, RMS, and mobile computing, are covered in Chapters 6, 7, and 8. The key aspect of wireless data that practitioners need to keep in mind is the limited bandwidths associated with RF channels. Consequently, it may be some time before video streaming and other multimedia applications that require 3G service can be efficiently deployed over wireless links.

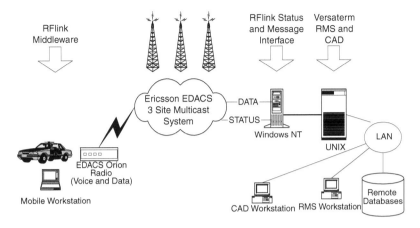

Figure 11.6 Middleware and the London Police Private Wireless Network using a private LMRS for data transport.

References

Blei, Jan, Mobile ISDN: Remote Access via GSM, World e-Police Conference Presentation, London, England, January 20, 2001.

Buckley, Sean, 3G Wireless scales new heights, *Telecommunications*, October 2000, 32.

CDPD Issues and Applications Presentation, IACP LEIM Conference, June 2, 1999.

Fenichel, Robert, Apco Project 25 — Here, Now and Into the Future, March 1999, Website: www.apcointl.org/bull/99/march/feature4.html.

Imel, Kathy and Hart, James, *Understanding Wireless Communications in Public Safety*, National Law Enforcement and Corrections Technology Center, NIJ, Rockville, MD, March 2000.

Jefferson, Steve, 3G Promises broadband without the leash, *Info World*, 22(48), 65, November 27, 2000.

Nettech Systems Inc. Website: www.nettechrf.com.

Pelton, Joseph, *Wireless and Satellite Telecommunications: The Technology, the Market and the Regulations*, Upper Saddle River, NJ: Prentice-Hall, 1995.

PSWN Program Symposium Compilation Report, August 1997–April 1999, PSWN Website: www.usdoj.gov/pswn/.

Rennie, Mark, Wireless Mobile Data, IACP LEIM Conference Presentation, May 1999.

Taylor, Mary, Epper, Robert, and Tolman, Thomas, *State and Local Law Enforcement Wireless Communications and Interoperability: A Quantitative Analysis*, National Institute of Justice, Research Report, NCJ 168961, January 1998.

Wireless Data over Cellular and PCS, Sierra Wireless Website: www.sierrawireless.com.

Wireless Data Services, Public Safety Wireless Network Website: www.pswn.gov, 1999.

Appendix

Sir Robert Peel's Principles of Policing

As British Home Secretary, Sir Robert Peel published the following principles of policing in 1829:

- The basic mission for which the police exist is to prevent crime and disorder.
- The ability of the police to perform their duties is dependent upon public approval of police actions.
- Police must secure the willing co-operation of the public in voluntary observance of the law to be able to secure and maintain the respect of the public.
- The degree of co-operation of the public that can be secured diminishes proportionately to the necessity of the use of physical force.
- Police seek and preserve public favor not by catering to public opinion but by constantly demonstrating absolute impartial service to the law.
- Police use physical force to the extent necessary to secure observance of the law or to restore order only when the exercise of persuasion, advice and warning is found to be insufficient.
- Police, at all times, should maintain a relationship with the public that gives reality to the historic tradition that the police are the public and the public are the police, the police being only members of the public who are paid to give full-time attention to duties which are incumbent on every citizen in the interests of community welfare and existence.
- Police should always direct their action strictly towards their functions and never appear to usurp the powers of the judiciary.
- The test of police efficiency is the absence of crime and disorder, not the visible evidence of police action in dealing with it.

Index

A

accidents, 139
address and jurisdiction verification, 125
Albuquerque Police Department, Websites, 42
analog telephone circuits, 190
APCO Project 25, 214, 216–218, 224
APCO Project 34, 229
application service providers (ASP), 74
ARDIS (Advanced Radio Data Information Service), 236
asynchronous transfer mode (ATM), 192–193
auto attendant feature, 178–179
Automated Fingerprint Identification System (AFIS), 108
Automated Regional Justice Information System (ARJIS), 39, 113–114
automatic call distribution (ACD), 178
automatic location information (ALI), 129, 174
automatic number information (ANI), 129, 174
automatic person location (APL), 152

B

bandwith limitations, 228
basic database elements, 98–101
basic principles of radio, 202–203
basic rate service (BRI), 191
BellSouth wireless data, 236–237
Berkowitz, David, 7
booking reports, 139
Braiden, Chris, 23, 25
Bratton, William, 26, 29, 106

Brown, Lee, 23, 27–28
Brown, Maureen, 34
building private data systems, 234
bulletin boards, 43–44
Bundy, Ted, 116
Business at the Speed of Thought, 62
business case for IT, 13–15
business process reengineering, 54–56

C

cable connections, 186
CAD architecture, 124
CAD systems, 18–19, 26–27, 40, 72, 119–132, 186
  address and jurisdiction verification, 125
  CAD architecture, 124
  call pathing, 125–126
  community policing, 131–132
  costs of, 132
  functionality and, 124–128
  interfaces, 128–131
  management information systems, 128
  manual processes and workflow, 120–123
call pathing, 125–126
Call-for-Service Process, 18–20
Canadian Police Information Center (CPIC), 182, 229
  and self-serve queries, 40
  Websites, 41
Candidate Submission Form (WAPS), 90–91
card file indexes, 97–98
Carnivore, 194–195
Carter, David, 28
case study
  Automated Regional Justice Information Systems (ARJIS), 113–114